The Postmodern Short Story

Recent Titles in
Contributions to the Study of World Literature

Imagining Africa: Landscape in H. Rider Haggard's African Romances
Lindy Stiebel

Seduction and Death in Muriel Spark's Fiction
Fotini E. Apostolou

Unorthodox Views: Reflections on Reality, Truth, and Meaning in Current
Social, Cultural, and Critical Discourse
James L. Battersby

Judgment and Justification in the Nineteenth-Century Novel of Adultery
Maria R. Rippon

The Late Modernism of Cormac McCarthy
David Holloway

The Colonial Conan Doyle: British Imperialism, Irish Nationalism, and the
Gothic
Catherine Wynne

In My Own Shire: Region and Belonging in British Writing, 1840–1970
Stephen Wade

Multicultural Literature for Children and Young Adults: Reflections on
Critical Issues
Mingshui Cai

Interfering Values in the Nineteenth-Century British Novel: Austen, Dickens,
Eliot, Hardy, and the Ethics of Criticism
Jeffrey Moxham

Interactive Fictions: Scenes of Storytelling in the Novel
Yael Halevi-Wise

The Life and Works of Ruskin Bond
Meena G. Khorana

The Hispanic Connection: Spanish and Spanish-American Literature in the
Arts of the World
Zenia Sacks DaSilva, editor

The Postmodern Short Story

Forms and Issues

Edited by
Farhat Iftekharrudin,
Joseph Boyden,
Mary Rohrberger,
and
Jaie Claudet

Under the Auspices of
The Society for the Study of the Short Story

Contributions to the Study of World Literature,
Number 124

PRAEGER

Westport, Connecticut
London

Library of Congress Cataloging-in-Publication Data

The postmodern short story : forms and issues / edited by Farhat
    Iftekharrudin . . . [et al.] under the auspices of the Society for the Study
    of the Short Story.
            p. cm. — (Contributions to the study of world literature,
    ISSN 0738–9345 ; no. 124)
        Includes bibliographical references and index.
        ISBN 0–313–32375–5 (alk. paper)
            1. Short story. 2. Short stories, English—History and criticism.
    3. Short stories, American—History and criticism. 4. English fiction—
    20th century—History and criticism. 5. American fiction—20th century—
    History and criticism. I. Iftekharrudin, Farhat. II. Society for the Study of
    the Short Story. III. Series.
PN3373.P697   2003
809.3'1—dc21   2003054722

British Library Cataloguing in Publication Data is available.

Library of Congress Catalog Card Number: 2003054722
ISBN: 0–313–32375–5
ISSN: 0738–9345

First published in 2003

Praeger Publishers, 88 Post Road West, Westport, CT 06881
An imprint of Greenwood Publishing Group, Inc.
www.praeger.com

Printed in the United States of America

∞™

The paper used in this book complies with the
Permanent Paper Standard issued by the National
Information Standards Organization (Z39.48–1984).

10 9 8 7 6 5 4 3 2 1

Contents

Acknowledgments

The editors gratefully acknowledge the help of the following individuals in the early and late stages of the preparation of this book: Rebecca Trainor, Aaron Nitzkin, Marcy Haynes, and Nicole Simpson. Thanks also to Nichole Stanford for her tireless proofreading. Of course, without the aid of the editors at Praeger Publishers—George Butler, A & B Typesetters and Editorial Services—and the authors whose work composes this anthology, this book would not have been possible. Thanks to all of you for contributing to our project.

Introduction

Farhat Iftekharrudin

Sociopolitical changes in the middle of the twentieth century provided the impetus for the emergence of an assortment of philosophical statements gathered together under the rubric "postmodernism." The affluence that followed World War II, causing the Western societies to become the power centers of the world, gave rise to rigid standards of conformity, technological advances, and a global economy by means of which the West sought social, cultural, philosophical, economic, and political conformity. Standardization was given priority over multiplicity until the demands of Western society came to dominate the world, overtly overshadowing the less affluent nations.

As modernism itself was a movement counter to Romanticism and a revolt against the prudishness of the Victorian period, postmodernism is a challenge to the rigidity of form, systems, and codes imposed by modernism. Postmodernism challenged existing modes of thought, economic ideology, and political assertions. The whole notion that modernity reflected the "real" was subject to investigation, which led to a new worldview—that oppressive modern conditions existed as a result of linguistic control and an adherence to a biased world history.

In *The Postmodern Condition: A Report on Knowledge* (1984), Jean-François Lyotard states that "the games of scientific knowledge became the games of the rich, in which whoever is wealthiest has the best chance of being right" (45). Thus, in the capitalistic modern world, cognition rather than acquisition becomes a commercial affirmation. That is, the financial ability to provide or acquire is the litmus test for cognitive legitimacy in the modern world. Lyotard asserts that "capitalism inherently possesses the power to derealise familiar objects, social roles, and institutions to such a degree that the so-called realistic representation can no longer evoke reality except as nostalgia or mockery" (143). Jean Baudrillard echoes Lyotard in "Simulacra and Simulations" where he states that "when the real is no longer what it used to be, nostalgia assumes its full meaning" (153). Baudrillard's claim is that the power base behind Western modernity is its insistence on the real in order to "convince us of the reality of the social, of the gravity of the economy and the finalities of production" (158). Once the populace is thus convinced, he continues, affluent nations can then suppress all other independent thoughts or behaviors. Baudrillard points out that when this concept of the "real" is threatened, the whole power base of modern capitalism is threatened.

Baudrillard argues that in order to maintain its power base, the highly technological industrial West continuously reinforces the "real" through the media and simulations. At the moment of simulation, reality loses its footing. Baudrillard contends that when "power risks the real, risks crisis, it gambles on remanufacturing artificial, social, economic, political stakes" (158). This reaction results not in maintaining the "real" but embarking on the "hyper real":

[W]hat society seeks through production, and over production, is the restoration of the real which escapes it. That is why contemporary "material" production is itself hyper real [*sic*]. It retains all the features, the whole discourse of traditional production, but it is nothing more than its scaled-down refraction. . . . Thus the hyperrealism of simulation is expressed everywhere by the real's striking resemblance to itself. (159)

In Baudrillard's postmodern world, it is "impossible to isolate the process of the real, or to prove the real" (157), thus blurring the line between the real and the simulated. Hyperreality takes over making the simulated the real. In such a postmodern condition, the clearly defined structures and demarcations created by capitalism, those defined by economic affluence, dissipate, leaving behind an uncentered, uncontrolling structure.

Unlike Baudrillard's postmodern theory erasing the distinctions between the real and the unreal, eradicating the boundaries resulting from capitalism, Michel Foucault's social theory addresses the suppressive nature of capitalistic power, which leads to marginalization and exclusion. Foucault argues that power and knowledge in the modern world have produced a method of subjugation where man, instead of being the subject, has become the object. Through his social analysis Foucault claims that his purpose is to "create a history of the different modes by which, in our culture, human beings are made subjects" (qtd. in Best and Kellner 36). Foucault's claim is that modernity with all its overt depiction of order and growth does not equate to historical progress: "Humanity does not gradually progress from combat to combat until it arrives at universal reciprocity, where the rule of law finally replaces war-fare; humanity instills each of its violence in a system of rules and thus proceeds from domination to domination" (151).

Undeniably, the modern worldview has resulted in significant progress, particularly in the field of science and technology, and capitalistic structures have provided the financial resources to sustain scientific advancements and have proven more successful than other forms of structures, such as communism. However, social theorists like Lyotard, Baudrillard, and Foucault point to the attendant vice that is also associated with capitalistic growth which, they argue, is the subjugation and domination of nations and cultures that have trailed behind or are unable to acquire a capitalistic mode. As a result, less affluent nations, in order to survive economically, must adhere to or even adopt Western ideologies (both political and social) thus sacrificing their own social order, culture, and language.

Although the grand objective of modernity is the equalization of power and knowledge through a strong economic system, some postmodernists argue that the system itself created a society in which male hegemony runs rampant. In that sense, in capitalistic nations themselves, there are populations that are marginalized, particularly all females of all colors, ethnic populations such as African Americans and Hispanics in the United States, indigenous people such as native Indians in the United States or Aborigines in Australia, individuals or organizations that fail to adhere to mainstream ideas or expectations, the uneducated, and others.

Unlike Lyotard and Baudrillard's social theories that consider postmodernism a deterrent to the underlying tyranny of Western industrialization, postmodern theorist Fredric Jameson's social theory suggests a less radical approach. He views postmodernism as an evolutionary product of a capitalistic society. In his 1983 essay "Postmodernism and Consumer Society," Jameson asserts that "radical breaks between periods do not generally involve complete changes of content, [but] rather the restructuring of a certain number of elements already given: features that in an earlier period or system were subordinate now become dominant, and features that had been dominant again become secondary" (177). This form of mediatory postmodernism may or may not solve the problem of marginalization that Foucault maintained was the outcome of capitalism, but it suggested no radical break from modernity itself.

In his 1971 book titled *The Dismemberment of Orpheus: Toward a Postmodern Literature*, Ihab Hassan also addresses the oppressive underpinnings of modernity, but the discussion moves from the social to the literary. Ihab Hassan points to a literary crisis that manifests itself through negativity and silence: "The negative . . . informs silence; and silence is my metaphor of a language that expresses, with harsh and subtle cadences, the stress in art, culture, and consciousness. The crisis is modern and postmodern, urgent and continuous" (12).

In defining his metaphor "Silence," Hassan states that it "refers to an avant-garde tradition of literature"; "silence implies alienation from reason, society, and history"; and "silence requires the periodic subversion of forms . . . resulting in anti-forms [that] oppose control, closure . . . and historic pattern" (13). In a sense this "avant-garde" literary reaction balances the control over form that modernity produced.

Like Hassan's theories, Jacques Derrida's theory of donnée (deconstruction) had great influence on the developing postmodern literary theory. Derrida, like most poststructuralists, questions the validity of a centering culture or language or of a totalizing structure. In his essay "Structure, Sign, and Play in the Discourse of Human Sciences," Derrida states that

even today the notion of a structure lacking any center represents the unthinkable itself. Nevertheless, the center also closes off the play which it opens up and makes possible. As center, it is the point at which the substitution of contents, elements, or terms is no longer possible [. . .]. Thus [. . .] the center, which is by definition unique, constituted that very thing within a structure which while governing the structure, escapes structurality. This is why classical thought concerning structure could say that the center is, paradoxically, within the structure and outside it. The center is at the center of the totality, and yet, since the center does not belong to the totality [. . .] the totality has its center elsewhere. The center is not the center. (109)

This philosophical thesis suggests the abandonment of a binding form, of a totalizing ideology. Derrida's theory opposes structuralist notions that stress language phenomenon through social or linguistic structures that adhere to a system of codes or rules. Poststructuralists, like Derrida, focus on the signifier over the signified. In his *Speech and Phenomena, and Other Essays on Husserl's Theory of Signs* (1973), Derrida argues the "indefinite" referentiality of "signifier to signified." He asserts that because of the "infinite implication" of "meaning of meaning," the meaning of the signified "always signifies again and differs"

(58). This endless loop (of signifier to signified back to signifier and signified and so on) disrupts modernist concepts of acquiring knowledge, and assigning meaning, for the written word in the text (the signifier) does not necessarily correlate to the signified. In this process of deconstruction, meaning within a text is infinite. The sociopolitical result of poststructuralist theory is the disappearance of the modernist "center" or "standard" or even the "subject."

Roland Barthes addresses the decentering of the subject in "From Work to Text" in *Textual Strategies* (1979) where he defines *text* as a "social space that leaves no language safe or untouched, that allows no enunciative subject to hold the position of judge, teacher, analyst, confessor, or decoder" (81). In his essay, "The Death of the Author," Barthes reiterates that "writing is that mental composite, oblique space where our subject slips away" (168). He further claims that in "leaving aside literature itself . . . linguistics has . . . provided the destruction of the Author. . . . Linguistically, the Author is never more than the instance of writing, just as *I* is nothing other than the instance saying *I*" (169). Barthes argues that without the author, texts become free of the limitations of the author's own past or ideologies. Thus, without the presence of the author, texts acquire multitudinous meanings.

Postmodernism is a complex entity that encompasses a wide range of philosophical, social, linguistic, and literary interests and attracts a variety of practitioners including social theorists, poststructuralists, and psychoanalysts. However, the combined viewpoints and theories, and the new vocabularies, create difficulties in the matter of definition. Ihab Hassan in *PARACRITICISM: Seven Speculations of the Times* states "I have not defined Modernism; I can define Postmodernism less" (54), but he tried: "Postmodernism may be a response, direct or oblique, to the unimaginable which Modernism glimpsed only in its prophetic moments. . . . We are . . . inhabitants of another time and another space, and we no longer know what response is adequate to our reality" (53). Postmodernism is a reaction, whether social or political, to the strictures imposed by modernism. In the literary arena, this reaction manifests itself in diverse forms. Postmodernist theories and texts, at the fundamental level, have adhered to heterogeneity as opposed to homogeneity, a set of uniform structures and forms on which modernity thrives. Postmodernism questions the whole process of acquiring knowledge, how we know what we know. Its assertion has been that a social, economic, political, and even literary crisis created by modernists' strict adherence to rules, systems, and forms exists that can no longer be addressed by the very rules, systems, and forms that created the crisis. The "center" that dictates the totality no longer holds and thus cannot be a reliable process for growth in human consciousness.

A close inquiry into the promise of modernity, that of a homogeneous society that is socioeconomically or sociopolitically balanced, reveals to the postmodernist a disheartening picture. There are serious gaps, some impossible to bridge, between the affluent and the economically deprived. This breech is not limited only to capital; it has resulted, globally, in depriving the less powerful of equal political voice, equal opportunities, and equal cultural recognition. Countries have actually become more fragmented, more cynical, more violent as their people seek answers through mockery, parody, and self-reflexivity, and fall back on indigenous cultures, beliefs, myths, and languages to make sense of current conditions and also to redefine themselves in terms of their own history and not in terms of the history depicted by modernism. Postmodern literary works are marked by this fragmentation, parody, and self-reflexivity. They are works that seek to redefine indigenous histories that create different realities counter to the accepted realities of the Western world that has no place, say, for magical realism because it defies logic and is not grounded in science. Postmodern works range from extreme textual reduction to prolific excess, a mockery against form.

Malcolm Bradbury in the *Modern American Novel* states that in the fiction of the sixties "history is seen not as a haunting progress, but as a landscape of lunacy and pain; the doubting of a rational and intelligent history leads to a mocking of the world's substance, a sense of inner psychic disorder, a cartooning of character, a fantasizing of so-called 'facts' or actualities, and a comic denominalization" (158). Bradbury further observed that one direction in which fiction moved was "towards fantastic factuality, attempting to penetrate the fictionality of the real" (158).

In "The Literature of Exhaustion," John Barth provides a definition for the aesthetics of postmodern fiction when he explains that writers faced "the used-upness of certain forms or exhaustion of certain possibilities" (29). His own groundbreaking work *Lost in the Funhouse* seems to provide an alternative to this problem of "used-upness" or "exhaustion of . . . possibilities." In the "Author's Note," Barth defines his fiction: "It's neither a collection, nor a selection, but a series . . . meant to be received 'all at once' and as here arranged" (xi). *Lost in the Funhouse* is an attempt to make "something new and valid" (109). In that vein, the first story, "Frame-Tale," immediately challenges all standard forms of fiction. It is a construct, bearing one incomplete sentence—"once upon a time there was a story that began"—printed so that it could be cut out and twisted to form a Möbius strip, thus giving the story not just a "one-, two-, or three-dimensional" feature as Barth suggests, but an endlessness of form and thought. To Barth, the major issue is "how an artist may paradoxically turn the felt ultimacies of our own time into material and means for his own work" ("Literature" 32).

Kurt Vonnegut's fiction of the 1960s demonstrates another way to approach what Barth calls "felt ultimacies of our times." Vonnegut's intentions are to reorder our perceptions of life and of the world and reevaluate our basis for meaning. In *Slaughterhouse Five*, Vonnegut reveals his concept of fictional form by means of the Tralfamadorian notion that all time is continuously and eternally present. This concept of time runs counter to the modern concept of the linearity of history. The description of the form of the Tralfamadorian text is of course Vonnegut's attempt to describe his own work and that of contemporaries like Donald Barthelme and Richard Brautigan. Jerome Klinkowitz makes the point in *The American 1960s: Imaginative Acts in a Decade of Change* that fragmentation in Vonnegut's works, "defying all traditional conventions and existing outside the continuum of linear time, is nothing other than [his] description of the appropriate form for fiction in the American 1960s" (57–58).

Donald Barthelme plays a mathematical game of permutation and combination with language. His primary concern is the way that language is used to enforce the way in which his works are to be read. Using techniques of deletion and various combinational forms of language and words themselves, Barthelme represents the fragmentary nature of our postmodern lives. His stories like "Robert Kennedy Saved from Drowning" and "Views of My Father Weeping" are, as Jerome Klinkowitz observed, "composed of Tralfamadorian-like 'clumps'— independent paragraphs whose principle of relation is more spatial than linear, because their effect depends upon the longer and wider view of the reader who considers them all at once, rather than in a sequential order building to a point" (59). For Barthelme, structure was the key to ultimate realities, and since fiction is composed of words, his focus was almost lexical. Klinkowitz's observation that "fiction breeds its own continuity" (*Disruptions* 1) clearly defines the structural pattern of Barthelme's works, for Barthelme employs structures, phrases, and words from contemporary diction and arranges them in the fragments that form the collages that create his new fiction: "The principle of collage," Barthelme explains, "is the central principle of all art in the twentieth century in all media" (15). And in a 1974 interview, he spoke with specific reference to fiction: "the point of collage is that unlike things are stuck together to make, in the best case, a new reality. This new reality, in the best case, may be or imply a comment on the other reality from which it came, and may also be much else. It's an *itself*" (qtd. in Bellamy 51–52). It is this "stuck together" form that gives his works their characteristic fragmentary appearance. The words of one of his own characters are closely associated with the approach of Barthelme himself: "Here is the word and here are the knowledge knowers knowing. What can I tell you? What has been pieced together from the reports of travelers. Fragments are the only forms I trust. Look at my walls, it's all there" ("See the Moon" 169). Through such an approach, Barthelme was able to capture successfully the fragments of contemporary American life. Barthelme's "fragments" and Vonnegut's "Tralfamadorian clumps" are characteristics of American postmodern fiction. These authors achieved continuity within their works primarily through the exploitation of language and through spatial rather than linear connections between each segment of their work. This form of fictional innovation is characteristic not only of the writing of the well-known Barthelme and Vonnegut, but also of many others, including, notably, Richard Brautigan, whose stories I emphasize here.

In 1964, a small magazine *Kulcher* in its spring issue gave Brautigan his first national exposure by publishing one of his short stories, "The Post Offices of Eastern Oregon." This short story reveals several of Brautigan's techniques that were to become central to the writer's art, such as synthesizing basic fancies with elegant poetic images. "Post Offices of Eastern Oregon" is about a little boy out for a day's hunting with his uncle. As they pass an old farmhouse the reader encounters the first of multiple images as he describes the empty house as "abandoned like a musical instrument"; and immediately following that another of the woodpile as "the color of years" (91). And when the boy and the uncle stop to look at a couple of dead bear on the front porch of an old house, the narrator informs us that "the house had wooden frosting all around the edges. It was a birthday cake from a previous century. Like candles we were going to stay there for the night" (93). It is not simply Brautigan's image-making power that supercharges the story; it is also the uniqueness of the images. Klinkowitz defines a typical Brautigan image as "a thought cast in such unfamiliar shape that no one in the straight culture could be expected to think of it first" (*American* 42). The images are startling poetic products and also vehicles of extension. Brautigan's narrative form is characterized by such extended images. The story itself is generated (or perhaps regenerated), as the narrator informs us, from an image, "a photograph in the newspaper of Marilyn Monroe, dead from a sleeping pill suicide" ("Post Offices" 96). There are multiple extensions here: a process of actual images creating a series of mental associations—news of the death of the recollection of dead bear to the recollection of a nude image of Marilyn Monroe on an Oregon post office wall to hunting in the Oregon countryside. Such mental associations lead to a reduction in narrative, a postmodern stylistic approach that operates on the theory that since life in the present culture is nonlinear and fragmentary, fiction can best reflect that life by breaking from the traditional linearity of narrative and moving to the nonlinear and the fragmentary.

In Brautigan's *Revenge of the Lawn* several stories exhibit a postmodern self-conscious construction of narrative. "The Literary Life in California/1964" contains a narrator who, after observing the indecisiveness of a book buyer, retrieves the buyer's "reluctance" off the floor. In a startling image the "reluctance" becomes a claylike object, slipping and sliding, but with sufficient substance that the narrator is able to take it home with him and shape it into a story. Then there are other stories that are purely metaphysical in experience such as "Blackberry Motorist," where blackberries for jam turn into black diamonds. Brautigan's castle here is a blackberry patch where pickers can plummet fifteen feet down. An initial innocence turns dark; a simple experience of picking blackberries for pies turns into a painful reminder of a lost era, where recapturing that which is lost requires an out-of-body experience.

In his stories Brautigan portrays age-old themes of human alienation, social envy, broken dreams, and loneliness in completely new presentations. "The Revenge of the Lawn" is a hilarious, yet dark and horrifying, account of the overbearing nature of human violence. The juxtaposition of the lack of emotion on the part of the narrator, a grandson, against the spontaneity of the violence he recounts creates the disturbing picture of how twentieth-century humanity has become anesthetized by violence. The grandson relates the story of his grandfather, a minor mystic, who prophesizes the exact date when World War I would start: June 28, 1914, but the prophecy was too much for him, and he was put in the state asylum, where he spent seventeen years believing he was six years old. The grandmother, a bootlegger, then takes a lover, Jack, who stays for thirty years. This lover is bent on destroying the front yard that the grandfather so lovingly nurtured, a place that is the origin of the grandfather's powers. Jack hates the front yard and curses it. The yard, turned barren by neglect, fights back, finding nails to place under the tires on his car, sinking the car during a rainy season, and using bees as allies to force Jack into twice driving his car into the side of the house.

In another story Brautigan uses violence or death to measure human failures. "The World War I Los Angeles Airplane" opens with the word *dead*. From there the narrator catalogs in numerical order (1 through 33) the entire life of the dead man, his wife's father. The structure of the story is a complete break from modernist standards of form. But reading the story reveals that the cataloging is a necessary component stressing the absurdity of the current human condition. The story is a study in human failure, every success followed by a greater failure. At the age of fifty-nine, the construction company Jack works for fires him from his bookkeeping job because he is too old and, they say, it is time to turn him out to pasture. The failures and disillusionment of an immigrant parent ironically runs counter to a basic American concept that defines the country as the land of opportunities. Stories like "The Revenge of the Lawn" or "The World War I Los Angeles Airplane" are postmodern in form, but they are not games of artifice; they are mirrors reflecting certain realities told with a sense of innocence that is frightening: "Always at the end of the words somebody is dead" (170). Brautigan's appeal lies in his ability to capture a basic vulnerability, to encapsulate a nakedness and transform that into sad burlesque.

Almost anything becomes a story in Brautigan's hands, and sometimes his stories may appear to be whimsical, but they are not; there is always a context and a degree of complexity. Take for instance "The Scarlatti Tilt," complete in two sentences: "It's very hard to live in a studio apartment in San Jose with a man who's learning to play the violin." That's what she told the police when she handed them the empty revolver (50). Through sheer economy of language, Brautigan captures a representative social insanity; "The Scarlatti Tilt" works as narrative only because it is a microcosmic embodiment of twentieth-century intolerance and social ennui. "The Gathering of a Californian," a slightly longer piece, acquires its completeness from the same economy of language. The opening and closing paragraphs of this story are only two sentences that capture first the suffocating and impersonal quality of California and, second, the dehumanization of those drawn into California. Synaesthetic similes make this compact and complete story larger than the half page it physically occupies. The entire collection is strewn with such synaesthetic images: "The door was tall, silent, and human like a middle-aged woman" ("1962 Cotton Mather Newsreel" 17); "There was the jar of instant coffee, the empty cup and the spoon all laid out like a funeral service" ("Coffee" 35); and "I smelled like the complete history of America" ("The Auction" 123). The subtle wit involved in these and other images soften the harshness of the anger, the pain, and the loss that permeates these stories. The epiphanic summation of these vignettes points to the failure within the system itself.

Writing counter to the conventional form, Brautigan creates a new dimension for his fiction, and that dimension belies rational order. Thus, the reader has to find cohesion in his stories through imaginative discourse. This is Brautigan's new aesthetic—spontaneous fiction that expands the vision and the experience through multiplicity, synaesthetic similes, juxtaposition of images, and extraordinary metaphors. Although his fictional form veers from the traditional, his thematic concerns on the whole do not. Of course, how far any author stretches from the conventional depends on where one sets the bounds. Brautigan's major deviation, like those of his contemporaries, is in the area of form—especially plot lines. Using the synthesizing power of the imagination Brautigan intends to create a "modern text, dissolving old natural narrative" (Klinkowitz, *American* 44). Bradbury stresses the point that Brautigan writes about the

ironizing of the world, the waning of pastoral myths of innocence and of escape from social constriction into nature; he shows the power of old images and then of the endeavors of the imagination to dissolve them, both through the struggle of his fictional outsiders, and of the poetic imagination itself. If the world wanes, the writer's exuberant comic imagination thrives; form in its collapse promises recovery, the fixities of time, space, and ideology dissolve. (170)

What evolves is a revitalized form of the genre itself where the reader comes to grips with the idea that Brautigan's works do not simply mirror life and that they are not pseudorealistic documents. They are serious commentaries on the decline of social, moral, and political values, a decline that is a serious threat to the American dream.

A major contribution to postmodern literature comes also from magic realists like Isabel Allende and Salman Rushdie. Under the umbrella of magic realism, Allende addresses the hegemony of patriarchal society. In her works, matriarchy assumes its primordial dominance. Octavio Paz in reflecting on the status of the woman in Mexican culture wrote "En efecto, toda mujer, aun la que se da voluntariamente, es desgarrada, chingada por el hombre [In essence, all women, including those who offer themselves voluntarily, are forced open, *fucked* by men]" (63; emphasis added). What is shocking about this statement is that such a viewpoint regarding females is not restricted to the women of Mexico; it is nearly universal. In a less abrasive language, Simone de Beauvoir's description of the "privileged other" renders a similar sentiment. Such pervasive social attitudes, of course, have influenced, controlled, and defined all aspects of male/female relationships in the male dominant modern period. The politics that engendered male hegemony has and continues to denigrate the female. However, postmodern emphasis on revaluating history, politics, and culture, and taking into account the disenfranchised and the marginalized is reflected in literature. Authors like Allende have challenged and subverted the patriarchal hegemony. Allende's women accomplish what Hélène Cixous recommended in "The Laugh of the Medusa," for not only do they put themselves into text, but they also involve their bodies; thus they transpose the male/female order with women becoming the powerful self as opposed to the privileged other. In this reconfiguration, the male becomes the *chingado* (the fucked).

In Allende's novel *The House of the Spirits*, Clara refuses her husband Esteban Trueba access to her womanhood; patriarchal authority dissipates with this single act of denial from Clara. The ease with which Clara dislodges male dominance and control is grounded in an archetypal act of seduction: Eve dislodged all of mankind from the Garden of Eden. That event, quite ironically but also quiet correctly termed "the Fall," is the precursor of all female politics: social, sexual, and religious. Allende's females take full advantage of their ancient, untold, innate ability, and conduct their affairs with an eerie dexterity. The female protagonists in Allende's *The Stories of Eva Luna* derive their indomitable strength from this innate, archetypal signature. Their politics of seduction involve both language and body and appear to derive from universal female genetic markers that trigger their dexterity in usurping manhood. Allende's women successfully reverse the male/female roles and thus render the male a shadow; consequently, the male becomes defined in terms of the nominative female. Belisa Crepusculario of the opening story entitled "Two Words" is keenly aware of the politics of both female body and word. Belisa went by that name "not because she had been baptized with that name . . . but because she herself . . . searched until she found the poetry of 'beauty' and 'twilight' and cloaked herself in it" (9).

Female politics emerges in the very first sentence of the collection. Belisa in naming herself creates her own beginning, and in refusing a baptismal name, in part denies the male a role in that beginning. She also "made her living selling words" a vital political tool:

For five centavos she delivered verses from memory; for seven she improved the quality of dreams; for nine she wrote love letters; for twelve she invented insults for irreconcilable enemies. She also sold stories, not fantasies, but long, true stories. . . . To anyone who paid her fifty centavos in trade, she gave the gift of a secret word to drive away melancholy. It was not the same word for everyone, naturally, because that would have been collective deceit. Each person received his or her own word, with the assurance that no one else would use it that way in this universe or beyond. (10)

The politics of words is so effective that her audience often traveled vast distances for the words that Belisa procured by sheer acclamation. Belisa Crepuscalario represents the tenacity and resiliency of not just words, but what words become in the possession of a female. The subtle politics embedded in this story emerge when Belisa as representative female declares ownership of words and, consequently, it renders the looming male incompetent. The colonel in the story comes to her with a declaration "I want to be President. . . . [S]ell me the words for a speech" (14–15). He needs words to win an election because he did not want to "gallop up to the Palace, and take over the government, the way [he] had taken so many other things without anyone's permission" (15). He wanted to alter the fact that "men fled at the sight of him, children trembled, and women miscarried from fright . . . so he decided to become President" (15). Besides the obvious political satire involved, the underlying suggestion is of greater note, which is that men "gallop" and possess "without permission." However this phallic tyranny that resonates throughout patriarchal society, as the story seems to suggest, is short-lived because every masculine threat, every possession, and every usurpation is a metaphorical ejaculation, subject to being *spent*.

The political substructures of "Two Words" reveal that the woman is central to revitalization, before and after ejaculation, particularly if the male is a tyrant. The Colonel cannot win the presidency without words, words that he must procure from a woman. In fact, Belisa Crepuscalario accepted her assignment not because of her fear of the Colonel, but because she was afraid that "the Colonel would burst into tears" if she declined. In this unflattering transformation of the Colonel from tyrant to a teary-eyed infant lies the female political "rub," the reversal of roles where man becomes dependent on woman. Belisa Crepuscalario is cognizant of that role as she

searched her repertory for words adequate for a presidential speech. . . . She discarded harsh, cold words, words that were too flowery, words worn from abuse, words that offered improbable promises, untruthful and confusing words, until all she had left were words sure to touch the winds of men and woman's intuition. (15–16)

Once again, the internal politics of the Allende story involves a blunt criticism of masculine language usage set forth in an absence-is-presence mode. In this case, however, it is the male gender that is present through deliberate exclusion. Thus, Belisa's actual political commentary focuses on what the male is as a result of his language usage: "harsh," "cold," and often useless because "flowery." Male political leaders also make "improbable promises" and "confuse" their audiences because they are incapable of touching human intuition. Therefore, it is the female who must equip the male with words of grace, intuition, and success. In actuality, then, when the Colonel speaks, Belisa is doing the speaking. In fact, the Colonel has to memorize the winning speech because he cannot read. The Colonel is illiterate, and his right-hand man, his chief adviser, is a lascivious mulato "who could not take his eyes from [Belisa's] firm wanderer's legs and virginal breasts" (15). The satire directed at patriarchal Latin American politics (and by extension all politics) is obvious; however, most of the political game that is played out in "Two Words" is cloaked in subtlety. Belisa charges the Colonel one peso for the speech, which includes the gift of two words "for his exclusive use." These two words, however, actually complete the female triumph and assert themselves as the dominant force.

The concept of the female body as an integral part of female language is prevalent throughout *The Stories of Eva Luna*. In the story "Clarisa," the protagonist by the same name, is a "miracle worker." Her miraculous works are unpredictable: "she does not heal the blind like Santa Lucia, or find husbands for spinsters, like St. Anthony" (42) but "she had a boundless understanding of human weakness" (46). Clarisa was a true politician with connections. She "knew people of note, women of breeding, wealthy businessmen, bankers, and public figures, whom she visited seeking aid for the needy, with never a thought of how she might be received" (47–48). With her verbal powers and "irrefutable logic" she "obtained scholarships for young artists from the Jesuits, used clothing for neighborhood prostitutes from the League of Catholic Dames, musical instruments for a Hebrew choir from the German Institute, and funds for alcohol rehabilitation programs from viticulturists" (48). And when her judge husband failed to produce two normal children in her, Clarisa helped herself by fornicating with Congressman Diego Cienfuegos "known for his incendiary speeches and for being one of the few incorruptible politicians in the nation" (48). This illicit relationship produced two boys. "'These two boys will grow up healthy and help me take care of their [mentally retarded] brother and sister,' she said with conviction, faithful to her theory of compensation" (99). Female language and body as inseparable components become powerful political tools as Clarisa uses them in conjunction to "procure a new modern refrigerator" and also to procure two healthy children for herself. The absolute ease with which Clarisa corrupts the incorruptible congressman is the power of sexual politics that men are destined to lose. Clarisa who has "boundless understanding of human weakness" is consciously and instinctually aware of this primordial sexual superiority. She, like Belisa Crepusculario, is also aware of the transformative power of words particularly as they use them to interact with their male counterparts. In certain stories like "Toad's Mouth" the female language is entirely the female body, which is used as a political text to gain superiority over the all-assuming male. Hermelinda in this story builds a profitable enterprise on an island of sheepherders by designing a game of Toad's Mouth where a man can easily lose his entire month's income:

Hermelinda would draw a circle [and] lay down on her back, knees spread wide. . . . The dark center of her body would be revealed as open as a fruit, as a merry toad's mouth. . . . The players took position behind the chalk line and tossed their coin toward the target. Some were expert marksmen . . . but Hermelinda had an evasive way of sliding her body, shifting it so that at the last instant the coin missed the mark. Those that landed inside the chalk circle belonged to her. [The award was] two hours alone with her behind the curtain in absolute ecstasy, seeking consolation for all past wants. . . . The men who lived those two precious hours, [said] that Hermelinda knew ancient love secrets and could lead a man to the threshold of death and bring him back transformed into a wise man. (63–64)

Seduction is perhaps the ultimate politics of the female body, the continuous "leading" of the man. Hermelinda, like Clarisa and Belisa Crepusculario, is "presence," and this presence is undeniable as it is associated with irresistible "ancient" female sexuality, a definite weakness for heterosexual males.

In *The Stories of Eva Luna*, females like Hermelinda, Clarisa, and Belisa Crepusculario are self-created individuals and entrepreneurs. The ease with which they assert and control their reality that leads to their immediate success threatens and confuses male hegemony. The textual politics of this collection is that these females, besides being the "presence" themselves, appear as representative females who subvert and parody a masculine world order.

In all of the short stories in *East, West: Stories* (1994), Salman Rushdie compresses the multitudinous levels of narrative for which his novels are famous. In each story, multiple realities function simultaneously, complicating the process of linear comprehension. The central themes in Rushdie's stories appear to be the inalienable rights of man in the face of social and religious taboos, cultural biases, and political agendas. In many of Rushdie's stories it is often difficult to locate these themes because the central ideas emerge often as refracted realities in parallel worlds. The versatility with which he captures a singular moment in each of the stories in *East, West* is a result of his dexterity with language itself. By infusing the English language, at the precise moment, with the dialectal variants of Asian immigrants, Rushdie has forged a new language that requires etymological reconfiguration to comprehend not only his texts but also the characters that inherit them: Postmodernism is Rushdie's umbrella and in telling his stories in this mode he creates myths both magical and real. *East, West: Stories* is a collection of nine stories grouped under three sections: East; West; and East, West. These divisions are superficial separations only. The stories of the East are also about the West. Those grouped under East, West are at once about both and neither.

The first story "Good Advice is Rarer than Rubies" under the section East focuses on a peripheral corrupt industry that has germinated around the British consulate which embodies its own indigenous form of corruption. The central issue is immigration and a British passport that is imperative. The applicants who crowd the British consulate on Tuesdays are uneducated women who live on the verge of poverty; they are the "Tuesday women" (5). To these women, the passport officials at the British consulate are the impediment to their perceived sense of freedom and affluence. The trivial questions they ask parody the absurdity and overintrusive nature of British investigation whose intent is to arrive at the truth. However, the system is a failure and the result is the birth of a black market industry for British passports, which is ironically an industry of exploitation itself, a mocking mirror of the system it intends to subvert through characters like Muhammed Ali, a gray-haired fraud, who classifies himself as proficient in giving advice and specializes in providing false British passports for poor women who pay him with their life savings. These women come from hundreds of miles away, a fact he has made sure of so that when they discover they have been tricked they are unlikely to return. Muhammed Ali, uneducated and poor himself, has found his own source of affluence in these women who are victims of the Western imperialistic system that discriminates against aspiring immigrants. Muhammed Ali's rationalization of his trade shows a parasitic side of the economically disadvantaged. He tells himself that he must live by his wits and so rationalizes away any compassion he might have for the women he swindles.

Into this malignant world enters Rehana, an *ayah* (a nanny in Western terms without similar wages or human rights), seeking a British passport. Rehana with her youth, beauty, and independence is the hopeful antidote in this degenerate circle of corruption. She deliberately mishandles her interview with the passport official choosing dignity over perversion.

The story "The Free Radio" also involves individuals who are uneducated and economically strapped, particularly the protagonist, a young rickshaw puller, who manages a living through sweat and grind; however, when he dares to dream, his desires do not comfortably package themselves to meet the conformities of society, economics, or politics. Ramani, the rickshaw-wallah, following his passion falls in love with a thief's widow with five children. He thus exceeds his own economic abilities as well as violates a multifaceted cultural taboo that disallows association with a female of a questionable background or an affair with a widow, particularly one with children. The tragicomic tone of the story is set in the opening observation of the narrator: "the boy was an innocent, a real donkey's child, you can't teach such people" (19). These qualifiers serve not only to describe the general, large, uneducated and uneducable population of the Indian subcontinent, but also serve as foreshadowing and irony. Ramani's innocence represents not only sexual innocence, but also political innocence. He acquiesces to the widow's demands that he not add to the existing five children and agrees to a vasectomy, which draws him into the political claws of the government. Residents of the Indian subcontinent (because of their actual experience or knowledge of the incident) can readily recognize the multiple levels of irony in Ramani's situation. With the promise of a free radio that never arrives, the Indian government actually performs countless numbers of vasectomies on not only "innocents" like Ramani, but also the poor elderly who can hardly contribute to the overpopulation of India. The government accomplished this task with the aid of thugs wearing "arm bands of the new youth movement" (22), a further irony. These ironies multiply almost endlessly and contribute to the tragedy of countries known to the Western world as Third World nations. The most tragic irony is that the "vasectomy" that renders Ramani impotent also represents the impotence of a government that has failed in its economic and educational plans for the country.

Ironies in this story move the plot along into postmodern realities. Ramani, who never gets the radio, imagines the radio into existence by cupping his hand over his ears and yelling out the news from All India Radio as he peddles the streets: "All the energy of his young body was being poured into that fictional space between his ear and his hand, and he was trying to bring the radio into existence by a mighty, and possibly fatal, act of will" (28). It is this same act of will that enables Ramani to escape into another reality, a romantic world, a conjured Bombay, to become a film star. Ironically and tragically, he attempts to replace his own sterilization with another sterile world, one that does not exist.

The story "Yorick" is a postmodern patchwork of fiction and drama. Beginning with an observation on the human elemental need to destroy, the story moves to a rewriting of *Hamlet* employing both Elizabethan language and Lawrence Sterne punctuation (dashes and asterisks). In this tour de force, Sterne's parson Yorick marries Ophelia and later kills the King of Denmark when he fornicates with Ophelia. Claudius detects the crime and executes Yorick. Yorick as ghost visits Hamlet and convinces him that Claudius is guilty of fratricide. Hamlet kills Claudius, mistreats his own Ophelia because "his cracking brain confuses her with the unbearable memory of the Fool's—foully odorous wife," and finally dies from a drink of poison himself. "Yorick" is a postmodern pastiche of parody, word games, and merged literary allusions. The story introduces Yorick's saga as having begun when the ancient text came into the possession of "Tristram, who . . . was neither triste nor ram, the frothiest, most heady Shandy of a fellow" (64). The game ends with the subtitle of *Tristram Shandy* stating that "such a cock-and-bull story is by this last confession brought quite to its conclusion" (83).

Entirely self-reflexive in form, "Yorick" is also self-critical as it parodies sixteenth- and eighteenth-century texts. The story's narrator is a jester merging with Yorick the court jester and ultimately with Rushdie the arch jester. However, Rushdie's humor is, as always, a cloak that is the key that unlocks the meaning of the story. Thus, "Yorick" is also a parable, for the plight of migrants as the following passage reveals:

All cats will look at kings; but to gaze upon a monarch is to place one's life in their hands; and lives held in such hands do often slip through fingers and are spilled. Now, Hamlet, count the spaces on your hands, I mean 'twixt finger and finger, and finger and finger, and finger and finger, and finger and thumb. On two hands, count eight chasms through which a life may fall. Only nine lives will ensure that one at least remain; and so our cat, king-watching, must have nine. (69–70)

The "cryptic key" ultimately unlocks Rushdie's own predicament: "I can no longer keep the great World from my pages, for what ended in Tragedy began in Politics. (Which [is a] small surprise)" (72).

In the second story, "At the Auction of the Ruby Slippers," the auction draws a microcosmic gathering. Present are memorabilia junkies, exiles, political refugees, religious fundamentalists, and even orphans. Here the Auctioneer assesses not so much the value of the ruby slippers as the accounting of the people themselves. Rushdie's postmodern game becomes clearer as each layer of the story gives way to the next and the next in rapid succession. "At the Auction of the Ruby Slippers" is a compilation of sketches illustrating each of the representational groups present. Each sketch is a voyeuristic depiction of absurdities of contemporary affluence-driven, agenda-oriented irrationalities. Exiles emerge from underground dodging bazookas. Political refugees, sporting silk and sequined apparel representing great works of art, appear together with religious fundamentalists. The ruby slippers offer magical resolutions, a panacea of sorts, that bring together diverse groups in "these . . . uncompromising times" (91) where our relativistic universe, becomes a microcosm of contemporary life, and the balance in this world is tenuous and fragile like the ruby slippers. The slippers themselves are the obvious symbol of intangibility, of the unreal, the fictional. For Rushdie the perception of the real world through the fictional is a symptom of our postmillennial culture.

These sketches of contemporary, Western absurdities inevitably point to the central concern of the story (and even of Rushdie himself): finding a home particularly for the émigrés who, like the "jump-suited Latino janitor" of this story, clean up the metaphorical "pools of saliva" around the shrine of the ruby-sequined slippers left behind by the affluence-driven Western culture. Or like the orphans, the untouchables, and the outcasts who come hoping that the ruby slippers will carry them back through time as well as space and reunite them with their dead parents. But the security forces deal with these people brusquely. To the émigrés, "home" is a scattered and damaged concept, so much so that the story raises a series of questions: What price tolerance if the intolerant are not tolerated also? (92) Are metaphors of homeliness comprehensible to them, are abstractions permissible? (93) Are they literalists, or will they permit us to redefine the blessed word? Are we asking, hoping for, too much? (93)

And the response: There is much to yearn for. There are so few rainbows anymore (93). The "they" and "them" in these questions are at once universal, addressing any immigrant and also in particular, addressing only Western countries (and in the case of Rushdie specifically Great Britain). Rushdie points out that in the true sense of "home" of setting roots, there is no place for émigrés. The only security today is "money [which] insists on democracy" (93). Only in that sense is their equality in dreams, and "thanks to the infinite bounty of the Auctioneers, any of us, cat, dog, man, woman, child can be a blueblood; can be—as we long to be; and as, cowering in our shelters, we fear we are not—*somebody*" (103).

East, West: Stories is about Rushdie's "grotesques" whether set in the East or the West. It is also about beliefs that expose human perversion in both Indians and the British. The stories in this collection document the peripatetic journey of Rushdie's nomads, the immigrants who fight an endless battle for recognition, for definition, for equity and balance but in the end remain suspended between the East and the West. Rushdie who revels in the art of nonlinear and fragmented narrative has successfully crafted stories in this collection that at the core embody a complex menagerie of concepts and ideas that trouble, challenge, and sometimes enrage his two audiences: India and Great Britain.

Although postmodern theorists have paid little attention to the short story in itself—likely because they make no genre distinctions in their writings—much of what they say can be applied to the short story, and, just as important, many short story writers have created a postmodern mode for their stories to provide structure and meaning. Postmodern stories are complex in form and content and make use of a variety of styles including parody, self-conscious fictionality, grotesquerie, and fantasy. They are antistories as Mary Rohrberger explains in *Story to Anti-Story* (1979, 7). Through a variety of fictional forms and themes, postmodern writers address historical, moral, and political issues of the late twentieth century. They also draw attention to the language crisis of the times, which has led many postmodern writers to experiment with fragmentation, economy of form and narrative, and also with excess. How we come to know what we know, or think we know, how that knowledge is recorded, and the legitimacy of the system that disseminates that information are central issues in postmodernism. So, postmodern writers and theorists question, on epistemological grounds, the validity of the "real," the authenticity of linear history. With the advancement in technology and the resurgence of sociopolitical awareness in the United States and abroad, the modernist notion of a central guiding principle in politics, economics, and culture needed to shift and change. In addition, with the advent of virtual reality, the line between real and postmodern illusion is hardly discernable. And though many short story writers still work within the modern epiphanic mode, many others have successfully captured a new postmodern avant-garde and translated it into a new aesthetics for literature.

References

Allende, Isabel. *The Stories of Eva Luna*. New York: Bantam, 1992.
Barth, John. "The Literature of Exhaustion." *Atlantic Monthly* Aug. 1967: 29–34.

————. *Lost in the Funhouse*. New York: Doubleday, 1988.

Barthes, Roland. "The Death of the Author." *Modern Criticism and Theory*. Ed. David Lodge. London: Longman, 1988. 167–95.

————. "From Work to Text." *Textual Strategies*. Ed. Josué V. Harari. Ithaca: Cornell UP, 1979. 73–81.

Baudrillard, Jean. "Simulacra and Simulation." *Modernism/Postmodernism*. Ed. Peter Brooker. New York: Longman, 1992. 151–62.

Bellamy, Joe. *The New Fiction: Interviews with Innovative American Writers*. Urbana: U of Illinois P, 1974. 51–52.

————. "See the Moon." *Unspeakable Practices, Unnatural Acts*. New York: Farrar, 1968. 169.

Best, Steven, and Douglas Kellner, eds. *Postmodern Theory: Critical Interrogations*. New York: Guilford, 1991.

Bradbury, Malcolm. *The Modern American Novel*. New York: Oxford UP, 1984.

Brautigan, Richard. *Revenge of the Lawn: Stories 1962–1970*. New York: Simon, 1971.

Derrida, Jacques. "Structure, Sign, and Play in the Discourse of the Human Sciences." *Modern Criticism and Theory*. Ed. David Lodge. London: Longman, 1988. 108–23.

————. *Speech and Phenomena, and Other Essays on Husserl's Theory of Signs*. Evanston: Northwestern UP, 1973.

Foucault, Michel. *Language, Counter-Memory, Practice*. Ithaca: Cornell UP, 1977.

Hassan, Ihab. *The Dismemberment of Orpheus: Toward a Postmodern Literature*. New York: Oxford UP, 1971.

————. *Paracriticisms: Seven Speculations of the Times*. Urbana: U of Illinois P, 1975.

Jameson, Fredric. "Postmodernism and Consumer Society." *Modernism/Postmodernism*. Ed. Peter Brooker. New York: Longman, 1992. 163–79.

Klinkowitz, Jerome. *The American 1960s: Imaginative Acts in a Decade of Change*. Ames: Iowa State UP, 1980.

————. *Literary Disruptions: The Making of a Post-Contemporary American Fiction*. Urbana: U of Illinois P, 1975.

Lyotard, Jean-François. "Answering the Question: What Is Postmodernism?" *Modernism/Postmodernism*. Ed. Peter Brooker. New York: Longman, 1992. 139–50.

————. *The Postmodern Condition: A Report on Knowledge*. Minneapolis: U of Minnesota P, 1984.

Paz, Octavio. *Laberinto de la Soledad*. Mexico: Fondo de Cultura Economica, 1963.

Rohrberger, Mary. *Story to Anti-Story*. Boston: Houghton, 1979.

Rushdie, Salman. *East, West Stories*. New York: Pantheon, 1994.

Schickel, Richard. "Freaked Out on Barthelme." *New York Times Magazine* 16 Aug. 1970: 15.

FICTIONAL NONFICTION AND NONFICTIONAL FICTION

One of the predominant themes of postmodernism is the blurring of lines between fiction and nonfiction. In "Playing It Straight by Making It Up: Imaginative Leaps in the Personal Essay," Marilyn Abildskov explores how, in the hands of able writers, "making it up" and "telling the truth" can exist simultaneously and comfortably beside one another. Writers of this genre know that it is obvious to the reader that they are lying to tell the truth. More precisely, these writers lie openly, Abildskov says, to tell the truth so that their ethical posture as storytellers exists in their ability to lie openly and artfully. This revealing of one's bluff takes a variety of forms and reminds readers, as Abildskov notes, "You are now in the realm of a certain kind of reality. Imagined reality."

In her essay "Facts and Fancy: The 'Nonfiction Short Story,'" Michele Morano explores short stories and essays that blur distinctions between fiction and nonfiction and offer the reader a meta-awareness of "genre negotiation." Morano identifies nonfiction short stories as having the "reality warp" of fiction complicated by nonfictional elements that induce "double vision" in the reader. In the late postmodern age, the nonfiction short story calls attention to a sense of divided selves among writers and divided reading subjectivities among audience members.

Michael Orlofsky defines the term *historgrafiction* as a postmodern blend of the words *historiography* and *fiction*, which denotes the literary treatment of persons or events from the past. Historgrafiction is primarily concerned with character and theme; in contrast, historical fiction is activated by plot, setting, details, or lifestyle. Orlofsky further notes that it is an important element in the postmodern questioning of traditional historical assumptions and "objectivity," and it releases authors to investigate the epistemological possibilities of previously submerged characters and points of view in real events from the past. In his essay, Orlofsky explores stories by Donald Barthelme, Raymond Carver, Robert Olen Butler, and Bharati Mukherjee, as well as offers a historical survey of writers' and critics' attitude toward history in fiction and the other arts.

Playing It Straight by Making It Up: Imaginative Leaps in the Personal Essay

Marilyn Abildskov

Practitioners, readers, teachers, or even the most casual observer from the sidelines of the circuslike discussions surrounding creative nonfiction's various forms—the essay, the memoir, or even certain kinds of journalistic reportage—know well how the genre invites an inevitable discussion of ethics. Can the writer of memoir "make something up"? Should the journalist "stretch" the truth? What are the boundaries of creative nonfiction and does the word "creative" mean the nonfiction writer can "fictionalize" at whim?

If one were to plot out key moments of the contemporary debate, surely certain incidents would make a collective list, including Annie Dillard's remark that she never actually owned a tomcat, let alone a tomcat with bloody paws, as described in the beginning of *Pilgrim at Tinker Creek*, a book of gorgeous acrobatic meditations and the recipient of a Pulitzer Prize—that the opening of *Pilgrim at Tinker Creek* was imagined, in other words, not experienced firsthand.[1]

But these admissions and the responses that follow too often ignore context, trivialize important ethical questions in the process, and banish from conversation, either intentionally or not, a discussion of aesthetics, which threatens to nudge aside what is or ought to be of vital concern: a cogent description of the effects those choices that writers of creative nonfiction make; a description of what meaning the choices inscribe onto a text.

In fact, it may be that the dichotomy of "making it up" versus "telling the truth" is a false one altogether since, in able writers' hands, we see the two sitting on the page, gracefully side by side, as essayists play it straight by making it up—artfully tipping their hands, in other words, and exposing the seams of the writing process along the way. That these writers lie to tell the truth is obvious. Put more precisely, they lie *openly* to tell the truth, so that their ethical posture as storytellers lies in their aesthetic authority, in their ability to lie openly *and* artfully.

This tipping of the hand, or revealing one's bluff, takes a variety of forms, but one of the most compelling is the way an author negotiates the territory of a title or first line, using the opening as an opportunity to tell readers they are now in the realm of a certain kind of reality: imagined reality. "What's so hard about the first sentence," said writer Joan Didion in an interview with *The Paris Review*, "is that you're stuck with it. Everything else is going to flow out of that sentence. And by the time you've laid down the first two sentences, your options are all gone" (411).

Or, one might argue that the options are starting to slip even earlier on, as a writer titles a piece. A title, which creates for the reader a first impression, is as much an entrapment as a first sentence, often setting up the terms by which a piece must operate.

In "Remembering, I Was Not There," an essay by Anne Panning published in *In Brief: Short Takes on the Personal*,[2] the title is both flexible and wide in its reach but not duplicitous, as a more genre-bending essay-story might be. Here, Panning "remembers" her parents before she was born, skillfully offering up portraits of each, a narrative of how the two met, and what she, as their now-grown daughter, thinks many years after these events have taken place.

The essay opens in 1963 with the writer's mother sewing one hundred cloth-covered buttons on the back of her newly purchased white satin wedding dress. "Do not marry him, I wish to warn her," Panning writes (54). "He's wild already, though oddly charming with his square black glasses, his white T-shirt. His hair rolls back at the forehead like an Elvis or better, a Buddy Holly with narrow boy's hips, the beginning of pockmarks" (54–55). The warnings this narrator-daughter offers her mother come many, many years too late; they are futile, of course. To stop the parents from marrying—to stop what has already taken place—it is impossible now. This is what Panning deftly admits. "They cannot hear me. I am born two whole years later, the first baby daughter with black hair like an Indian's, cloudy gray eyes that would magically turn gold years later" (55).

Still, the desire remains. And it is this impossible desire, the product of imagination meeting up with reality, that the essay refuses to fight, that the essay submits to instead, allowing imagination to mingle with present-day knowledge and then cohabitate. "I wish to sit them both down, say don't. You will destroy yourselves, everything dear. You will make your lives harder than they have to be" (55).

The urgency comes from just that: what has to be. And so, this impossible situation—the narrator-daughter wanting to warn her parents never to unite—creates a double bind, one that only heightens the essay's poignant plight: the impossibility of going back in time for you as well as anyone else; the futility of watching others' mistakes; the burden of being the product of others' unfulfilled desires. All this is accomplished, as Panning remembers what she was not present to remember, literally, all this happens as Panning engages in an imagined dialogue that she makes no effort to disguise.

If beginnings are traps, on the other end of the essay, endings are—or can be—the opposite of trap: a release, one might say. Didion states, again from *The Paris Review*: "the last sentence in a piece should make you go back and start reading from page one. That's how it should be" (411). The fourteenth-century Japanese writer Kenko, in his *Essays in Idleness*, puts it just as simply: "In all things, it is the beginnings and ends that are interesting" (115).

In the memoir, "The Bend from Home," excerpted in *In Brief* as a stand-alone essay, Dermot Healy calls the reader's bluff with a kicker at the end that forces a rereading of what has come before. The piece contains twenty-eight lines broken into fifteen short paragraphs. The story is told in a straightforward way, but in the final four sentences Healy pulls the rug out from under readers and undercuts the "reality" of what he has set up so carefully; but to what effect? This ending does not undercut Healy's storytelling authority, does not make the reader question what Healy as narrator knows or does not know, does not make the reader question Healy's ability to play it straight. The essay is too short and beguiling for any of that kind of questioning to take place.

Instead, the "trick" appears purposeful, skillful, part of an illusion on stage meant to please rather than ruin the earlier trick of the story offered for the naive eye. It is as if Healy has pulled a rabbit out of a hat and then tipped his hat to the audience and whispered just how that rabbit came to be, all so deftly that the audience cannot fail to appreciate both sides of the trick, the rabbit and the revelation afterward, for both, it turns out, are excellent stories.

Healy's narrator, after all, by tipping his hand at the end, remains credible, the type we have come to expect the essayist or memoirist to be, someone we trust who will give us the story straight. But at the same time, he is offering the reader a sense of something else: the fluidity of stories, the way we think we are there when certain family stories are told, the ones told so often, how could it be otherwise? He is giving us the story as he knew it for so long and then the revised version, the factual truth. He is, in showing us this double version of reality, allowing us to perceive something of the fluidity of a community as well, the way stories flow from one house to the next, the way autobiographies are not made of factual stories alone. His trick, in other words, is purposeful. It adds rather than detracts or disrupts; it makes the story richer than it might otherwise be, commenting, as it were, on the nature of storytelling at the same time it delivers its tale. As readers, we can, perhaps, imagine confusing our own birth stories—the family myths that become the stories, which are, so often, neither grand nor mythological at all—with someone else in our own small circles, after all, but we cannot imagine confusing those stories with someone in the neighborhood, so isolated were ours.

Healy's essay, then, implicitly suggests that we live in a house of stories, shared. And if the "we" of whom he speaks implicitly are Irish, this text is certainly a piece of cultural commentary that illuminates life in Ireland as well.

To illuminate, to report, to remember, to record: these are a few of the impulses to which writers of all genres submit. And this: to imagine. Why then do we so often speak of imaginative acts as somehow specific to or belonging to the domain of fiction alone? Why do we act as if this business of "making it up" or relying on imagination is not as natural a part of nonfiction's bent toward "reality"? The tradition of the essay has a long history of marrying memory to imagination, the latter often tipping its hand—and hat—to the former, so that the process of writing becomes part of the essay's subject matter itself, giving the genre an intensely reflective feel as if writing and experience were happening at once.

Charles Lamb in his essay "Dream Children: A Reverie" tips his hand at the very start, suggesting by his title that the children in his essay are not made of flesh, but of dreams, of reverie. The first line of the essay goes like this: "Children love to listen to stories about their elders, when they were children; to stretch their imagination to the conception of a traditionary great-uncle, or grandame, whom they never saw" (169).

Still, the scene he creates of a first-person narrator gathering little ones around to hear stories about their great-grandmother has such force and is sprinkled with such rich detail that it almost seems real, at least momentarily. As the narrator tells these family stories, the children sit at his feet, listening, responding. "Here Alice put out one of her dear mother's looks. . . . Here John smiled, as much as to say, 'that would be foolish indeed'" (170). These small gestures, surely, add to the texture of the essay as a reverie that has come alive, and they are part of the reason why, at the essay's end, the reader feels a certain melancholy thrill when the narrator who has spoken to these children of his dear Alice is now left sitting quietly alone in his bachelor armchair, watching as his dream children recede, listening as they say "We are not of Alice, nor of thee, nor are we children at all. The children of Alice call Bartrum father. We are nothing; less than nothing, and dreams" (172). The fact that these children are the narrator's imagined life with Alice, whom he had loved, is hinted at in the essay's title and tagged in its conclusion. There is no "trick," so to speak, played out here, just the very real and powerful tapping into an imagination that wishes it were so. Knowing what will happen—that the children will vanish as all dreams must—does not tarnish the pleasure of experiencing the bittersweet reverie for ourselves.

Imagination is the primary experience dramatized in Virginia Woolf's essay "Street Haunting" in which the narrator goes out for a walk in the London streets to buy a pencil and finds herself falling into reveries about the people she sees, thus bringing herself out of her self and into an imaginative life, one that is, for the duration of the walk, celebratory.

Woolf goes into the minds of passersby when she writes of a dwarf in a shoe shop and, "thinking that feet, after all are the most important part of the whole person," she concludes that women "have been loved for their feet alone" (259), and in doing so, she mirrors the larger aims of the essay about layers of exterior and interior worlds, the surface of the imagination and consciousness underneath, and the pleasure of being in two places at once. Woolf's fictionalizing, if we call it that—the leaps she makes into others' minds—is brief and fleeting enough, though, that the essay remains an essay, hovering over, then landing back on the firm ground of reality.

"The Boys of My Youth," in Jo Ann Beard's collection of essays by the same name, opens in a scene, the kind that gives the essay the feel of a short story in nearly every respect. The narrator and her best friend Elizabeth are teenagers watching from Elizabeth's bedroom window a boy they adore, Dave Anderson, as he plays basketball in his driveway across the street. Beard's details are exquisite, from the description of Dave Anderson ("smooth brown hair cut straight across his forehead, like the Dave Clark Five Dave") to the description of Elizabeth's bedroom (with "antiqued Provincial furniture and a princess telephone") to the description of teenage girls' antics, which involve phoning Dave Anderson up, then hanging up the minute he says hello (152–53). This time, though, the girls do not hang up right away and Dave Anderson doesn't either. Instead, he says, in a controlled ninth-grader voice, "I know who this is" (153) and the girls jam the receiver back into place and behave crazily, leaping off the bed and running into each other and fastening the curtains shut with a bobby pin.

The essay goes on from there to contextualize the friendship between narrator and Elizabeth, to show how the two met in French class, which is rendered dramatically by Beard, once again in a present-tense scene. Once again the details light up all over the place as Beard describes the first week of junior high as one where everyone is "terrified of their lockers and the hall monitors" and says this is the "year of the tent dress and loud prints, so all the girls look like small hot-air balloons" (154). The French teacher is Mrs. McLaughlin, who "weighs about ninety-eight pounds" and "smells like cigarette smoke" and on this first day of class is wearing "a pale green mohair suit, cinnamon hose, and dark green lizard skin high heels" (154). The cheerleaders sit on her desk and trade jokes before class, Beard writes, but everyone else is terrified of her.

When Mrs. McLaughlin asks the narrator, whose French name is Colette, "Ou est la bibliotheque?" the narrator, who is in a "pink plaid dress made of spongy material" tilts her head to the side and pretends she can almost think of it as her heart clatters and a roaring in her head begins. Mrs. McLaughlin asks again, "Colette? Ou est la bibliotheque, si'il vous plait?"

"Now, *s'il vous plait* I've heard of," Beard writes. "It means either please or thank you" (155).

Eventually Mrs. McLaughlin moves on to Elizabeth, whose French name is Georgette, and Georgette watches the wall while her left cheek, still visible, "turns red beneath the curtain of her hair" (155). She answers quietly. Mrs. McLaughlin laughs out loud, says she sounds like Porky the Pig. And then, time passes and a friendship's seedlings are sown, as Beard writes: "The minute hand crawls around the face of the clock, others are called on, dialogue is read out of the book, words are written on the board. At some point I look over at Georgette just as she looks at me. I shake my head, almost imperceptibly, in disbelief; she widens her eyes for an instant, mimicking a look of abject terror" (156).

There it is: a present-tense scene. But in the next breath, Beard does a curious thing by shifting gears and fast forwarding to when the narrator and Elizabeth are all grown up and talking on the phone from their respective jobs in Chicago and Iowa and commenting on the slippery quality of memories in general, French class in particular. "That was ninth grade, not seventh," Elizabeth says of the French class incident. "We were already friends when that happened" (156).

In a less able writer's hands, such a move might be jarring, but it is not here, because the commentary that revises memory is encoded within another scene; and this scene, like that which takes place in Mrs. McLaughlin's classroom is equally rich. The commentary on the fragility of memory is meant to illuminate, not obscure, and illuminate not for the sake of getting the writer out of some theoretical ethical bind but illuminate for the sake of story, for creating a richly textured piece that uses the appearance of seams as part of its overall theme.

We find out that what we just heard was what Beard, as the writer, thinks happened, how she remembers meeting her best friend Elizabeth when the two were young. Beard has called attention to her own unreliability, but she has done so straightforwardly and artfully so that the reader goes along, listens as the narrator asks Elizabeth, if the two didn't meet in French class then, where did they meet, and derives great pleasure as Elizabeth says, "We just met, that's how we met" (157). Yes, the reader thinks, this is how memory works—we don't know when we met the most important friends in our lives; we have simply always known one another. Yet the pleasure of imagining that these two met in French class lingers and the fact that they met under humiliating circumstances will continue one of the essay's most powerful themes: the vulnerability of these female lives later on.

The scene of the two women talking continues. There is the sound of paper rifling on the other end of the phone. Elizabeth says, "I'll try to remember and call you after lunch. I have to proofread this thing this afternoon" (157).

Beard continues, using the landscape of this phone conversation between the women as adults to weave in details about their teenage years and then move back again, this time to convey the fact that the two women now have one more thing in common regarding boys: divorce. "She can proof a manuscript and talk on the phone at the same time; so can I. In school, we had a policy of never studying unless it was absolutely necessary, and still got high-to-mediocre grades. This convinced us that we were smarter than the average citizen, and actually, we're still thinking that way. It might be one of the reasons our husbands divorced us" (157–58).

Beard, Healy, Panning, and others—these are writers willing to tip their hands, either at the outset, the end, or somewhere in the middle, calling the reader's bluff by sitting up and announcing they are, indeed, fictionalizing or making things up but not as a way of playing games, but, instead, as a way of playing it straight. These imaginative moves in their essays momentarily expose storytelling's seams but never threaten to tear at those seams by lingering or gawking or tugging for too long.

Do we call such texts essays? Stories? Some hybrid form with elements of each? Do we call these forays into the imagination fictive techniques?

Robert Scholes notes that the critic Tzvetan Todoro has argued that a literary genre differs from the classifications used in zoology since in literature "each work modifies the whole set of possibilities." Writes Todoro: "Each new work changes the species" (128).

A few weeks ago, in a city I visited for the first time, I went to a zoo that is much praised for its abundant representatives of animal life. In front of one exhibit, what caught my attention were the animals we call humans, and in this case, they appeared to be mother, father, young daughter, and son. I overheard the mother say to her son, "Look at the monkeys, honey," to which her husband, who was carrying the couple's infant daughter, turned and whispered loudly, "Dear, I do believe those are apes." And the woman, in a clipped and biting tone that suggested maybe she was exhausted or had had enough of her husband's corrections and was not particularly interested in distinctions of any kind, especially those between mammals—or am I just imagining this?—said: "Close enough."

Close enough.

Sometimes our descriptions are close enough. Sometimes it is close enough to say that the nonfiction writer is using "fictive" techniques when, on balance, those techniques saturate a piece. Sometimes, too, a narrative essay and short story are so close they are nearly impossible to tell apart—like the endless varieties of small brown birds that those of us who are only casual bird watchers think look so strikingly similar, so very much alike.

But when a piece of writing published as nonfiction includes imaginative leaps and those leaps are in service of making the truth, as the writer knows or believes it, clearer in every possible way, perhaps we should create a new label for this kind of text. Perhaps there are more precise ways of describing those leaps of the imagination than saying these are fictive devices, and perhaps this new term might embrace this reality: that the act of imagination knows no bounds; that the act of imagination is especially not genre bound; that imagination is very much a part of reality—every reality, including those conveyed in the essay. That we have ever thought otherwise—that we speak of "imagination" as solely a resident of fiction's domain—seems not only ludicrous but diminishing of essayistic moves that have a tradition yet remain unnamed.

This "new" category, which is not new at all, might begin to capture, perhaps, something of the flavor of what these texts all along have engaged so eagerly and artfully in—these "straightforward tricks," so to speak—and also something of the flavor of what the term *fictional non-fiction* suggests. For is not memory an act of imagination? And when we are in memory, as so many personal essays demand, are we not in some in-between place? Something between the stark labels that fiction and nonfiction represent?

Each text is a different creature, of course, and each creature is, the reader hopes, very much alive. One hopes, then, that there is more than enough room at the inn for these creatures, more than enough room on our library bookshelves and also more than enough faith on readers' parts to rise above the quagmire those hypothetical questions about "making things up" versus "telling the truth" tend to raise and embrace the artistry that particular texts convey, appreciating them, these imaginative pieces, as creatures that live alongside others—others that were probably born as well in that wild place where memory and imagination and craftsmanship reside, a place where writers of all genres live and thrive.

Notes

1. Annie Dillard's remarks were recorded in Sarah Heekin Redfield's "Surveying the Boundaries: An Inquiry into Creative Nonfiction," part of the "Truth and Consequences of Creative Nonfiction" issue of *Poets & Writers* Sep./Oct. 1999.

2. Editors Judith Kitchen and Mary Paumier Jones address the controversy surrounding the issue of fictionalizing in nonfiction in their preface by saying that the selections for *In Brief* share this common belief: "that there is a real world—and that we live in it." This may seem obvious, they continue, but recent years have seen a burgeoning not only of creative nonfiction but of academic theorizing about it.

The result has been much talk about how, because truth is subjective, it doesn't matter if you make things up—even in nonfiction. We buy the first part: truth is subjective and, by definition, there is nothing we are more subjective about than our own lives. But we do not buy the specious logic of the conclusion. If a writer calls a piece nonfiction, there is an implied contract with the reader: "This is factual as best I can remember and re-create it."

References

Beard, Jo Ann. *The Boys of My Youth*. New York: Little, 1998.
Didion, Joan. "Joan Didion." *The Paris Review Interviews: Women Writers at Work*. Ed. George Plimpton. New York: Random, 1998.

Healy, Dermot. "The Bend for Home." *In Brief: Short Takes on the Personal*. Ed. Judith Kitchen and Mary Paumier Jones. New York: Norton, 1999. 46–47.

Kenko. *Essays in Idleness*. Trans. Donald Keene. New York: Columbia UP, 1967.

Kitchen, Judith, and Mary Paumier Jones, eds. *In Brief: Short Takes on the Personal*. New York: Norton, 1999.

Lamb, Charles. "Dream Children: A Reverie." *The Art of the Personal Essay*. Ed. Phillip Lopate. New York: Doubleday, 1994. 169–71.

Panning, Anne. "Remembering, I Was Not There." *In Brief: Short Takes on the Personal*. Ed. Judith Kitchen and Mary Paumier Jones. New York: Norton, 1999. 54–58.

Scholes, Robert. *Structuralism in Literature*. New Haven: Yale UP, 1974.

Woolf, Virginia. "Street Haunting." *The Art of the Personal Essay*. Ed. Phillip Lopate. New York: Doubleday, 1994. 256–69.

Facts and Fancy:
The "Nonfiction Short Story"

Michele Morano

In the introduction to his essay collection *Somehow Form a Family*, Tony Early confesses to a dilemma faced by many contemporary prose writers: he doesn't know how to categorize the short works contained in his book. Early writes, "I hesitate to call the ten pieces collected here essays because only one of them . . . strikes me as an essay in what I came to understand years ago as the essay form. At its heart this book is a collection of stories." However, the label of *story* doesn't quite fit, either. The pieces are true, Early states, with the caveat that "memory, like imagination, is largely a function of individual perception" (xviii).

Early's unease with the genre label of these short prose works speaks to the nature of the creative nonfiction essay: it often combines all the narrative style of a short story with a claim to the factual of an author's life. Writer and editor Lee Gutkind describes the term *creative nonfiction* as "being indicative of the style in which the nonfiction is written so as to make it more dramatic and compelling. We embrace many of the techniques of the fiction writer, including dialogue, description, plot, intimacy of detail, characterization, point of view; except, because it is nonfiction—and this is the difference—it is true" (37). The irony, of course, is that given the stylistic similarities between nonfiction and fiction, readers generally rely on genre labels to know whether material purports to be "true." Had George Orwell's classic essay "Shooting an Elephant" initially been published as a short story, I suspect it would still be cropping up in the fiction sections of literary anthologies. Similarly, if not for the label on the book jacket, any one of Tim O'Brien's stories from *The Things They Carried* could pass as an essay.

This is not to say that genre distinctions are meaningless; quite the opposite is true. From the writer's perspective, crafting a short story is a very different creative act from crafting an essay. Presenting a piece of short prose as an essay or a story means offering the reader a set of parameters for receiving the work, a contract of sorts that indicates something about the author's creative intent and the interplay between imagination and experience. As most writers understand, however, our works go out into the world and develop meaning quite apart from authorial intentions. From the reader's perspective, a work's label of *short story* or *essay* sometimes competes with other information—be it intra- or extratextual—that complicates genre. In these cases, I find that pinning down distinctions between fiction and nonfiction is much less interesting than exploring the characteristics of works that blur genre boundaries. To the end of identifying and generalizing from such works, I will first sketch out some general attributes of the short story and the essay and then examine pieces of short prose that function as "nonfiction short stories." In the process, I hope to offer some insights about the particularly postmodern nature of this subgenre.

To state the obvious, the short story is characterized by fancy. That is, it lures its reader into a world born of the writer's imagination, a world that, no matter how autobiographical, has been transformed by imaginative alchemy into something purer and more valuable than reality. As Joyce Carol Oates writes, "the short story is a prose piece that is not a mere concatenation of events . . . but an intensification of meaning by way of events." A story, she explains, captures a character's "distinct shift in consciousness" and "deepening of insight" (48–49). Susan Lohafer explains in her seminal work on short story theory that a story is an experience that happens between meals. It is brief and complete, luring us temporarily into an alternate reality that displaces the world in which we live. Lohafer notes that we are "in" a story the moment we cross the ontological gap between our world and the story's; that is, the moment when we adjust to what she terms a "reality warp" (56).

In contrast, an essay does not so much warp the reality of the reader's world as ponder it. Because the narrative "I" is also an authorial "I," we understand the elements of the essay to be facts and the relaying of those facts to represent the work of a consciousness that has processed them. Scott Russell Sanders has written that the essay is "the closest thing we have, on paper, to a record of the individual mind at work and play" (189–90). That record ranges widely from expositional interrogation to narrative pieces like Tony Early's essays, which read "like stories." As Phillip Lopate notes, "the essayist must be a good storyteller," writing in service of "narrative possibility" and guided by "storytelling momentum" (xxxviii).

The potential interiority of the short story, coupled with the narrative elements of even the most expositional essay, points to potential crossover between the two forms, one that goes beyond confusion over what to label a piece of writing. In certain short stories, the reality warp may be incomplete or challenged, while in some essays, the presence of a reality warp upsets the one-to-one correspondence between the narrator's world and the reader's. In either case, the result can be termed a nonfiction short story.

Tobias Wolff's "Firelight," which appears in his short story collection *The Night in Question*, offers an example. The piece involves an adult narrator relating the boyhood experience of spending a Saturday afternoon with his mother, looking at apartments they have no money to take. At the final apartment on their list, a Mr. Avery welcomes the mother and son into his home where a fire blazes in the hearth, a wife offers homemade brownies, and a daughter with honest-to-God "boobs" lounges in the living room. The boy is seduced by this domestic scene. As his mother talks with Mr. Avery, he allows his imagination to transform the apartment into a home in which he belongs and the people into characters in his own life. After some time, the boy reluctantly accompanies his mother back into the cold twilight and toward the boardinghouse where they live. The story ends with the adult narrator describing his own home, a place not unlike the one he and his mother visited years before. "But," he tells us, "in the very heart of it I catch myself bracing a little, as if in fear of being tricked. As if to really believe in it will somehow make it vanish, like a voice waking me from sleep" (199).

This is a story whose structure moves through the traditional stages of conflict and resolution, in the process illustrating the narrator's accumulated insight. Nonetheless, readers may quite naturally experience "Firelight" as nonfiction, in spite of its placement in a collection of short stories. Anyone who has read Wolff's memoir *This Boy's Life* will recognize elements of "Firelight." The situation of a boy and his single mother struggling financially and living in a Seattle boardinghouse, the sense of undiminished hope that the mother wears like a shawl, the boy's desire to ease his mother's life while simultaneously rebelling against her—these elements and more are common to the story and the memoir. In addition, the narrator's movement between childhood and adulthood, between naivete and earned wisdom, is reminiscent of *This Boy's Life*. In short form, this style feels very essayistic, very much like a record of a mind working to understand itself. As the adult narrator of "Firelight" relates his memory of the short time spent with the Avery family, he describes the storytelling process he engaged in then, saying "I even managed to forget they were not my family, and that they too would soon be moving on. I made them part of my story without any sense that they had their own to live out. What that was, I don't know. We never saw them again. But now, so many years later, I can venture a guess" (195). This passage relays the narrator's understanding of how experience and imagination form story and how memory and imagination work together in the act of storytelling to create a richer, more layered narrative. Given its similarities to Wolff's nonfiction and its stylistic signature, "Firelight" invites the reader to perceive the narrator and the author of this passage as momentarily collapsed into one.

The question becomes, then, What difference does it make whether we understand Wolff's narrator to be, at times, Wolff himself? When we read a short story, we abandon ourselves to its fancy, even when everything about the story seems as if it could be true. The most factual of stories warps reality, allows us to feel coaxed into a writer's imaginative house of mirrors, where real events are transformed by degrees of reflection. In an essay, on the other hand, the mirror of the author's mind seems to reflect accurately; things appear more or less as they really are. To mix metaphors, we could say that a short story exists in the subjunctive mood, in the mood of "might have," "could be," or "should," while the mood of the essay is more certain—"is" or "was"—even when the author openly struggles with an experience or idea.

Reading "Firelight" as a nonfiction short story allows—or perhaps forces—the reader to straddle two modes of thought: the hypothetical and the definite. I am reminded of an interview with Rick Bass, in which he talks about consciously deciding whether to treat certain material from his life in fiction or in nonfiction. Sometimes, he says, he can see the material handled either way, which gives him a kind of "double vision" (qtd. in Lyons and Oliver 75). Perhaps this is exactly the gift afforded by the nonfiction short story: double vision, whereby the reader sees an imaginative space infused not just with verisimilitude but with reality, a place where fact and fancy are locked in a complicated embrace.

This embrace can be seen even more clearly in Lorrie Moore's "People Like That Are the Only People Here." Included in her short story collection *Birds of America*, this piece was published originally in the *New Yorker*, where it created a stir. Even before I pulled the magazine from my mailbox, I had heard about the story from writer friends lauding the way Moore blurs boundaries, the way she explores real-life events in her fiction. That Moore herself denies such blurring is something I will return to in a moment.

The story concerns a woman whose baby son is diagnosed with a rare form of kidney cancer. It is a horrifying situation, made all the more poignant by the detailed treatment of parental perspective and emotion. The protagonist—referred to throughout as the Mother with a capital "M"—is a fiction writer and teacher who struggles for most of the story against the possibility of writing a nonfiction account of her family's tragedy. Her Husband (referred to throughout with a capital "H") encourages her to write a memoir, arguing that the family will need the money his wife can earn from it. The material of the story, that is, foregrounds questions of genre.

While the story is written in the third person, the interior life of the Mother is often presented as an unmediated address to the reader:

The Mother drags deeply, blowing clouds of smoke out over the disfigured cornfields. When a baby gets cancer, it seems stupid ever to have given up smoking. When a baby gets cancer, you think, Whom are we kidding? Let's all light up. When a baby gets cancer, you think, Who came up with *this* idea? What celestial abandon gave rise to *this*? Pour me a drink, so I can refuse to toast. (*Birds* 225)

Throughout the story, the Mother's thoughts infiltrate the narrator's voice until the two replicate the familiar tone of a confidant, the stance of someone who's been there, done that, and is now telling about it. Which brings me to the other piece of information I received before having seen the *New Yorker* story: Lorrie Moore's own baby, my friends explained, has also had a life-threatening illness. Coupled with the parallels between the Mother and the author—both writers and teachers, both living in the Midwest, which they satirize brilliantly, and both having written novels about teenage girls—this information predisposed me to experience the story as something more, or at least something other. To be fair, few readers outside the world of literary gossip would have known about some of the autobiographical elements before beginning the story. But anyone who read the original magazine publication would surely have been influenced by its presentation.

In the *New Yorker*, the story is clearly labeled as such by the word *fiction*, which appears in small type above the large title. However, vying with that label is a photograph of Lorrie Moore, placed in the middle of the page and framed by columns of text. It is a candid photograph in which an unsmiling Moore is caught with her left hand moving toward her face. The hand is blurred, the facial expression serious. This is the pose of someone who might have received horrific news a second before the shutter clicked. Moreover, the photo's caption reproduces this dialogue from the story: "Are you taking notes?" "No." "You're not?" "No, I can't. Not this! I write fiction. This isn't fiction" (*New Yorker* 58). Clearly the intent of the *New Yorker* was to play with the connection between author's life and material, to urge the reader to receive the story in a genre-straddling way.

The Husband repeats the refrain "Take notes" throughout, as the Mother struggles with what it means to set this experience down in language. At one point, after a page break that begins a new section, Moore writes:

How can it be described? How can any of it be described? The trip and the story of the trip are always two different things. . . . One cannot go to a place and speak of it; one cannot both see and say, not really. One can go, and upon returning make a lot of hand motions and indications with the arms. The mouth itself, working at the speed of light, at the eye's instructions, is necessarily struck still; so fast, so much to report, it hangs open and dumb as a gutted bell. All that unsayable life! (*Birds* 237)

The expositional stance of the narrator in this passage seems to transcend fiction, to get at the heart of nonfictional difficulties. Privy to even the slightest information about the real-life source of Moore's material, or influenced by the author's photograph and caption in the *New Yorker*, the reader would have to work hard *not* to attribute this passage to the writer herself. For her part, Moore has vehemently denied that the story is at all nonfictional, saying "It is autobiographical but it's not straddling a line. Things did not happen exactly that way; I reimagined everything. . . . And the whole narrative strategy is obviously fictional. It's not a nonfiction narrative strategy" (qtd. in Garner).

Moore's intentions notwithstanding, there are two narrative arcs in this story, and one of them may be experienced by even the most genre-conscious reader as nonfictional. First there is the story of the baby's cancer, with its descent into the hell of Pediatric Oncology—Peed Onk, for short. There is an operation, the looming cloud of chemotherapy, and a final, tentative respite when the baby qualifies for a national experiment in which he will be monitored with ultrasound. There is the escape from the hospital, with its bald-headed boys and tired, heroic parents, and there is the narrator's final bit of dialogue: "I never want to see any of these people again" (*Birds* 150). In addition, there is the interior arc of the Mother's attempt to understand her experience and, more importantly, to grapple with its translation into literature. For all that she scoffs at the idea of taking notes throughout the story, the piece ends with her acquiescence, with her accepting narration—nonfictional or otherwise—as a tool for coping. After she and the Husband leave the hospital, we have a section break and then this final two-line dénouement: "There are the notes. Now where is the money?" (*Birds* 250).

Who speaks these last lines? Not the Mother, exactly, although we might say that they occur in her head. But in the absence of any mention of her, and since the story has led us to expect her interior commentary to be accompanied by actions or external dialogue, we might conclude that the lines belong to the third-person narrator, that the "shift in consciousness" and "deepening of insight," to borrow Oates's phrases, occur within the mind not of the Mother but of the writer who tells her story. Add this to the interior commentary throughout, to the photograph, and to its intriguing caption (not to mention any gossip provided by writer friends) and the final lines of the story contribute to the magnetic pull of the label *nonfiction*.

In the end, then, "People Like That Are the Only People Here" creates a reality warp that takes us into the world of "Peed Onk," and that may nonetheless make us resist the story's full categorization as fiction. The reader may find herself, as I did, alternating between the mantra, "It's a story," and the sense that as Moore's mind worked on and played with the material of her life, the reality warp of her story became punctuated by nonfiction. The reader may become more conscious of the writer in a story such as this one, more conscious of the act of translating experience into narrative. By affording the reader an opportunity to read with double vision, the nonfiction short story may encourage a kind of metareading, in which the curtain seems pulled back enough to show the wizardly writer exercising her craft.

Reading "Firelight" and "People Like that Are the Only People Here" as nonfiction short stories means being hyperaware of the breadth of fiction to encompass elements of nonfiction, without discounting either. Wolff's and Moore's stories are fictional works that nonetheless straddle genre, encouraging the reader to negotiate between fiction and nonfiction in the process of reading. A similar negotiation takes place with nonfiction works that straddle genre, although the effect may be different. Essays by Jo Ann Beard and Diane Ackerman provide additional models of genre crossover, in which the narration of events from actual life warps reality and momentarily challenges the label of nonfiction.

The essays in Beard's collection *The Boys of My Youth* meld the narrative arc of stories with the consciousness of a mind at work and play. In particular, the title piece is a beautifully written tale of the narrator's history with "boys," as well as the history of her best female friendship. In this essay, Beard takes us through childhood flirtations, adolescent pranks, teenage parties, and adult marriages and divorce. She also takes us through the writing process, chronicling the fact-checking process with her best friend Elizabeth. Sometimes Elizabeth corrects the year of an event; sometimes she concedes that the narrator has it right; and sometimes the two admit defeat in the face of information that is irretrievably lost, such as how they originally met. Throughout the essay, Beard makes clear that remembering involves compromise, piecing together, and that writing about the past is a tricky business. At the same time, her descriptions are so precise and her narrative so perfectly paced that the story she tells seems as reliable as any piece of nonfiction could be. In characterizing a middle-school event, for example, Beard writes:

Eighth grade, spring, between classes. The hallway is damp and swampy, loud with clanging lockers and the clamor of overstimulation; popular kids are being hailed, unpopular ones hooted at. A drinking fountain, a line in front of it, me in an impossibly short skirt and white knee socks. The dress code has been lifted for three months now, the boys wear pants as tight as long-line girdles and the girls wear hip-hugger skirts that are less than a foot long. Getting a drink at the fountain involves a cross between kneeling and squatting. (163)

Beard's narration uses the techniques of good fiction but maintains a one-to-one correspondence between the story she tells and the real world inhabited by both author and reader.

Later in the essay, however, this correspondence breaks down. Beard describes her experience at an artist colony, during which she is working on an essay and telephoning Elizabeth daily for input. At one point, after offering the reader a long and particularly vivid scene of a summer party when they were seventeen, Beard relates a conversation with Elizabeth:

I tell her I'm working on a party scene.
    "Which party?" she asks suspiciously. "What am I doing at it?"
    "It's sort of a composite of all parties, you know?" There's silence at the other end. "It's just a *party* party, is all, with those guys who all had the same names." (193)

Beard then admits that neither she nor Elizabeth can remember much about the guys at the party, the very guys she has described in detail only a page before. It is a humorous moment, not least of all because Beard is playing with the facade of honesty. But it is also a disconcerting moment, one that calls into question all the gorgeously detailed memories that have come before. It even calls itself into question—can we trust that Beard remembers her telephone conversation with Elizabeth on that day?

This is a small but important example of what I mean by an essay creating an unexpected reality warp. One moment the reader is immersed in an atmospheric, *real* 1970s party, and the next moment she is made aware that the party represents the work of imagination as much as reality, that it contains at least as much fancy as fact. The reader is suddenly "in" the story, to borrow Lohafer's phrasing, and yet at the same time not. However much imaginative work Beard has done to breathe life into her memories, the narrative "I" continues to reference the author directly, from beginning to end of the essay. The double vision this requires of the reader allows for an understanding of the way memory both influences and subordinates itself to the craft of writing.

In his *Biographia Literaria*, Samuel Taylor Coleridge offers this felicitous claim: "The fancy is indeed no other than a mode of Memory emancipated from the order of time and space" (305). We might say that fiction and creative nonfiction operate on a continuum of memory, with fuller emancipation coming on the fictional end and a stronger adherence to time and space coming on the nonfictional end. Somewhere in between, the nonfiction short story foregrounds memory's emancipation and yet also makes the reader hyperaware of the anchors of real time and real space in narrative.

This phenomenon is particularly evident in my final example of a nonfiction short story, an essay that creates a reality warp almost from its first page. Diane Ackerman's "In the Memory Mines" is a haunting piece in which fact and fancy bleed into each another. The essay treats the discrepancy between what Ackerman's conscious mind remembers of early childhood and what she has not always remembered but has discovered hidden away in her subconscious, during sessions of hypnosis. The essay begins:

I don't remember being born, but opening my eyes for the first time, yes. Under hypnosis many years later, I wandered through knotted jungles of memory to the lost kingdoms of my childhood, which for some reason I had forgotten, the way one casually misplaces a hat or a glove. Suddenly I could remember waking in a white room, with white walls, and white sheets, and a round white basin on a square white table, and looking up onto the face of my mother. (1)

Because her first waking moments are experienced under hypnosis, the reader may or may not accept Ackerman's description of them as factual. Nonetheless, the essay's beginning presents the description as truthful according to Ackerman's perspective. As the opening scene continues, the description widens to include not just the limited perspective of a newborn but the view back through time of the narrator: "What I couldn't know was how yellow I had been, and covered with a film of silky black hair, which made me look even more monkey-like than newborns usually do, and sent my pediatrician into a well-concealed tizzy" (1). Stylistically, this sentence combines the perspective of a past self with that of the author, indicating how much the writer now knows. This is a common fictional and nonfictional technique, and it serves to reinforce the authority present in the essay's opening.

The description of the situation continues, as the narrative follows the doctor out of the room, through his subsequent consultations with colleagues over the baby's hairy coat, into his decision not to alarm the mother by emphasizing an abnormality he does not understand. At this point, the reader may well question Ackerman's access to this information—did she speak with the doctor as part of her research? Did the doctor eventually relate his dilemma to the mother, who told the story to Ackerman later on? Because the answers to these questions are plausible, the reader may continue to perceive the details as factual and to give Ackerman the benefit of the nonfiction doubt. Until, that is, the interior perspective of the doctor slides into more specific musings:

New York State seemed to him suddenly shabby and outmoded, like the hospital on whose cracked linoleum he stood; like the poor practice he conducted on the first floor of his old, street-front, brick house, whose porch slats creaked at the footstep of each patient so that, at table or in his study, or even lying down on the sofa in the den wallpapered with small tea roses, he would hear that indelible creaking and be halfway across the room before his wife knew he hadn't merely taken a yen for a dish of ice cream or gone to fetch a magazine from the waiting room. (2)

Clearly this passage moves into something other than nonfiction. Ackerman has begun by describing an experience of hypnosis which she believes to be true, and she has followed that experience along fairly natural paths into the imaginative configuring of events and outcomes. The doctor is transformed from a person in the background of Ackerman's earliest waking moments into a fictional character with an interior life that transcends the author's own story. A reality warp results, signaling to the reader a departure from the nonfiction contract.

The effect of this reality warp reverberates throughout the essay. Ackerman moves from the doctor's mind into her mother's, weaving family background into the woman's drowsy contemplations of her baby. That background in place, Ackerman then moves into a chronology of her consciousness—at two years old, at four, through the beginning of school attendance at six, and, finally, to her father's death that same year. She moves from the reality warp of the fictive opening into memories that are neither mediated by hypnosis nor, at least overtly, the product of imaginative forays. The essay acts like an essay, but with the fancy of its opening infusing every page. The reader might well find herself wondering: Who is this narrative "I" that is so comfortable (a) admitting to what she cannot remember, (b) writing about it anyway, (c) slipping into various points of view, and (d) returning to her essayist self, all without apology?

The most satisfying answer is that she is the author of a nonfiction short story. Ackerman's subject is memory, an entity that continuously negotiates between experience and imagination. Perhaps the greatest fiction of the essay form is that it allows us to believe that recovering the past in a factual way is possible, that our own lives are not lost to us as they move from present to past tense. The nonfiction short story exposes this fiction, and yet it does not undo the form. Rather, it brings the reader into a kind of collusion with the author. Ackerman's descriptions of the doctor's musings and her mother's train of thought are seductive. They pull us in, ask us to see the larger picture because without it, how can we understand the narrator's story? And they ask us to contemplate the difference between "facts" and "truth" in a way that makes us more aware of what it means to write the nonfictional "I."

Short stories that straddle the genre of the essay subvert or complicate the reality warp so that the narrative "I" seems at times to transcend character and refer directly to the author; in so doing, these pieces help readers become aware of the writer's negotiation between personal experience and the creation of characters' lives. In contrast, essays that straddle genre create some degree of reality warp, in which the authorial "I" temporarily falls away or illustrates itself to be born of imagination, in the process highlighting the impossibility of separating fact from fancy. In both cases, nonfiction short stories prompt readers to negotiate between the expectations posed by genre and the subversive moments that induce double vision, encouraging the reader to experience fiction and nonfiction simultaneously.

As the foregoing examples illustrate, nonfiction short stories do not necessarily work on readers in the same way, and in some cases they require prior knowledge on the reader's part in order to push genre boundaries. Nonetheless, one common denominator of the nonfiction short stories I have identified is a strong sense of divided narrative self. Each piece illustrates the attempt of an authorial persona to understand a prior or parallel incarnation of itself, and in so doing complicates the expectations of genre labels. These works offer readers a more active role than stories or essays generally do in constructing meaning; they make readers aware of the tension between fact and fancy, foregrounding authorial negotiations between selves during the writing process. With the proliferation of creative nonfiction literature in recent years and the mutual influences of fiction and nonfiction upon each other, audiences are primed to engage in the kind of divided reading subjectivity that nonfiction short stories require. In the late postmodern era, nonfiction short stories propel both writer and reader toward awareness—and meta-awareness—of the quintessential literary subject: the mind's eternal struggle to represent itself.

References

Ackerman, Diane. "In the Memory Mines." *The Best American Essays 2001*. Ed. Kathleen Norris. Boston: Houghton, 2001.

Beard, Jo Ann. "The Boys of My Youth." *The Boys of My Youth*. New York: Little, 1998.

Coleridge, Samuel Taylor. *Biographia Literaria*, Vol. 1. *The Collected Works of Samuel Taylor Coleridge*. Ed. James Engell and W. Jackson Bate. Princeton: Princeton UP, 1983.

Early, Tony. *Somehow Form a Family*. Chapel Hill: Algonquin, 2001.

Garner, Dwight. "Moore's Better Blues." Salon Oct. 1998. Dec. 2001 <http://www.salon.com/books/int/1998/10/cov_27int.html>.

Gutkind, Lee. "The Creative Nonfiction Police." *Writer's Chronicle* (Dec. 2001): 36–39.

Lohafer, Susan. *Coming to Terms with the Short Story*. Baton Rouge: Louisiana State UP, 1983.

Lopate, Phillip. Introduction. *The Art of the Personal Essay*. Ed. Phillip Lopate. New York: Anchor, 1994.

Lyons, Bonnie, and Bill Oliver. *Passion and Craft*. Chicago: U Illinois P, 1998.

Moore, Lorrie. "People Like That Are the Only People Here." *Birds of America*. New York: Knopf, 1998.

———. "People Like That Are the Only People Here." *New Yorker* (Jan. 1997): 58+.

Oates, Joyce Carol. "The Origins and the Art of the Short Story." *The Tales We Tell*. Ed. Barbara Lounsberry et al. Westport: Greenwood, 1998.

Sanders, Scott Russell. "The Singular First Person." *The Secrets of the Universe*. Boston: Beacon, 1991.

Wolff, Tobias. "Firelight." *The Night in Question*. New York: Random House, 1996.

Historiografiction: The Fictionalization of History in the Short Story

Michael Orlofsky

Postmodernism is history's self-fulfilled prophecy. One of postmodernism's diagnostic traits is its use of historic forms, texts, periods, and characters to new purposes. If the argument holds that our culture has been unable to learn from its past, then the inevitability of our repeating it is the context of postmodernism—which is not necessarily a bad thing.

The term *historiografiction* itself is a postmodernist construction assembled from the words *historiography* and *fiction*, and which I use to denote the literary treatment of persons or events from the past. It is a corrective to the label *historical fiction*. The latter is useless, for example, in an effort to address Donald Barthelme's story "Robert Kennedy Saved from Drowning" or Raymond Carver's retelling of Anton Chekhov's last hours in "Errand." The difference as I see it is this: historiografiction is primarily concerned with character, perhaps secondarily with theme; historical fiction, on the other hand, is activated by plot, setting, details, or lifestyle. In addition to the pieces by Barthelme and Carver, I would like to examine aspects of historiografiction in Bharati Mukherjee's "Management of Grief" and Robert Olen Butler's "A Good Scent from a Strange Mountain."

Each of the four stories presents the historic in unique ways. In Barthelme's story, Robert Kennedy clearly is the protagonist—a public, yet in the final analysis, a very enigmatic figure; conversely, in Carver's "Errand," Chekhov's death is like a force of nature that makes measure of several other characters. In an entirely different treatment, Mukherjee moves fictional characters through real events: the aftermath of a midair explosion aboard Air India Flight 182 in 1985 that killed 329 people. In "A Good Scent from a Strange Mountain," Butler presents a revisionist image of Ho Chi Minh in his role as a foil against the main character Dao. Throughout these narratives the authors have expanded the possibilities of history without diminishing its veracity.

Historiografiction

The impulse among writers toward historiografiction has been around for a long time. It goes back at least as far as Homer and his retelling of the struggles on the killing fields outside the walls of Illium. Shakespeare has given voice to a host of English kings, as has Browning to Florentine artists. Yeats has sung of Irish nationalists, and Eliot has elegized martyred priests. Furthermore, in one of the earliest examples of literary criticism in English, *An Apology for Poetry* (1595), Sir Philip Sidney writes that philosophy and history are best realized by the poet, and by extrapolation to our own day, the writer. As a matter of fact, one is hard-pressed to find a better description of the postmodern attitude toward history than Sidney's:

The historian . . . laden with old mouse-eaten records, authorizing himself (for the most part) upon other histories, whose greatest authorities are built upon the notable foundation of hearsay; having much ado to accord differing writers and to pick truth out of partiality; [and is] better acquainted with a thousand years ago than with the present age. (139)

Sidney says that the philosopher teaches by way of bloodless precept, the historian by way of heedless example—but the poet utilizes the best of both disciplines, and "no other human skill can match him." He continues:

The philosopher, setting down with thorny argument the bare rule, is so hard of utterance, and so misty to be conceived, that one that hath no other guide but him shall wade in him till he be old before he shall find sufficient cause to be honest. For his knowledge standeth so upon the abstract and general, that happy is that man who may understand him, and more happy that can apply what he doth understand.

Now doth the peerless poet perform both: for whatsoever the philosopher saith should be done, he giveth a perfect picture of it in some one by whom he presupposeth it was done; so as he coupleth the general notion with the particular example. A perfect picture I say, for he yieldeth to the powers of the mind an image of that whereof the philosopher bestoweth but a wordish description. (140)

However, Marguerite Alexander observes that historical fiction has been diminished over the last two centuries, basing her assessment on Georg Lukacs's argument that the French Revolution and the Napoleonic Wars made history a mass experience. The playing fields of history were leveled, and the masses came to consciousness as a historical force—with the subsequent rise in the nineteenth century of realism in literature. Alexander says that "serious realist fiction has been firmly rooted in its own time" while historical fiction "has been further marginalized by the insistence of the *modernist* movement on the inner, subjective world and on the primacy of the writer's own experience" (125; emphasis added).

Part of the postmodern reaction against modernism is historiografiction. But old-school modernism in no way has gone gently into that good night. Fredric Jameson writes that postmodern authors will not have an easy task assuming the reins from the modernists:

We also have to take into account the immense weight of seventy or eighty years of classical modernism itself. There is another sense in which the writers and artists of the present day will no longer be able to invent new styles and worlds—they've already been invented; only a limited number of combinations are possible; the most unique ones have been thought of already. So the weight of the whole modernist aesthetic tradition—now dead—also "weighs like a nightmare on the brains of the living," as Marx said in another context. (658)

Jameson says that artists will be forced to accept the death of art and aesthetic, and face "the failure of the new, the imprisonment of the past" (658).

But as I said at the start, that is not necessarily a bad thing. The past was a big place, a lot of people lived there. That is a lot of stories, as well as a lot of perspectives on the floodtide of history.

The conflict for the contemporary author is twofold. The gospel of the writing workshop is to "write about what you know." On the other hand, an author's imagination may be stoked by the idea of the writing about some of those who have crossed over before us—and who would have thought that death had undone so many, eh? The postmodern oddment is this: each of us is, a posteriori, worthless after deducting the black market price of our body's trace elements and organ meat; yet, a priori, each of us is of inestimable value. The paradox casts a different light of interpretation on the lives of those who have passed into history. It is a familiar conflict: the human being is "in apprehension like a god! the beauty of the world! the paragon of animals." Yet even the loamy remains of mighty Alexander himself, "might they not stop a beer-barrel?"

Here's more on the subject by the author John Gardner:

When one begins to be persuaded that certain things must never be done in fiction and certain other things must always be done, one has entered the first state of aesthetic arthritis, the disease that ends up in pedantic rigidity and the atrophy of intuition. Every true work of art—and thus every attempt at art . . . must be judged primarily, though not exclusively, by its own laws. (3)

Later in the same text, Gardner criticizes the writing theory that begins "write about what you know":

"Write about what you know." Nothing can be more limiting to the imagination, nothing is quicker to turn on the psyche's censoring devices and distortion systems, than trying to write truthfully and interestingly about one's own hometown, one's Episcopalian mother, one's crippled younger sister. For some writers, the advice may work, but when it does, it usually works by a curious accident. (18; emphasis added)

What I like about the postmodern writers is that they have developed the literary and esthetic confidence to take risks to see where their characters want to go, rather than restricting those characters to the author's world. Bob Shacochis, author of the story collection *Easy in the Islands* (1985), says much the same:

Today's novels tend to be set at the mall, the university, the farm; in the small town, the neighborhood; on the Upper West Side; within the nuclear family—in short, the places where writers feel most comfortable. No one seems to have the strength or the desire required to write in a bold and sweeping manner about our lives and our homeland, or about how our lives and our homeland fit into a bigger picture. Rather, the modern writer favors the present tense and the first person, rejecting the macrocosm for the microcosm, exercising an imagination that never leaves home or worse, never leaves the self. (15)

Historiografiction is the attempt to escape the self. Furthermore, the postmoderns may be the first generation of writers who self-consciously, or self-conceitedly, expropriate history to their own ends—telling the truth, in other words, but telling it at a slant.

Paula Geyh, Fred G. Leebron, and Andrew Levy discuss the contemporary synthesis of literature and history in their *Postmodern American Fiction* (1998):

The postmodern instability of literary forms is apparent in the collapse of many of the traditional distinctions between literature and other kinds of discourse. One of the most crucial distinctions to undergo revision during the postmodern era is the standard that defined literature as subjective, fictional creation of imaginary reality, and history and journalism as objective, factual records of real events. Yet we know the past only through "textualized remains" that are themselves incomplete, fragmentary, and in many cases already deeply subjective (diaries, letters, memoirs). . . . If the historical evidence is partial or suspect, the history that is made from it must also be, no matter how historians try to bridge the gaps. And the interpretations historians make are determined or at least influenced by their interests, assumptions, and prejudices, however objective these historians might wish or appear to be. For artists, journalists, government officials, and authors alike, the question of whose history constitutes History—whose history survives, and whose does not—has become a central issue of postmodern politics. (xxiv)

Ihab Hassan calls history a people's "active knowledge" (134). It seems to me that journalists are the scribes who record that active knowledge, at least since the inception of a popular press in the eighteenth century. And in no small degree journalists have helped inaugurate and define the postmodern consciousness. Tom Wolfe in *The New Journalism* (1973) was one of the first writers to codify the characteristics of this new reportage. In analyzing a news feature by Jimmy Breslin about an extortion trial in New York, Wolfe writes, "Well—all right! Say what you will! There it was, a short story, complete with symbolism, in fact, and yet true-life, as they say, something that happened today, and you could pick it up on the newsstand by 11:00 tonight for a dime" (13–14). The techniques that the New Journalists expropriated from fiction writers were scene-by-scene construction, realistic dialogue, the third-person point of view, and the recording of what Wolfe calls the "status details" of a person's life (32).

This is the power that fiction has to bring the past to life. It's a cross-pollination of the best sort. T. Minh-Ha Trinh says that story *is* history:

Something must be said. Must be said that has not been *and* has been said before. . . . It will take a long time[,] for living cannot be told, not merely told: living is not livable. Understanding, however, is creating, and living, such an immense gift that thousands of people benefit from each past or present life being lived. The story depends upon every one of us to come into being. It needs us all, needs our remembering, understanding, and creating what we have heard together to keep on coming into being. The story of a people. Of us, people. Story, history, literature (or religion, philosophy, natural science, ethics)—all in one. (652–53)

Although Hassan argues that defining postmodernism is antipathetic to the movement itself, he has nonetheless identified many features of postmodernism in order to "gauge the climate of its discourse." Of these features, several apply to historiografiction, including decanonization, hybridization, but particularly constructionism.

Decanonization applies to all the "master codes, all conventions, institutions, authorities . . . we revise or subvert norms; we deconstruct, displace, decenter, demystify, the logocentric, ethnocentric, phallocentric order of things." Hybridization is the "mutation of genres in parody, travesty, pastiche." It is also "promiscuous or equivocal forms: paracriticism, paraliterature, happening, mixed media, the nonfiction novel, the new journalism. Cliché, pop, and kitsch mingle to blue boundaries, 'dedefine' the modes of representation" (132).

Hassan writes that constructionism is tropic, figurative, it must construct reality in post-Kantian "fictions." Such effective or heuristic fictions *imply the growing intervention of mind in nature and history"* (133; emphasis added). This "intervention" is the most revealing aspect of historiografiction, which the following four stories make manifest.

"Robert Kennedy Saved from Drowning"

Donald Barthelme was postmodern before postmodernism was cool. As his colleague John Barth says, "some of us who have been publishing fiction since the 1950s have had the interesting experience of being praised or damned in that decade as existentialists and in the early 1960s as black humorists. . . . Now we are praised or damned as postmodernists" (196). I don't think many of us realized it at the time, but when we first read Barthelme's "Me and Miss Mandible" (1961), the story was a manifestation of an esthetic that would become a new literary period.

Barthelme's "Robert Kennedy Saved from Drowning" appeared in the *New American Review* two months before the senator from New York was assassinated in the early summer of 1968 while campaigning during the presidential primaries. The poignancy of the story in part arises from its theme, in which a public figure like Kennedy (referred to as K. in the story) ultimately is unknowable. Robert Kennedy was dead before his time, and whatever impact for better or worse he may have had on American politics was stillborn.

The story is a montage of news clippings, press releases, anecdotes, and casual observations that Barthelme fashions into a biographical study. Jerome Klinkowitz says that in spite of the montage effect, the story is "a conventional epistemology. Gathering together notes from various sources, the story attempts to tell what the man was, to put down on paper the meaning of his life . . . but the conclusions are ambiguous" (69).

The scenes show K. working at his desk, dealing with subordinates, reaching for the bottle of Scotch at a party, debating issues such as public transportation, responding to international crises, campaigning, or reading to his children. Yet a clear picture of the character never emerges: "He is neither abrupt with nor excessively kind to associates. Or he is both abrupt and kind. . . . His reactions are impossible to catalogue. . . . Important actions often follow, sometimes within a matter of hours. (On the other hand, these two kinds of responses may be, on a given day, inexplicably reversed.)" (76–77).

Klinkowitz says:

Although Barthelme has assembled all varieties of reports, including considerations of the dreck he claims is so revealing, the point of "Robert Kennedy Saved from Drowning" is that the conventional epistemology fails. Unlike "Karsh of Ottawa" [a photographer referred to in the story], we are unable to get the "one shot in each sitting that was, you know, the key shot, the right one." And the spirit of Kennedy, unlike Churchill or Hemingway, is never captured—unless that spirit be the enigma itself. (70–71).

Another of the reports about K. comes from a friend who comments that the man operates in an existential isolation, "that essentially he's absolutely alone in the world. There's this terrible loneliness which prevents people from getting too close to him . . . he's very hard to get to know, and a lot of people who think they know him rather well don't really know him at all" (80).

In the final vignette, the narrator saves K. from drowning. Dramatic tension climaxes in the rescue, but if the reader expects a glimpse into K.'s personality through the chink in the monomyth caused by his close encounter with death, then there is only disappointment. Be that as it may, the conclusion of the story is in keeping with its theme—that each person ultimately is beyond understanding, be he famous or historically obscure. Ironically, the skewed light of publicity on K. serves only to cast deeper shadows.

The point of view in the story shifts from third person to first person in the rescue episode, yet even that attempt toward personalization fails to bring K. any closer to the narrator:

K. in the water. His flat black hat, his black cape, his sword are on the shore. He retains his mask. His hands beat the surface of the water which tears and rips about him. The white foam, the green depths. I throw a line, the coils leaping out over the surface of the water. He has missed it. No, it appears that he has it. His right hand (sword arm) grasps the line that I have thrown him. I am on the bank, the rope wound round my waist, braced against a rock. K. now has both hands on the line. I pull him out of the water. He stands now on the bank, grasping.

"Thank you." (85)

"Errand"

This story originally appeared in the *New Yorker* in June 1987 and was the last of Raymond Carver's stories to be published while he was alive, and it is generally accepted as his homage to Chekhov. The story opens in March 1897 while Chekhov and his friend Alexei Suvorin are at a Moscow restaurant. The two men have just been seated at their table in the Hermitage when Chekhov suffers a severe pulmonary hemorrhage and blood begins "gushing" from his mouth. Later, after another hemorrhage, Chekhov checks into a clinic, and while recuperating there his visitors include his sister Maria as well as Leo Tolstoy.

The story presses ahead to July 1904. Martin Scofield notes that Carver seems to have gleaned details from Henri Troyat's biography on Chekhov, and the first half of the story does read like a historian's account. It shows a concern for place, date, witness, chronology, and interpretation. Carver makes mention of an eyewitness account of Chekhov's visit to Dr. Karl Ewald in Berlin and the lung specialist's frustration over his inability to help the ill writer. This is followed by a reporter's observations at the Potsdam *bahnhof*: "Chekhov had trouble making his way up the small staircase at the station. He had to sit down for several minutes to catch his breath" (384).

Chekhov and his wife, Olga, arrive in Badenweiler, a Black Forest spa popular among Russians who promenade the grounds and take the waters. Chekhov, however, "went there to die." Carver includes an excerpt from one of Chekhov's letters to his mother in which he inexplicably claims "that I'll be completely cured in a week." He also introduces Dr. Schwöhrer, Chekhov's physician in Badenweiler, who prescribes cocoa, oatmeal, and strawberry tea for the consumptive writer.

It is Dr. Schwöhrer whom Olga summons on a stifling midnight on July 2. The following events are based on Olga's memoirs. In his hotel bedroom Chekhov is delirious with fever, and Schwöhrer gives him an injection of camphor to increase his heartbeat. He orders oxygen. At this point, Chekhov suddenly becomes lucid and says, "What's the use? Before it arrives I'll be a corpse" (385). After pausing to look at the dying Chekhov, the doctor goes to the phone and orders a bottle of the hotel's best champagne and three glasses. Carver uses Schwöhrer's gesture of ingenuousness as the narrative's key symbolic act—in a story that until that juncture has been absent of unifying metaphors.

A disheveled young manservant delivers the champagne, takes in the scene, and awkwardly departs with Schwöhrer's tip in hand. It is three in the morning. The doctor removes the cork from the bottle of Moët, pours it into the three glasses, and they drink:

They didn't touch glasses. There was no toast. What on earth was there to drink to? To death? Chekhov summoned his remaining strength and said, "It's been so long since I've had champagne." He brought the glass to his lips and drank. In a minute or two, Olga took the empty glass from his hand and set it on the nightstand. Then Chekhov turned onto his side. He closed his eyes and sighed. A minute later, his breathing stopped. (387)

A few moments pass when—and this is recorded in Olga's memoirs—the cork pops out of the bottle and champagne froths onto the table. At this point, the history in the story gives over to the fiction. In its final pages, Carver structures the story around images of the champagne, a large black moth, a vase of roses, and a mortician. He has also introduced a new character who assumes the story's point of view—the maitre d's assistant, "the young man" who delivered the champagne:

In the second, largely fictional half, Carver maintains the same understated and dispassionate tone; there is no feeling of moving from historical to fictional events. The activity of the short-story writer and the historian are in many ways very similar: the historian also has to judge the pace of his narrative, to balance major events against details, to phrase the narrative to achieve drama and mood as well as factual accuracy. . . . Carver simply is increasing the imaginative element, while keeping as close as possible to what facts there are and keeping the semblance of factual account in his fiction. (Scofield 10)

At daybreak, the young man returns to Room 211 to fetch the ice bucket and glasses, but he also carries a vase containing three yellow roses. He is clean-shaven and pressed, and in deference to Olga suggests that rather than her taking breakfast in the garden she receive her meal in her room. Olga is distracted, and the young man notices Chekhov's inert body lying in bed. In time, Olga orders her thoughts and asks the young man to summon a mortician, discretely. This is the errand by which the story takes its title. "The young man's picking up the cork—his act of appropriation crowns his independent contribution to the action—is simultaneously the culmination of Carver's own appropriation in his own fiction and his contribution to significant narrative" (Scofield 11).

Many critics have commented on Carver's affinity to Chekhov, including Peter Henning, Charles May, Lionel Kelly, and William L. Stull. Carver uses his art to make sense of the loss of Chekhov. Art, even postmodern art, can give structure to reality, to history. Furthermore, you cannot escape the question "Has Carver associated himself with the young man on the errand? The young man's sensibilities seem changed by his brief encounter with the dying man and his wife although he "was afraid of seeming to intrude even more by drawing any further attention to himself" (389). The aching realization, of course, is that by the time of the story's publication (June 1, 1987), Carver himself was desperately ill with lung disease. Three months later in September he experienced lung bleeding, and in October he had two-thirds of his left lung removed. Carver ultimately succumbed to cancer on August 2, 1988.

In "Errand," Carver writes that the name of the young man has not survived, and that he probably died in World War I. Ironically, Carver's postmodern expropriation of history has established the young man's presence in *literary* history.

"The Management of Grief"

A second major approach in historiografiction is the insertion of imagined characters into real events. Bharati Mukherjee does this in response to an explosion on a plane bound for England. Epistemologically, what is interesting for readers removed by time and distance from the historic settings of these stories is that the fictional characters assume as much reality as the anonymous participants in the actual events. What historiografiction offers is an exploration of that most human of questions What was it like to be there? and its corollary What would I have done?

"The Management of Grief" (1988) is about an Indian immigrant's efforts to cope with the staggering loss of her husband and sons who are killed over the Irish Sea when an explosion blows apart their transatlantic flight. There is evidence to suggest that it was a terrorist act. Mukherjee presents the thoughts and feelings of an unassuming character thrown into the crosshairs of terrorism and the historical moment. The story is in reaction to a real event, the crash of Air India Flight 182 in 1985 in which many first- and second-generation Canadians of Indian descent died.

The protagonist, Shaila Bhave, works as a bill processor in a Toronto travel agent's office, and she labels herself a dutiful wife who keeps her head veiled and her voice shy and sweet. Ironically, she and her husband Vikram emigrated from India to Canada to avoid conflict, but history comes slouching toward Toronto. And the people who die in the crash are the first to die from it. However, some characters in the story prefer to call the movement of history by other terms, such as *fate* and *God*:

Some, I know, prefer ignorance, or their own versions. The plane broke into two, they say. Unconsciousness was instantaneous. No one suffered . . . Kusum [an Indian neighbor who lost her daughter in the same crash] says that we can't escape our fate. She says that all those people—our husbands, my boys, her girl with the nightingale voice, all those Hindus, Christians, Sikhs, Muslims, Parsis, and atheists on the plane—were fated to die together off this beautiful bay. She learned this from a swami in Toronto.
"I have my Valium," Shaila comments (338).

Without her husband and children Shaila becomes emotionally numb. She is even denied their bodies for burial because most of the corpses were never found in the Irish Sea where the plane went down (only 131 of 329 were retrieved). Further, the objects of middle-class life are for her mere detritus: radio headphones, a pocket calculator, bathrobes, gas grills, model airplanes, and her pink split-level house. Shaila says about herself, "I am trapped between two modes of knowledge. At thirty-six, I am too old to start over and too young to give up. Like my husband's spirit, I flutter between worlds" (343).

In an effort to find herself in the world, Shaila returns to India and begins an odyssey to hill stations, beach resorts, tea dances, and especially holy places that she had ignored in years past. However, on the third day of the sixth month of her journey, and while offering flowers and sweetmeats to an animist god, she encounters the spirit of her husband:

He is squatting next to a scrawny sadhu in moth-eaten robes. Vikram wears the vanilla suit he wore the last time I hugged him. The sadhu tosses petals on a butter-fed flame, reciting Sanskrit mantras, and sweeps his face of flies. My husband takes my hands in his.
You're beautiful, he starts. Then, *What are you doing here?*
Shall I stay? I ask. He only smiles, but already the image is fading. (344)

Shaila returns to Canada. There she is asked by a Canadian government social worker to help the relatives of some of the crash victims. Of particular urgency are the circumstances of an elderly Sikh couple whose sons died in the bombing. The social worker asks Shaila to interpret in an effort to get the couple to sign bank forms and powers of attorney so that the government can set up a trust fund for them, invest their money, and provide a monthly pension. The old man and woman refuse to sign anything, yea, they refuse to believe that their sons are never coming back. The husband says, "God will provide, not government."

As Shaila and the social worker drive away, Shaila thinks, *"In our culture, it is a parent's duty to hope"* (344).

At the end of "The Management of Grief," Mukherjee universalizes the loss felt by her main character. History does not stop, and Shaila has only two choices: either stasis or movement. While on an errand, she hears the voices of her family in a park on a beautiful winter day. She looks at the clear blue sky. " I thought I heard the rustling of larger forms, and I waited a moment for voices. Nothing. Then, . . . I heard the voices of my family one last time. *Your time has come*, they said. *Go, be brave*" (50).

As the title of the story implies, grief is managed, it is rarely erased.

"A Good Scent from a Strange Mountain"

Robert Olen Butler calls his story an "aesthetic dialectic" between the imagined character Dao and the historical figure Ho Chi Minh. Dao is almost a centenarian, and he has summoned his family and friends for a traditional Vietnamese leave-taking because he senses that his own death is near. Ho Chi Minh visits Dao in his room in New Orleans on three successive nights. Dao takes pains to assure himself that Ho is not a spirit—Dao smells the sweetness of confectioners' sugar on Ho's hands, and his daughter reports that the doorknob to his room, after one of Ho's departures, is sticky.

Commenting on the story, Butler says:

These things are true: Ho Chi Minh was once a pastry chef under the great Escoffier at the Carlton Hotel in London; he once worked retouching photographs in Paris; he showed up at the Hall of Mirrors during the signing of the Treaty of Versailles to enlist Woodrow Wilson's support in winning certain modest rights for the Vietnamese in French Indochina; after the Second World War he once again hoped that America would be an ally in his cause. (qtd. in Kenison and Stone 366–67)

From these facts, Butler says he distilled images of Ho adding blush to the cheeks of Frenchmen, of his discomfort in a rented suit and bowler, and of his hands coated with pastry flour.

The commingling of history and fiction that is historiografiction allows for the dialectic that Butler refers to—the real Ho and imagined Dao represent two spheres of human endeavor: the political and the spiritual. Ho chose the path of political revolution; Dao chose the path of spiritual reawakening. Dao says that while he was drawn to the past and the religion of his father, Hoa Hao Buddhism, Ho "was being called not from his past but from his future" (240). However, in light of their choices in life, both men are burdened with restless souls.

The story begins, "Ho Chi Minh came to me again last night, his hands covered with confectioners' sugar" (235). Dao remembers when he first knew Ho in 1917, during his prerevolutionary days when he was Nguyen Ai Quoc, and when both men worked at the Carlton Hotel, Dao as a dishwasher and Ho as a pastry chef's assistant. They were best friends and saw snow for the first time together. When he appears in Dao's room many decades later, Ho's hands are powdered with sugar. Both men seem troubled in each other's presence. Ho because something about the sugar recipe is not quite right. Dao because he has overheard his son-in-law and grandson talking about the recent murder in New Orleans of the editor of a Vietnamese-language newspaper who had editorialized about accommodating the communist government in Vietnam. The son-in-law, Thang, and his son, Loi, are both members of the former Army of the Republic of Vietnam, and Dao believes they are implicated in the assassination.

The tension and suspicion that the editor's murder bring into Dao's home sour his hopes for his family at a time when his own psyche seems almost refulgent with spirituality: "I am a Hoa Hao Buddhist and I believe in harmony among all living things, especially the members of a Vietnamese family." He goes on to explain, "We follow the teachings of a monk who broke away from the fancy rituals of the other Buddhists. We do not need elaborate pagodas or rituals. The Hoa Hao believes that the maintenance of our spirits is very simple, and the mystery of joy is simple too" (241–42).

Ho, too, is concerned about family—the larger family of Vietnam itself. But his agenda is crowded and he is not at peace. His political victories are as nothing for "[t]here are no countries here" (245).

History has bullied both Dao and Ho Chi Minh. The former sought harmony, the latter, revolution, as means to an end. Yet, Dao doubts that there is harmony among the Vietnamese in the New World. His family members argue in front of him, bitter about the exile of their people, bitter for trusting the Americans, bitter about the Thieu administration. The vitriol makes Dao weep. He feels he has lived too long and wishes to "let go of life somewhere in my dreams" and return to his village square accompanied by the souls of his dead wife and son. Ho Chi Minh calls the Americans fools for not better understanding his people's petitions for surcease from French colonial rule. Yet, there is a nagging sense that Ho and his countrymen were victims of larger historical and political forces.

The final conversation between Dao and Ho is the most revealing. Dao expresses his concern to Ho that his son-in-law and grandson were involved in a politically motivated killing. At first Ho is silent. Then he speaks up:

> "You have never done the political thing," Ho said.
> "Is this true?"
> "Of course."
> I asked, "Are there politics where you are now, my friend?" (248–49).

The smell of sugar on Ho's hands becomes very strong and he leaves Dao's room without comment.

A key to the story rests in its title. Butler says that the phrase came his way in a back alley in Saigon when he asked an old man to translate the Chinese characters on the Buddhist shrine in the man's bedroom. "This . . . is the mystery of life, all that we need ever to consider: 'A good scent from a strange mountain'" (qtd. in Kenison and Stone 367).

Butler concludes "A Good Scent from a Strange Mountain" in Dao's consciousness as he reflects on the Carlton's kitchen: "I was only a washer of dishes but I did listen carefully when Monsieur Escoffier spoke. I wanted to understand everything. His kitchen was full of such smells that you knew you had to understand everything or you would be incomplete forever" (249).

The crux of the story, and of postmodernism in general, of course, is the capacity or incapacity of human knowledge to understand its portion in the skein of history.

Concluding Thoughts

What conclusions can be drawn from these historiografictions? For starters, the impetus for fictionalizing history has been strong in the cultural imagination. Among postmodern writers, historiografiction is an epistemological imperative based on the question Whose history is it anyway? Contributing to the imperative is the concept of literary exhaustion. If all the best forms and stories have been told, as Jameson suggests, then the postmodern has been forced to scribe through the ashes searching for embers. Frequently, the embers are characters ignored by formal histories, such as the anonymous young man in Carver's "Errand":

Since the 1960s, histories of those who had been previously ignored or forgotten, "history from below" or from the margins, have proliferated . . . these narratives challenge the age-old assumptions that have distinguished history from literature. These narratives also tend to thematize the fragmentary, disjunctive, and often contradictory nature of historical evidence and hence of history itself, rather than presenting history as a continuous, unified story[. . . . They] call attention to the fact that conventional *literary* history rarely offers a complete and unitary record of the past it has been constructed to represent. (Geyh, Lebron, and Levy xxv)

However, these historiografictions go beyond telling a story from a previously unchampioned point of view—they also explore the limits of knowing. Some may argue in the abstract about the death of history, in conference with the death of literature, but history and storytelling do not stop. Esthetically, historiografiction provides a sense of emotional closure, thematic completeness, or narrative structure—which history sometimes lacks, but which art needs. Lastly, historiografiction can be strongly revisionist. Our culture, nation–states, institutions, laws, morality, and leadership may not have been perfect in the past, but as Tolstoy says, we're on the road to perfection. Which isn't necessarily a bad thing.

References

Alexander, Marguerite. *Flights from Realism: Themes and Strategies in Postmodernist British and American Fiction*. London: Edward Arnold, 1990.

Barth, John. "The Literature of Replenishment: Postmodernist Fiction." *The Friday Book*. New York: Putnam, 1984. 193–206.

Barthelme, Donald. "Robert Kennedy Saved from Drowning." *Sixty Stories*. New York: Dutton, 1982.

Butler, Robert Olen. "A Good Scent from a Strange Mountain." *A Good Scent from a Strange Mountain*. New York: Grove, 2001. 235–49.

Carver, Raymond. "Errand." *Where I'm Calling From: New and Selected Stories*. New York: Atlantic Monthly, 1988. 381–91.

Gardner, John. *The Art of Fiction*. New York: Vintage, 1985.

Geyh, Paula, Fred G. Leebron, and Andrew Levy, eds. *Postmodern American Fiction*. New York: Norton, 1998.

Hassan, Ihab. "Beyond Postmodernism." *Rumors of Change: Essays of Five Decades*. Tuscaloosa: U of Alabama P, 1995.

Jameson, Fredric. "Postmodernism and Consumer Society." *Postmodern American Fiction*. Ed. Paula Geyh, Fred G. Leebron, and Andrew Levy. New York: Norton, 1998. 654–63.

Kenison, Katrina, and Robert Stone, eds. *The Best American Short Stories, 1992*. Boston: Houghton, 1992.

Mukherjee, Bharati. "The Management of Grief." *The Best American Short Stories of the Eighties*. Ed. Shannon Ravenel. Boston: Houghton, 1990. 333–50.

Scofield, Martin. "Story and History in Raymond Carver." *CRITIQUE: Studies in Contemporary Fiction* 40.3 (spring 1999). 12 Dec. 2001. GaleNet. Literature Resource Center. <http://galenet.gale.com>.

Shacochis, Bob. "The Enemies of Imagination." *Harper's Magazine* Nov. 1995: 13–15.

Sidney, Philip Sir. "An Apology for Poetry." *The Critical Tradition: Classic Texts and Contemporary Trends*. Ed. David H. Richter. Boston: Bedford, 1989. 131–59.

Trinh, T. Minh-Ha. "Woman, Native, Other." *Postmodern American Fiction*. Ed. Paula Geyh, Fred G. Leebron, and Andrew Levy. New York: Norton, 1998. 649–54.

Wolfe, Tom. *The New Journalism*. New York: Harper, 1973.

WOMEN'S IDENTITY IN THE POSTMODERN WORLD

An often overlooked but nonetheless integral aspect of postmodern writing pertains to gender. Too often, a long shadow is cast by "big" postmodern authors such as Robert Coover and Donald Barthelme, but the female voice has emerged strongly in recent decades. In her essay "Closure in Sandra Cisneros's 'Woman Hollering Creek,'" Rose Marie Cutting focuses on the final story, *"Bien* Pretty," which she argues creates a feminist form of postmodern "closure" for the entire collection. Cutting further demonstrates that postmodern theory declares that cultural beliefs and behaviors usually considered "natural" are actually social constructs, and the stories in Cisneros's collection lead to the conclusion that gender is socially constructed and that women are not trapped in a "prison of gender."

"The Silence of the Bears: Leslie Marmon Silko's Writerly Act of Spiritual Storytelling" by Brewster E. Fitz offers an intertextual reading of a short autobiographical passage from Silko's *Storyteller*. Fitz argues that in using a postmodern logic of paradox and undecidability, the reader puts forward the argument that Silko constructs a mixed conceptual space. In this space she can "tell" in writing, that is, silently, what she cannot tell orally.

In "The Feminine Consciousness as Nightmare in the Short-Short Stories of Joyce Carol Oates," Wayne Stengel explores a number of the author's briefer pieces. Stengel relates to us that Oates's short-short stories often demonstrate that being a woman in contemporary America can make one the unwitting object of the desire of others, can create incestuous transference between family members, or can make one physically, or psychically, wounded by the presumptions of desire. Stengel further states that in Oates's mingling of feminine fear of desire with the strains of Gothic literature in our culture, we begin to understand "the formal constraints and intensities of these short stories that can seem, superficially, autodidactic, hallucinatory outpourings of the bereft, the repressed, or the mutilated."

Although such early liberation opened many doors for women, Karen Weekes, in her essay "Postmodernism in Women's Short Story Cycles: Lorrie Moore's *Anagrams*," notes that "expanding opportunities . . . have not necessarily caused a concurrent expansion of personal fulfillment or happiness." Weekes makes the case for the short story cycle as the ideal medium to "feature one contemporary female's perspective, present a multiplicity of roles from which she must choose, and emphasize the intense emotional pressure surrounding these decisions." This "multiplicity" of identity can rightfully be termed "The Postmodern Condition."

Closure in Sandra Cisneros's "Woman Hollering Creek"

Rose Marie Cutting

Sandra Cisneros's collection of short fiction—*Woman Hollering Creek and Other Stories* (1991)—ends with a short story entitled *"Bien* Pretty," a story that creates a feminist form of postmodern "closure" for the entire collection. In keeping with the postmodern predilection for a play of fragments revealing fractured identities, Cisneros creates not one but three short sections to conclude her final story. Taken together, these three fragments offer at least temporary closure for the problems that trouble the protagonist of the story, and the three sections provide closure for the images and symbols that convey the themes. When read backward in relationship to the other major works in *Woman Hollering Creek*, the three concluding sections of *"Bien* Pretty" reiterate and offer a form of closure for the major themes, motifs, stylistic techniques, and types of closure offered by the pieces of fiction that precede *"Bien* Pretty."

Postmodern theory declares that cultural beliefs and behaviors usually considered to be "natural," "essential," and unchanging are actually social constructs. Jane Flax describes feminism as a postmodern philosophy for the following reason: "The single most important advance in feminist theory is [that] the existence of gender relations has been problemitized. Gender can no longer be treated as a simple, natural fact" (43–44). Most of the stories in Cisneros's collection explore issues of gender and clearly demonstrate that gender is socially constructed; moreover, the major stories generally show female protagonists who learn important lessons: men and women are not two "exclusionary categories," and women are not trapped in a "prison of gender" (Flax 45).

Lupe, the protagonist of the last story in the collection, becomes a postmodern heroine when she succeeds in understanding and releasing rigid gender identifications that bring her unhappiness and a sense of victimization. Although she is ostensibly a "liberated" woman, Lupe's pursuit of heterosexual romance has resulted in unhappiness more than once. At the beginning of *"Bien* Pretty," she moves from California to Texas to escape contact with a former lover who has left her for another woman. In spite of past pain, Lupe jumps into an affair with a Mexican national, Flavio, who returns to Mexico when he is called on to take up his role as father to the seven sons he has produced by two women in Mexico (156–57).

The first segment that concludes *"Bien* Pretty" focuses on Lupe's desire to live a life of passion and intensity. In all but one of the major stories in the collection, the female protagonists seek passion and intensity through heterosexual romance. Like Lupe, all of these protagonists suffer betrayal and rejection and plunge into grief and anger. Previous critics (Lewis; Thomson) have argued that many of Cisneros's heroines struggle to create some degree of freedom or empowerment out of their travail. This theme of freedom and empowerment comes to a climax in the conclusion to the final story in *Woman Hollering Creek*.

Cisneros's collection presents sketches and stories in three sections: section one focuses primarily on female children; section two on female adolescents; and section three is largely devoted to adult female characters. The first of the longer stories is found in the second section. In "One Holy Night," a pregnant, unmarried teenager has been sent to her relatives in Mexico to await the birth of her baby. Betrayed by the older man who seduced her, the protagonist remains trapped in the role of the imprisoned princess whose only option is to wait passively for the birth of her child and for a prince to rescue her.

"One Holy Night," however, in no way presents a simple, coherent conclusion. Multiple endings, all fragmentary conclusions that play off against each other, reveal the postmodern predilection for representing conflicting identity states through fragmentary and conflicting passages. The young protagonist of "One Holy Night" is undoubtedly confused and conflicted, but she has learned the basic premise of postmodern thought—"skepticism about generalized and universal claims of any sort" (Di Stefano 74). In particular, she is especially skeptical about gender stereotypes.

The young girl knows that her society constructs a female who is supposed to be passive (34). But she also knows she has actively pursued, not simply waited for the romance and sex that she believed would bring passionate intensity into her life. She recognizes the exact moment when she falls in love; she chooses to go to the room of the man she is attracted to; she touches him first when they have sex. Sadly, this sexual initiation does not fulfill her romantic expectation that her virgin identity would disappear to reveal a state of woman-hood (29). In fact, she discovers sex may not be such a big deal after all. Nevertheless, she has gained a fluidity of identity that allows her to feel proud of her transgressions against society's rigid conception of female gender. The teenager knows she is supposed to feel shame for having unmarried sex, but she does not. Because sex is no longer a romantic mystery fed to young girls, she wants "to stand on top of the highest building and yell *I know*" (28–30).

In the first fragment that concludes "One Holy Night," the narrator affirms her sense of superiority to the girl cousins who have never ex-perienced sex and are afraid to discuss it. The same short paragraph, however, exhibits her ambivalence and conflicted attitude. She warns her cousins that sex is a disappointment for which they will be sorry. In the next sentence, she shifts to an opposing mood, remembering the pleasure she felt while lying beside her sleeping lover and staring at and admiring his male physique (34–35). While the male sleeps, the female enjoys the dominant role that society says belongs to him.

In the second concluding section, the young girl reveals a mixture of both hope and disillusion. She still believes she can control her fu-ture sufficiently to choose the number, sex, and names of her future children. But the baby must be named "Alegre . . . because life will always be hard" (35).

Disillusion dominates the third and last fragment. The narrator de-scribes the metaphors her friends assign to "love": waiting to catch a falling piano pushed off a tall building or the image of a top, spinning so fast that "all the colors in the world" combine into a "white hum." These metaphors for the power and intensity of love are juxtaposed again in her own sad image of a crazy man walking around with a har-monica in his mouth, not able to play it, just wheezing though the in-strument all day (35). The multiple images the narrator ponders in her last words align her narrative with the postmodern belief that there are no simple or final answers to complex human experiences.

The first major story in section three of Cisneros's book, the title story "Woman Hollering Creek," features another pregnant woman. In this story, Cleofilas has been brought to Texas by her prince. Initially, she feels like a Cinderella rescued from the dusty town in Mexico where she kept house for her father and six brothers. Like Cisneros's other protagonists, Cleofilas identifies strongly with the belief that women will find the highest intensity and reason for living in romantic and sexual passion. Like the young girl in "One Holy Night," Cleofilas has been waiting for "true love." This gendered view of love has been fostered by the *telenovelas* (the Mexican soap operas). Watching these programs has taught Cleofilas that even suffering and pain can be sweet: "Because to suffer for love is good" (44–45).

When Cleofilas's husband beats and bullies her, however, she mobilizes other aspects of her identity. Like the teenager in "One Holy Night," she looks through the romantic image to see the actual man who smells bad and has disgusting habits as well as tenderness (49). Her husband's abuse drives Cleofilas to contemplate suicide, but a stronger and healthier aspect of her identity prompts her to escape. She learns to assert herself, hiding enough money to take the bus back to her family in Mexico. Cleofilas's escape is facilitated by Felice, a Mexican American woman who opens Cleofilas's eyes to the knowledge that women can live without men, can earn their own money, can even buy their own pickup trucks. Felice demonstrates the wide range of identities available to women; independence and choice are not reserved for the male gender.

"Never Marry a Mexican," the second major story in the third section, features Clemencia—an ironically named Mexican American protagonist—who was seduced when she was a nineteen-year-old student by Drew, her married Anglo teacher. Clemencia claims the status of agent rather than victim by pursuing a series of affairs with married men, a form of revenge against Drew, against men and their wives, and against white society. This dedication to revenge is capped by Clemenicia's seduction of Drew's sixteen-year-old son. Rather than accept her status as a brown female who has been used and tossed aside by a white man, Clemencia attempts to move outside of her preestablished gender role by proving that females can succeed in dominating men through seduction.

"Never Marry a Mexican" clearly demonstrates Cisneros's postmodern distrust of the simple, unified subject. Clemencia's behavior with regard to Drew reveals "fragmented selves and oppositional consciousness" (Di Stefano 74) that belie the illusion of unity she tries to project. Clemencia is an artist who paints Drew over and over, claiming that this allows her to control the way her former lover's identity is presented (75). Yet, of course, her sixteen-year-long obsession with Drew disproves her claims of autonomy.

"Eyes of Zapata," the next major story in the collection, focuses on Ines, the historical mistress of Zapata. Like Drew, Zapata is unfaithful. He has many affairs with other women, and he marries and has children by another woman (99–100). Like Clemencia, Ines refuses the role of discarded victim. She is a *bruja* (witch) who can use her dreams to continually pull Zapata back to her, and she may even be responsible for killing the children of Zapata's legal wife by means of a spell (99–100). Refusing to accept society's disdain for the mistress, or its image of her as victim, Ines functions as a powerful example of a woman who constructs her own identity and willingly transgresses limits constructed for her. By giving Ines the opportunity to narrate her own story, Cisneros has given voice to the woman and type of woman that official historical tales have silenced. In her analysis of postmodern literature, Andreas Huyssen emphasizes the significance of such voices: "It is certainly no accident that questions of subjectivity and authorship have resurfaced with a vengeance in the postmodern text. After all, it does matter who is speaking or writing" (264).

"Little Miracles, Kept Promises" is the fifth of the major stories. Written in the postmodern form of a collage of prayers and letters left on a church altar, this multivocal series of fragmentary stories offers an exemplary sample of postmodern form. "Little Miracles, Kept Promises" ends with a letter and offering to Our Lady of Guadalupe written by Chayo. Chayo (whose postmodern complexity of identity is evident in her double name—Chayo/Rosario) has cut off her long braid of hair as a gift to Guadalupe when she discovers she is not pregnant (125–27).

Chayo's letter to Guadalupe narrates a tale of resistance to the female roles her family wishes to impose on her. They want her to spend time with them instead of studying or painting; they pressure her to marry, to have children, to be like her mother and grandmothers. Rejecting this ethnic version of gendered identity, Chayo rejects motherhood. She would not mind being a father, she thinks, because then she could have a life beyond motherhood as constructed by Mexican American society (127). Chayo sees herself as painfully fragmented and fractured, as struggling out of the prison that gender creates. She sees herself as a woman straddling both worlds (125). Chayo's letter only hints at the story of the affair that led to her fear of pregnancy. But her fear that her sexuality will trap her connects her story with the other major stories in which heterosexual romance leads to suffering.

"*Bien* Pretty," the last story of the collection, helps resolve the conflict that women experience between their desire for romance and sex and their desire for autonomy. In the first of the three sections that close "*Bien* Pretty," Lupe struggles toward self-affirmation even while she accepts the ambivalence and complexity of her own desires. Before

Flavio left her to return to Mexico, Lupe's affair with him did actually bring her the intensity that she extols in the first of the closing segments of her story, but in spite of betrayal and suffering, Lupe never repudiates the search for such intense states. On the contrary, she understands well why she and Cisneros's other female characters seek the romantic experiences that give them a heightened sense of life. Lupe's advice to women is to live "[w]ith rage and desire, and joy and grief, and love till it hurts, maybe" (163).

Lupe's praise of intensity is accompanied by an essential piece of advice: women can safely pursue this state only when they have learned a core lesson, a lesson Lupe learned through her efforts at healing from her own unhappy love affair. Lupe calls on all women, but especially the women of her culture to learn and practice this lesson. They must stop weeping "Soy infeliz" over their affairs and instead follow the advice in a feminist song: "'Es verdad que te adoro, pero mas me adoro yo.' I love you honey, but I love me more" (163). Since identity is multiple rather than unitary, it is possible for women to learn to choose or to create "healthy" identities, even if these identities will never achieve perfect integration (Harding 247).

The second segment that concludes "Bien Pretty" offers closure for the theme of cultural conflict and cultural synthesis that permeates all of the pieces of fiction in Woman Hollering Creek, a theme that frequently dominates the shorter pieces. Lupe's story concludes with an act of cultural transformation. In keeping with postmodern thought, Lupe constructs rather than accepts cultural icons as fixed entities. She takes an image from a traditional Mexican myth and transforms it into the image that suits her need to reverse gender roles—an image that allows her to repudiate the fiction of gender as "natural." Lupe returns to a painting of twin Mexican volcanoes, one for which she used Flavio as the model, and she uses the transforming power of her work to image a new identity for women: she redoes the whole thing and reverses the roles of Prince Popo and Princess Ixta. "After all, who's to say the sleeping mountain isn't the prince, and the voyeur the princess, right? So I've done it my way. With Prince Popocatepetl lying on his back instead of the Princess" (163).

This paragraph of Lupe's narrative provides closure for the five other stories in the collection where Cisneros likewise revises Mexican myth or legend to empower a female character. As artist, Lupe assumes the role usually assigned to the male: the empowered agent who gazes at the body of the Other. Her painting offers a climax to the other stories in which the female learns to look directly at the male instead of casting down her eyes modestly while he looks at her: the teenager looking at her sleeping lover in "One Holy Night"; Cleofilas learning to really see her husband in "Woman Hollering Creek"; Clemencia painting Drew in "Never Marry a Mexican"; Ines narrating her story while gazing at the sleeping Zapata.

Lupe's transformation of Mexican legend demonstrates how Cisneros solves the dilemma created in short fiction by an author's attempts "to make us believe it conforms to reality . . . even as the mythic and aesthetic laws of the story drive the characters relentlessly toward the end" (May 67). The underlying mythic and archetypal elements that Cisneros uses are deliberately chosen so that she can alter them; these changes grant her characters the possibility of envisioning new identities rather than the passive, suffering, or evil roles often assigned to women in myth or legend.

The young girl in "One Holy Night" was courted by a man who claimed to be a Mayan prince, a leader of his people who would take her as his princess and produce a son to restore the greatness of the Mayan people. She views her sexual encounter with this man as the act of being accepted into an ancient world initiated by "Chaq, Uxmal Paloquin," while she plays the role of "Ixchel, his queen" (29–30). She later learns his name is, in reality, "Chato, which means fat-face"; moreover, he is not even Mayan. The romantic myth is ruthlessly exposed to reveal a serial killer who has seduced and killed eleven other females over seven years (33–34).

"Woman Hollering Creek" rewrites the La Llorona story, the Spanish and Mexican story of a weeping woman who haunts rivers and streams because she drowned her children, a folktale that has given rise to a postmodern variety of contemporary adaptations (Doyle 56; Rebolledo and Rivero 192–95; Saldivar-Hull 203–20). From the time she arrives in Texas, Cleofilas is fascinated by the creek near her house, a creek named "La Gritona" (Spanish for "Woman Hollering"). She asks the inhabitants about the meaning of the name but none of them can explain its origin or significance. Her own vulnerability causes Cleofilas to ponder whether the woman hollered from anger or pain (46–47). Realizing she is trapped in a marriage with a violent husband, Cleofilas begins to hear the beckoning calls of La Llorona (51). But she resists the pull to drown herself and her baby, and she learns a new and far more positive meaning for "La Gritona" when Felice drives her to the bus station to escape back to Mexico. Driving over the stream, Felice hollers as loud as anyone else (55). As Ellen McCracken has noted, Cisneros has transformed a symbol of victimization into a "symbol of action" (17). Even the identity ascribed to mythic figures can be transformed by the postmodern heroine.

In "Never Marry a Mexican," Clemencia's white lover Drew likes to cast himself in the role of Cortez and call her his "Malinalli" or "Malinche" (74). The historical Malinche (Dona Marina) was an Aztec woman who was Cortez' translator and mistress. Malinche has functioned as a powerful archetype in the literature written by Mexicans and Mexican Americans because of her role as symbolic "mother" of the Mexican people. According to some historical accounts, the cast-off Malinche was married off to one of Cortez' soldiers when Cortez' wife came to the New World (Rebolledo 63–64; Rebolledo and Rivero 192–93). Clemencia, in contrast, refuses to disappear or suffer quietly when Drew goes back to his wife. As Gwendolyn Diaz says, the Latina "rescues her identity" from the cultural division of being "either the good Virgin/Madonna or the bad Malinche/Prostituta" (135).

Ines's story in "Eyes of Zapata" re-creates the mythic image of the *bruja*, another of the most prominent female archetypes in the literature written by Latinas (Castillo 145–61; Rebolledo 83). The *bruja*'s special powers allow her to transgress human limits, giving her power over both genders. Ines keeps Zapata tied to her, drawing him from his wife and his other women. While he is sleeping beside her on one of these visits, she tells him about her magic where she seduces him, even from afar, and then twists him until his dreams match hers (99).

Women who possess the power of the *bruja* may pay a terrible price for transgressing gender roles. Ines's mother was a *bruja* who was brutally murdered specifically because she demanded the independence allowed males in her culture. She was attacked, gang-raped, murdered, and left as a warning to other women (111). From childhood, Ines is feared, hated, and hunted because of her special powers. The villagers want to burn her when the harvest is bad (104). As an adult, she suffers Zapata's betrayal, struggles through violence and near starvation during the civil war, and keeps herself and her daughter alive by whatever means she can summon. Cisneros's story allows Ines to speak in full of her human vulnerability and suffering, her struggles to develop her *bruja* powers, her use of these powers for healing, survival, and perhaps, at times, for revenge. Ines is a magnificent heroine, a complex and very human female character who yet possesses and develops extraordinary and mythic powers.

Similar to the manner in which the *bruja* becomes a fully rounded character, marked by complexity and conflict, so too does the central religious icon in the Mexican American spiritual tradition take on a complicated double identity in "Little Miracles, Kept Promises." Chayo's letter, which closes the story, is the longest of the letters. Writing to Our Lady of Guadalupe, Chayo explains that she had previously blamed this religious figure for the suffering her mother and the other women in her family experienced in their lives. Repudiating the Guadalupe tradition because of its connection with an ideal of passive female suffering, Chayo could not acknowledge the existence of multiple traditions and multiple effects on her culture. Once she comes to acknowledge this complexity, Chayo is able to offer a "rearticulation of the Virgin of Guadalupe as an image of feminist strength" (McCracken 139).

During the years when she rejected Guadalupe, Chayo had yearned instead for a goddess who could be imaged "bare breasted . . . swallowing raw hearts and rattling volcanic ash" (127). Studying the history of the Guadalupe tradition, Chayo gains a new and important insight: in accepting Guadalupe, she is not simply praying to the Christian version of Mary but also to "our mother Tonantzin"—whose temple at Tepeyac is the site of Guadalupe's basilica. Guadalupe's shrine is sacred ground, regardless of which goddess is worshipped there (127–28). Moreover, Chayo's new understanding of the complexity of identity does not simply extend to Guadalupe; she begins to admit that her mother and grandmother have power, too, the power of "understanding someone else's pain" (128).

The third and final section of "*Bien* Pretty" closes the story and the story collection with a scene in which Lupe creates a daily ritual of euphoria. The teenager's fate in "One Holy Night" is an exception, but Cisneros concludes the stories of all of her adult protagonists by moving them into a state of euphoria. John Gerlach, in his book on closure in the short story, discusses the function of euphoria:

Certain mental states are associated with natural termination. Statements of bliss, satisfaction, or euphoria are terminal in their own right, even if divorced from problems and their solutions. No further movement is required for a character attaining nirvana. It does not matter if the bliss is ironic, if a character deludes himself—the presence of this form of natural termination will nevertheless close the story. (9)

"Woman Hollering Creek" ends with Cleofilas recounting the scene when Felice drove her over the stream named "Woman Hollering." The self-confident Felice startles Cleofilas by yelling loudly in laughing tribute to the name of the creek. True to her own name, Felice lets out a joyful Texas whoop that reveals she knows she has the right to holler as loudly and assertively as Tarzan (55–56). Felice teaches Cleofilas a lesson of hope and even joy by transforming the lamentation of the "weeping woman" into the shout of a laughing "mariachi." In the short last paragraph of the story, Cleofilas describes how she moved out of her state of terror and depression; she joins Felice in remaking the myth of the weeping woman into the tale of a laughing woman.

Concluding her narrative in "Never Marry a Mexican," Clemencia gives in to the temptation to telephone her former lover Drew at two o'clock in the morning. Surprisingly, the act of calling Drew actually releases Clemencia into a state that allows her to claim the significance of her name. After Drew hangs up on her, she excuses her conduct to the man she still calls "Love" by saying "Good or bad, I've done what I had to do and needed to" (83). In the final paragraphs of her story, Clemencia stops demanding reparation for the injustice done to her and moves into a loving understanding of the tie between the long-married couple. She offers clemency, even affection, to the couple and to herself.

In the short concluding paragraph, Clemencia, the archetypal betrayed and revengeful mistress, wishes compassion for all people. Here are her last words: "Sometimes all humanity strikes me as lovely. I just want to reach out and stroke someone, and say There, there, it's all right, honey. There, there, there" (83). Thomson finds this "a curiously conflicting statement" for a character so obsessed with seduction and revenge (421). However, Cisneros's sympathy for Clemencia is clearly expressed in the logic of Clemencia's transformation from revengeful seductress to good mother/lover, a transformation dictated by the use of euphoria as a form of "natural" termination for the whole series of stories focused on adult female characters.

"Eyes of Zapata" ends with a sweeping transcendent vision. As a *bruja,* Ines has developed skill at achieving trances in which she leaves her body and flies in the form of a *tecolote* (owl). Often she uses this visionary "flying" to watch over Zapata while he is away from her, and over time this power to transcend the limits of her own life brings her a sense of freedom, joy, and ecstasy (97–99).

In the story's concluding segment, Zapata is sleeping beside Ines on one of his visits. While he sleeps, Ines soars high in the sky, "farther" than she's flown before. She is able to look down on a vision of her life, seeing the future and then the past. She sees Zapata's death and her own funeral; she sees the loss of the revolution. She sees that change and permanence are the same. She sees the fragments that make up a universe: animate and inanimate, human and nonhuman, beautiful and ugly, sick and healthy, all are part of a complex tapestry; all have their rightful place.

At dawn, Ines returns from her vision to address Zapata with love: "My sky, my life, my eyes, Let me look at you. Before you open those eyes of yours. . . . Before we go back to what we'll always be" (113). "Eyes of Zapata" is the most powerful story in Cisneros's collection;

Ines is the heroine who haunted Cisneros's dreams (Ganz 27; Sagel 74). In spite of her pain, Ines's vision concludes with the bliss that comes from her acceptance of personal love and also her visionary acceptance of all existence.

Chayo is likewise moved to ecstatic spiritual insight in the conclusion to "Little Miracles, Kept Promises." Imitating the litanies of the Catholic church, Chayo praises Guadalupe by chanting the indigenous names of the Aztec foremothers of Guadalupe, the Spanish names that Mexicans use to honor Guadalupe, and the English names used to invoke Mary. In the conclusion to her prayer, Chayo identifies Guadalupe with the power of God. The postmodern heroine transgresses the traditional exclusion of the feminine from the divine. She ends her prayer by endowing Guadalupe with the names used by the world's religions to address the highest power: "the Buddha, the Tao, the true Messiah" (128). In the last sentence of the story, Chayo explains that learning to love Guadalupe has taught her to love herself (128). Like Ines, Chayo/Rosario ends her story with an affirmation of personal love—this time directed toward herself—and with an empowering spiritual vision.

The third and final segment of "*Bien* Pretty" shows Lupe seeking euphoria and intensity by means of a vision more accessible to the ordinary person than the one that Ines creates. At twilight every evening, Lupe hastily puts aside her painting brushes and rushes up to the roof of her garage. There she stands and watches the despised *urrachas* (grackles) as these birds arrive to settle in the trees by the side of the San Antonio River (164). The simple act of settling for the night seems to arouse ecstatic energy in the birds: "And every bird in the universe chittering, jabbering, clucking, chirruping, squawking, gurgling, going crazy because God-bless-it another day has ended, as it if never had yesterday and never will again tomorrow" (165). As a postmodern heroine, Lupe uses her freedom to choose the vision she wants rather than submit to one constucted by others. She separates herself from those who habitually look down and see only the excrement left on the ground by the birds. Sharing the soaring dance of song and flight of a flock of birds marking the end of each day, Lupe concludes her story and Cisnero's collection of short fiction on a literal and metaphorical high note.

References

Castillo, Ana. *Massacre of the Dreamers: Essays on Xicanisma*. Albuquerque: U of New Mexico P, 1994. 145–61.

Cisneros, Sandra. Interview. Videocassette. Santa Fe: Lannon Foundation, 1997.

————. *Woman Hollering Creek and Other Stories*. New York: Vintage, 1991.

Diaz, Gwendolyn. "Postmodern Pop: The Construction of Context in the Fiction of Sandra Cisneros." *Actes du VI congres europeen sur les cultures d'Amerique Laine aux Etats-Unis: confrontations et metissages*. Ed. Elyette Benjamin-Labarthe et al. Bordeaux: Maison des pays Iberiques, 1995. 133–40.

Di Stefano, Christine. "Dilemnas of Difference: Feminism, Modernity, and Postmodernism." *Feminism/Postmodernism*. Ed. Linda J. Nicholson. New York: Routledge, 1990. 63–82.

Doyle, Jacqueline. "Haunting the Borderlands: La Llorona in Sandra Cisneros's 'Woman Hollering Creek.'" *Frontiers: A Journal of Women's Studies* 16 (1996): 53–70.

Flax, Jane. "Postmodernisms and Gender Relations in Feminist Theory." *Feminism/Postmodernism*. Ed. Linda J. Nicholson. New York: Routledge, 1990. 39–62.

Ganz, Robin. "Sandra Cisneros: Border Crossings and Beyond." *MELUS* 19 (spring 1994): 19–29.

Gerlach, John. *Toward the End: Closure and Structure in the American Short Story*. University: U of Alabama P, 1985.

Harding, Sandra. "Feminism, Science, and the Anti-Enlightenment Critiques." *Feminism/Postmodernism*. Ed. Linda J. Nicholson. New York: Routledge, 1990. 83–106.

Huyssen, Andreas. "Mapping the Postmodern." *Feminism/Postmodernism*. Ed. Linda J. Nicholson. New York: Routledge, 1990. 234–77.

Lewis, L. M. "Ethnic and Gender Identity: Parallel Growth in Sandra Cisneros' Woman Hollering Creek." *Short Story* 2 (fall 1994): 69–77.

May, Charles E. "Metaphoric Motivation in Short Fiction." *Short Story Theory at a Crossroads*. Ed. Susan Lohafer and Jo Ellyn Clarey. Baton Rouge: Louisana State UP, 1989. 62–73.

McCracken, Ellen. *New Latina Narrative: The Feminine Space of Postmodern Ethnicity*. Tucson: U of Arizona P, 1999.

Rebolledo, Tey Diana. *Women Singing in the Snow: A Cultural Analysis of Chicana Literature*. Tucson: U of Arizona P, 1995.

Rebolledo, Tey Diana, and Eliana S. Rivero. *Infinite Divisions: An Anthology of Chicana Literature*. Tucson: U of Arizona P, 1993.

Sagel, James. "Sandra Cisneros." Interview. *Publishers Weekly* Mar. 1991: 74–75.

Saldivar-Hull, Sonia. "Feminism on the Border: From Gender Politics to Geopolitics." *Criticism in the Borderlands: Studies in Chicano Literature, Culture, and Ideology*. Ed Hector Calderon and Jose David Saldivar. Durham: Duke UP, 1991. 203–20.

Thomson, Jeff. "'What Is Called Heaven': Identity in Sandra Cisneros's Woman Hollering Creek." *Studies in Short Fiction* 31 (1994): 415–24.

The Silence of the Bears: Leslie Marmon Silko's Writerly Act of Spiritual Storytelling

Brewster E. Fitz

Wovon man nicht sprechen kann, darüber muss man schweigen.
[What we cannot speak about we must pass over in silence.]
—Ludwig Wittgenstein

"This is my helper," he told Tayo. "They call him Shush. That means bear."
—Leslie Marmon Silko, *Ceremony*

The short "autobiographical" passage in *Storyteller* that begins with the sentence "When I was thirteen I carried an old .30–30 we borrowed from George Pearl" (77) and ends with the verse "Sleeping, not dead, I decided" (79), is both a coming-of-age hunting story and a bear story. Like the other bear stories found in Silko's writing, it is informed by silence, liminality, paradox, and an uncanny ambiguity.[1] In this essay I shall offer a reading of this short story from *Storyteller*, in which I argue that, among other things, it is an account of young Leslie Marmon's becoming not just a hunter, but also a writing storyteller, a writer priest endowed with the writerly art of spiritual storytelling.

Liminality and undecidability are indicated both in the details and in the temporal and spatial setting of the story. At the age of thirteen Leslie Marmon is on the threshold between childhood and adulthood. She depicts herself hunting at a time of year between fall and winter: "patches of melting snow" lie about, but the sunny afternoon suggests

winter has not yet arrived (78). This is her first time to hunt with a
high-powered rifle, but neither this rifle nor the status of hunter is per-
manently hers. Both are borrowed, so to speak. Thus, she is cautious to
pass over in silence any possible sign that she might not yet be ready to
handle the high power, not yet ready to pass from adolescence into the
world of adult hunters. The gun is heavy and hurts her shoulder, but
she makes no protest because she is happy to be hunting for the first
time. It turns out that during her first hunt, young Leslie experiences a
power much greater than that of the old .30–30 or of her father's larger
caliber rifle. She returns from Mt. Taylor not with a stag but with a
story of a giant sleeping bear, an animal known especially among Native Americans for its great spiritual and physical power. But, just as
she doesn't say anything about the old .30–30, lest she not be allowed
to hunt, so she does not tell her story. In writing what she did not say,
she leaves the impression that not only does she become a hunter, but
that she also remains in a betwixt and between—similar to the silent—
ursine liminality inhabited by Old Betonie's helper Shush in *Ceremony*,
or by the anonymous person addressed in "Story From Bear Country."

Silko's description of seeing this giant bear shares some details with
a scene from an early novella, *Humaweepi, the Warrior Priest* (1971), in
which the young protagonist's vision of a giant sleeping bear is part of
what may be read as a coming-of-age ritual. Humaweepi, an orphan,
has been raised outside of the pueblo by an elderly uncle. At the age of
nineteen he accompanies his uncle on a long trip into the mountains.
The old man leads his nephew to a lake, the unexpected appearance of
which stirs in the young man the desire to ask a question, which is,
however, never voiced.[2] It is shushed in Humaweepi's experience of his
uncle's gestures and singing as natural phenomena. Humaweepi sees a
lake he has never seen before. He wants to ask his uncle about it, but the
old man is singing and throwing corn pollen to the winds.

In this lake Humaweepi sees what from a distance appears to be a
boulder.

Having obeyed his uncle's silent sign to come closer, he sees that
the boulder is "[t]he bear. Magic creature of the mountains, powerful
ally to men" (Rosen 165). Humaweepi's response to seeing this bear is
to sing a prayer asking it for power and protection, after which he realizes that he is completing a coming-of-age ritual from which he will
emerge a warrior and a priest.

Whereas Silko's fictive warrior priest in her early novella first sees
a boulder off in the distance, then from up close a giant sleeping bear,
to which he intones a song, young Leslie in *Storyteller* first sees a giant
bear from a distance and without approaching it, conceives a silent

question, "Dead or just sleeping, I couldn't tell" (77). Part of the purpose of writing the story of the giant bear, which young Leslie at first decided to leave untold, was to tell how she later decided the bear was sleeping, not dead. Another part of the purpose, however, appears to be to tell what she cannot tell because she cannot speak of it. The juxtaposition of this story from *Storyteller* with a later telling of a different version in "An Essay on Rocks" (*Yellow Woman* 187–91) suggests that rather than resolving whether the bear was sleeping or dead, the writing storyteller points to the ambiguity and silence underlying all of her writing. In the essay, Silko rewrites the bear story so that she resembles Humaweepi; she approaches for a closer look at what she had seen from a distance: "Once while I was deer hunting I saw a giant bear sleeping on a rock in the sun; when I got closer there was only the great basalt boulder amid the patches of melting snow" (191). But, insofar as Silko portrays herself as seeing the bear from afar, rather than from up close, she marks a difference between herself and Humaweepi, the warrior priest. Rather than the silently posed question from *Storyteller*, "Dead or just sleeping, I couldn't tell" (77), the question that Silko, the writer priest silently poses in the novella and in the essay is whether the vision is a bear or a boulder, or both a bear and a boulder.

In "An Essay on Rocks" Silko relates the vision of the bear almost as an afterthought in an account of how she had at first perceived a rock in a distant arroyo near her house outside of Tucson to be "a black form," "a blackened carcass or a floor safe half buried in the sand" (187). Upon approaching she sees "only a black rock the size of an auto engine alone in the middle of the arroyo half buried in white sand" (190–91). This essay is accompanied by photographs of the rock from different distances. In uncanny transitions, Silko subtly leaves undecided whether "the angle of the sun or the shift in shadows on the snow next to the rock" and her imagination are responsible for her perceptions, or whether some power residing in the rock as well as in herself is responsible for the vision (191).

In the case of a power possibly residing in the rocks and in the writer herself, Silko, in another essay entitled "On Photography" (*Yellow Woman* 180–86), posits that her imagination, as she has come to understand it, is informed by a special power that she thinks shows itself in the silent art of photography, an art whose practice she shares with her father and which she relates to magic: "My father Lee H. Marmon, learned photography in the army. But to me it is still *magic*" (180; emphasis added). Silko goes on to offer a scientific explanation of this magic in terms of contemporary physics: "The more I read about the behavior of subatomic particles of light, the more confident I am that photographs are capable of registering subtle electromagnetic changes in both the subject and the photographer" (180). In resorting to modern Western science to explain the magic of photography, Silko is putting in question the conceptual boundary between photographic subject and photographer, much as the boundary between subject and object, or observer and observed, is put in question by postmodern philosophers who speculate epistemologically about Werner Heisenberg's uncertainty principle.[3] Here Silko is scientifically positing that a photograph comprises not just traces of the chemical reaction that occurs when a photographer exposes a portion of film to visible light reflecting off the photographic subject, but it also comprises traces of the "invisible" electromagnetic radiation produced by an interaction between the photographer and the subject being photographed. Now, in telling of rocks that appear from a distance to be different objects, Silko is implicitly stating that she, like the photograph, can "register" visually what usually appears invisible to the naked eye. In other words, Silko is writing that at special times, in special places, she is endowed with a "magic photographic" vision that allows her to see the invisible from a distance. Silko's story of the giant bear sleeping in the sun could thus be taken as a story about her first experience of this special vision at the time of her first hunt.

Of course, there is no photograph of a boulder or of a bear accompanying the bear story in *Storyteller*. There is a photograph of the young Leslie standing between five slain deer and her Uncle Polly and her Uncle Walter. What registers the vision of the invisible bear in the pages of *Storyteller* is writing. Just as photography (etymologically, light + writing) is envisaged magico-scientifically by Silko as silent traces of the visible and the *in*visible, so writing can be understood as silent traces of the effable and the *in*effable—of the tellable and untellable—as well as of the visible and the invisible. It would follow that writing, like photography, could be considered by Silko to be *magic*, especially when it *registers* her vision of a giant bear, "[m]agic creature of the mountains, powerful ally to men" (*Ceremony* 165).

As she tells how she discerned whether the bear is "dead or just sleeping," Silko shushes other questions that are inextricably interwoven into this story about telling the untellable and seeing the invisible. In order to do this, young Leslie will need the power to tell silently—to write, a power that the warrior priest, who has not been to school, apparently does not have.

This power to write entails the power to silence one's reader. In the passage that follows the question "Dead or just sleeping," as in the "Essay on Rocks," Silko passes over in silence questions that some of her readers might voice. Without literally writing these questions, she never-theless acknowledges their conceptual appropriateness. For example, she mentions the possibility of visual problems that could have been caused by physical strain on the eyes or on the imagination. The five years of prehunting experience are mentioned to shush the reader who might want to voice the question, Real or just imaginary? In order to keep this question quietly dormant in her text and in her reader, the writing storyteller tells how she as a young hunter allowed her heartbeat and her breathing to slow—how, in order to assure herself of her power of perception, she, the observer, became almost as motionless as the giant bear observed. She moves only her eyes in a silent quest for an older uncle or cousin to witness her vision. But there is no one to witness or to bring her back, so to speak, from the special place and time from which she can see this bear. That she will be able to do only in writing.

Before the young hunter shifts her eyes back to the giant bear, she consults her memory to confirm that this bear in size alone surpasses all other known bears. In having the young hunter refer to her knowl-edge of the physiological dimensions of bears, either from oral hunting stories, in which bears do have a tendency to grow larger as the story is retold, or from written zoological accounts that are informed by the objective spirit of scientific observation, the writing storyteller cau-tiously avoids stating another question about this bear that lies dor-mant in the text: Preternatural or just natural?

Having suspended in silence both questions that a reader in the spirit of scientific inquiry or in the spirit of common sense, might feel obliged to ask, the writing storyteller depicts the young hunter as mo-tionless as the bear, suspended in a space and time, so to speak, whence she wonders how she might "tell" the only explicitly worded question "Dead or just sleeping." It turns out that she will leave this question undecided for two years. In doing so, young Leslie nevethe-less carefully acts as if the bear were just sleeping, thereby showing a wise hunter's great respect for the bear whose power is even greater than that of the borrowed .30–30.

The old borrowed .30–30, which the young hunter knows is not powerful enough to stop this giant bear dead in its tracks, were it real and natural—much less preternatural—and just sleeping, could, how-ever, annihilate the vision of the bear, were it just imaginary. One can see this by envisaging the following scenario: The young hunter fires the .30–30 over the bear's head. The bear does not move. The young hunter approaches to examine the "dead" bear up close and discovers either that there is nothing there or, as in the abbreviated retelling in "An Essay on Rocks," that "there was only the great basalt boulder amid the patches of melting snow" (191). Of course, the bear could also remain lying there either because it was hibernating above rather than below ground, or because it was dead.

Rather than allowing the young hunter to risk a confrontation with a real sleeping bear, be it natural or preternatural, or with a dead bear, or with no bear at all, the writing storyteller walks her young self away from the place where she viewed the bear from a distance. From this distance in a spiritual photograph, so to speak, she has registered the bear power within and without herself. She seems to be operating almost according to some law that resembles Heisenberg's uncertainty principle. Having "measured" the bear from afar, she cannot simultaneously measure it up close. She leaves behind in uncertainty what is visible, leaving the feeling that something portentous, uncanny, and very powerful is blowing in the wind behind her at Chato, this ancient site of volcanic eruptions. Here the young writing storyteller's glancing back brings to the surface the previously shushed question Real or just imaginary? as well as the question Preternatural or just natural? It also recalls other stories from bear country, such as "He was a small child" (*Ceremony* 128–30; *Storyteller* 207–09), in which a child, apparently Shush, who has wandered away from his human family and joined a bear family, must be called back by a medicine man. Although this calling back is accomplished according to prescribed ceremonial steps in order to keep the child from being left suspended in an ursine betwixt and between, it seems that the child can never return. Young Leslie, however, apparently does not require a medicine *man* to call her back. The writerly and spiritual power awakening within her enables her to return and shush her changed self. Like Shush, who helps old Betonie lead Tayo through the Navajo Red Antway in *Ceremony*, like Humaweepi the warrior priest, the young hunter will not be the same when she returns. But unlike Shush, she will not literally be sentenced to silence or ursine grunts. She will be able to write. She will have silently and carefully taken the first steps toward becoming a writing storyteller, a writer priest whose writerly spirituality brings not only herself but also her ancestors back from states that are figured in *Storyteller*.

Nevertheless, the space into which she brings herself and her ancestors remains a liminal and a mixed space, whether it be the space of the page of her recent essays or the space of *Storyteller*. From this space there emerge questions and rumors that Silko still must shush as she continues to write from her home outside Tucson. Thus, rather than force an end to the ambiguity, the young writer priest reasons according to a magic dialogic. Unlike Humaweepi who lays beads from his medicine bundle on the "gray granite rock" that is the magic bear's head, Leslie defers an examination of the giant bear up close, thereby deferring both the telling and the ending of her bear story. What the young hunter cannot tell, in either sense of this word, the writing storyteller also leaves undecided in writing. She leaves not only the sleeping bear, but also the questions about this giant bear's status, as well as the question about the sanity of a young hunter who passes over such a story in silence: "I never told anyone what I had seen because I knew they don't let people who see such things carry .30–30's or hunt deer with them" (78).

Even when the somewhat older storyteller on the following page in lines set up as verse, repeats the story, the ambiguity remains. When her uncle Polly is rewarded by an appearance of "the old man of the mountain," Leslie finds herself again in the liminal setting of two years earlier. Her patience in waiting for an answer without telling is rewarded as she "deliberately" moves up close to the place where she saw the giant bear, but she finds no bones: "Sleeping, not dead, I decided" (79).

For the young hunter finding *no bones* on Chato is "telling." She sees *nothing*, but feels in the wind *something* that causes her to hurry around the hill to find her uncle Polly. Rather than allowing a reader to understand that the lack of bones eliminates the ambiguity reading, Silko effects a spiritual reading in which finding "no bones" annihilates the fact of physical death for the bear registered in the spiritual photograph. The spiritual and writerly narrative point of view of the writing storyteller not only refuses to let the giant bear die, it also refuses to annihilate it according to the logic of scientific inquiry or to the logic of the letter.[4]

Of course, Silko must be aware, that finding "no bones" there, or in other words, seeing *nothing* there, if read in the spirit of classical Western epistemology, could indeed be taken to show either that the bear was sleeping there or that *no bear* was there two years earlier. The heretofore shushed decision of the fifteen-year-old hunter cannot put an end to the ambiguity of the story.

Silko, who no longer lives at Laguna, yet who adamantly refuses from a distance to give up her vision of the Laguna oral tradition; Silko, the internationally known Native American writer who is celebrated by modern and postmodern critics, can best exercise the photographic or magic power she has as writing storyteller to rewrite Laguna spirituality by shushing the story of her writerly spirituality or madness in a silent glyph where uncertainty is given ontological status owing to its invisibility. Like the giant bear lying in the sun in the liminal setting on Chato, like the "blackened carcass or floor safe" Silko saw lying near "crumbling volcanic tufa" (187), the Laguna tradition is hibernating on the written page of *Storyteller.*

In the "Program" included in the first issue of *Glyph*, a deconstructionist and postmodern journal of textual studies, Samuel Weber tropes the saying of Ludwig Wittgenstein that opens this essay: "Wovon man nicht sprechen kann, darüber muss man schreiben" [What we cannot say, we must write] (xi). By replacing *schweigen* with *schreiben* (to pass over in silence with to write), by using a postmodern logic of undecidability, I have attempted here to envision the mixed conceptual space in which Leslie Marmon Silko uses her writerly art of spiritual storytelling to tell what cannot be told.

Notes

1. Silko's "bear stories" are found in "Humaweepi, the Warrior Priest," in *Ceremony* ("He was a small child"; 128–30), and in *Storyteller* ("Story From Bear Country"; 204–07). "He was a small child," which appears to offer insight into the ursine nature of Old Betonie's helper Shush, also appears in *Storyteller* (207–09).

2. This unasked question could be whether the lake is Kawaik, the Keresan name for the lake beside which Laguna is said to have been built and after which the pueblo was named. Thus, there is the possible sign that Humaweepi and his uncle have taken a temporal as well as a spatial journey in their ascent up the mountain.

3. For example, Douglas Hofstadter opens the way for his readers to remain undecided about undecidability: "By the way, in passing, it is interesting to note that all results essentially dependent on the fusion of subject and object have limitative results. In addition to the limitative theorems, there is Heisenberg's uncertainty principle, which says that measuring one quantity renders impossible the simultaneous measurement of a related quantity. I don't know why all these results are limitative. Make of it what you will" (699).

4. I am alluding here to the exegetic logic expressed in Paul's words "the letter killeth but the spirit giveth life" (2 Cor. 3.6). Silko makes no bones about her strong dislike of Christianity, despite her acknowledgment that her beloved grandmother A'mooh was a devout Presbyterian. It is ironically fitting that in her autobiographical bear story, as well as in other passages from *Storyteller*, Silko, the writer priest, treats the Laguna written word as though it were endowed with the ontological power to create, to give life.

References

Hofstadter, Douglas R. *Gödel, Escher, Bach: An Eternal Golden Braid*. New York: Vintage, 1979.
Rosen, Kenneth, ed. *The Man to Send Rain Clouds: Contemporary Stories by American Indians*. New York: Viking, 1974.

Silko, Leslie Marmon. *Ceremony*. New York: Penguin, 1986.

———. *Storyteller*. New York: Arcade, 1981.

———. *Yellow Woman and a Beauty of the Spirit: Essays on Native American Life Today*. New York: Simon, 1996.

Weber, Samuel. "Program." *Glyph I* (1977): vii–xi.

The Feminine Consciousness as Nightmare in the Short-Short Stories of Joyce Carol Oates

Wayne Stengel

The short stories of Joyce Carol Oates have frequently combined elements of the gothic with a feminine fear of desire, the body, or sexuality. This paradigm is nowhere more vivid than in a concise, highly elliptical variety of Oates's story of no more than five, and often under three, pages. In the afterword to her 1995 collection of short stories *Haunted: Tales of the Grotesque*, Oates identifies several qualities of the grotesque that she finds in many categories of horror in art: (1) the inaccessibility, unreality, and mysteriousness of human subjectivity; (2) the blunt physicality of gothic horror; (3) the attractiveness of evil and its ability to make its perpetrators active accomplices in a powerful action; and (4) the awareness by both men and women that individuals do have their role and place on a biological food chain (303–07).

Applying these precepts to five of Oates's short stories, "Fatal Woman" from *Night-Side* (1977) and "Happy," "The Mother," "Little Blood-Button," and "Nuclear Holocaust" from *Raven's Wing* (1986), makes a fascinating case for Oates's linkage of feminine desire and the horrific. In "Fatal Woman" a young girl, who confesses that she has always been a femme fatale realizes, with increasing terror, that she has been the object of sexual desire for several generations of males in her community. In "Happy," a young girl describes herself slipping inexorably, and against her will, into the sexual hold of her new stepfather over both her and her aging mother. In "The Mother," a middle-age housewife describes, with both horror and passion, her sexual desire for her teenage son, intensified by the boy's growing appetite for young women in his world. With "Little Blood-Button" and "Nuclear

Holocaust," we find Oates at her most elusive and experimental in the short story form. These are angry, crazed three-page monologues, the first from a prostitute livid at the men who have left a blackened cyst on her upper lip, and the second from a deranged mental patient who sees the anger of Jesus as a means of bringing nuclear holocaust to punish and bless civilization in the same instant.

These stories articulately demonstrate that being a woman in contemporary America can make one the unwitting object of the desires of others, can create incestuous transference between family members, or can make one physically or psychically wounded by the presumptions of masculine desire. In Oates's mingling of feminine fear of desire with the strains of Gothic literature in American culture, we begin to understand the formal constraints and intensities of these short stories that can seem, superficially, autodidactic, hallucinatory outpourings of the bereft, the repressed, or the mutilated. As Oates herself says of the short-short story form, "Very short fictions are nearly always experimental, exquisitely calibrated, reminiscent of Frost's definition of a poem—a structure of words that consumes itself as it unfolds, like ice melting on a stove,"or human desire itself (Shapard and Thomas 83).

One of the most important and prototypic of all Oates's short stories is "Fatal Woman" from *Night-Side*. In this four-page, short-short story, Oates locates several themes, defined and redefined in a large number of her stories and novels throughout an extraordinarily prolific career. Initially, "Fatal Woman" is an unabashed first-person account of a femme fatal, a woman who recounts her lifelong ability to attract, mesmerize, and then release the men in her life from the powerful hold of her physicality. The story quickly develops a macabre and then grisly tone as the narrator begins to understand, perhaps through the cadence of her own telling, that she is as much victim of the men in her grasp as their seductress. Grotesquely, this fatal woman has been pursued by several generations of men. As she grows older—and presumably remains physically unchanged—many young men, including her son-in-law, desire her. Oates concludes her tale with the narrator's hamartia, revelation, her gaining of knowledge that she has become a sexual vampire, a monstrosity who fears that her body like the haunted manor house in Gothic literature can be invaded by intruders at any time. Deliriously pleased with her sexual power at the story's beginning, her body's ability to make her ecstatically happy produces a parallel sense of doom by story's end.

Some criticisms of Oates, as well as Oates's speculations on her own writing, have frequently disdained feminist approaches to interpreting her works. Yet these very short-short stories in which sexual desire eats its own children are consistently, sympathetically feminist in scope and tone. In these tales women are conditioned to use their beauty and sexuality to interest and entice men and then remain prisoners of male libidinous impulses all their lives. The supernatural horror of "Fatal Women" is that sex and sex play become the means to trap women in their own bodies and into perpetual subservience to men. Excerpts from "Fatal Woman" reveal the increasing hysteria with which the narrator's consciousness of her unappeased sexuality becomes a nightmare vision for her.

The first time, the very first time, I became aware of my power over men, I was only twelve years old. . . . There must be something about me, an aura of some kind, that I don't know about. Only a man would know. It's the strangest thing. . . . If I take pity on him I can somehow "release" him and allow him to look away and talk to others; it's hard to explain how I do this—I give a nearly imperceptible nod and a little smile and I will him to be released, and it works, and the poor man is free. . . . I take pity on men most of the time. . . . It seems a woman's body sometimes might be flirtatious by itself without the woman herself exactly knowing. (256–60)

A seminal Oates short-short story like "Fatal Woman" also reveals her incantatory, hypnagogic power as a storyteller. In many ways, Oates, the most obsessively naturalistic writer in American fiction since Theodore Dreiser, is also one of America's greatest surrealistic writers. The supernatural force of this narrator's voice is finally a supranatural power revealing that no boundaries exist for this visionary voice: all voluptuous women's bodies in this story become one body; all male predators are one masculine violator. The nightmare of this story is the narrator's recognition that for women bound exclusively by their physicality or in awe of masculine knowledge, human subjectivity and differences between individual consciousness become blurred and amorphous, as do conceptions of good and evil. For these prisoners of the body and sexuality, all men and women flow into one another, controlling and horrifying, desiring to be controlled. In much of her best short fiction, Oates's authority as a visionary writer is at a conscious level, exacting war with her dominant naturalistic determinants: her beliefs that gender, class, race, age, physical strength, even considerations of geography and landscape do determine human possibility. The intense formal brevity of a short story like "Fatal Woman" results from a woman's momentary dream of dominance immediately undermined and destroyed by male surveillance, voyeurism, or violation.

In "Happy," from *Raven's Wing*, at five pages an even shorter story than "Fatal Woman," the femme fatale is an aging mother sexually rejuvenated by a late marriage to a sixtyish second husband. This new husband immediately insinuates his stepdaughter into his newfound sexual domain. Told from the fearful, repulsed perspective of his recently acquired stepdaughter, "Happy" is about the horror of mother–daughter relationships when men claim sexual rights and control over their second wives, and extend these rights to their wives' grown children. Flying home for Christmas, the graduate student narrator of "Happy" meets her new stepfather for the first time and is immediately frightened by the debilitating physical effects this whirlwind romance and second marriage has produced in her mother. The brute physicality of her stepfather's handshake and both mother and stepfather's assertions that all three of them know and understand exactly what he has done for the narrator's mother terrify the narrator:

Her mother hugged her again—God I'm so happy to see you—veins in her arms ropier than the girl remembered, the arms themselves thinner, but the mother was happy, you could feel it all about her. The pancake makeup on her face was a fragrant peach shade that had been blended skillfully into her throat . . . giggling, Jesus, she said, it just makes me so happy, having the two people I love most in the world right here with me. Right here right now. . . . He makes me feel like living again, I feel, you know, like a woman again, and the girl was too embarrassed to reply. As long as you're happy, she said. . . . He shifted his cane chair closer, leaned moist and warm, meaty, against her, an arm across her shoulders. There's nobody in the world precious to me as that lady. I want you to know that, he said, and the girl said, Yes, I know it, and her mother's new husband said in a fierce voice close to tears, Damn right, sweetheart. You know it. (103–05)

"Happy," like "Fatal Woman," seems explicitly a story about the imposition of masculine knowledge on the feminine mind and body. Oates's feminist Gothicism lies not only in the threatening sexuality of the rapacious stepfather, but in all three of the stories' characters recognition—in the classical Greek sense—that need, sexual desire, and happiness in contemporary American culture is so narrowly defined in masculine terms that satisfaction, contentment, happiness in certain American families implies incestuous authority.

"Damn right, sweetheart. You know it," the last defiant words of this short-short story, spoken as the law of the father, the new household god, in a voice close to tears, is both promise and threat. The phrase is recorded through the nervous system of a young woman, pleased for her mother's happiness at feeling like a woman again, but horrified by her parent's aging, haggard appearance, and, apparently, a sensibility without the will or the force to know what should constitute her own mental or physical happiness. The mother's power as a fatal woman over her new husband draws her closer to her blood daughter, but entangles this young woman, pinned, in Oates's words, against the warm, moist, meaty arms of the predator stepfather, in a web of complicity, fear, and sexual threat. The phrases "I want you to know," "I know it," and "you know it," in the final paragraph signify what is to be this family's learning curve. Father knows best, and mother and daughter will suffer for it.

"The Mother," also from *Raven's Wing*, is, at first reading, a more conventional, if equally brief, tale of the clash between mother love and a masculine way of knowing or understanding this force. In essence, the story is a retelling of the Phaedra legend in a monologue from a contemporary American woman. This feminine consciousness, trapped in veils of secrecy and repression, lies awake in bed next to her sleeping husband as their teenage son returns home, night after night, from early morning couplings with the young girls the mother envisions as her son's lovers. The great agon in this intense, four-page battle of wills is between a feminine force who is passionately, sexually possessed by the beauty of her son's body and the resistance of the young man to his mother's knowledge of his sexual life, particularly when he is excitingly knowing other women, other blood. The story reaches its sexual and epistemological climax in its last lines with the mother's recognition that she can hurt and violate her son's flesh but never penetrate his sexual mystery or hold over her. Only the young girl whom she believes has sex with her son might gain this kind of rapture. Yet this young girl's "cry of deliverance, cry of triumph," that a lover might savor in intercourse with her son—or possibly, the sound of her son's sexual arousal with this girl, which she hears in the rhythmic, terrified yet ecstatic telling of her own perverse love—may be no more a release than sex with the sleeping husband beside her once was. All of these instinctual sounds signify the fitful, unsatisfying release that all Oates's fatal women give to the men clamoring around them.

Why do you lie to me, she is saying to her son, her fingers closing about his arm as they have a right to close, her nails digging gently into his skin, so you think I don't know what your life is now? The things you do? You and your girls? You alone? In your room? With the door locked against your mother? (233)

Once more, the obsessive qualities of Oates's feminist Gothic nightmare are resonant in "The Mother." The blunt, intimidating physicality that Oates finds in much of the literature and art of the grotesque and the horrific in this story come from this fatal mother herself. Cursed with an unspeakable desire for her virile son, she becomes a mutilating monster who wants to abuse her son's flesh and experience his masculine knowledge of his girlfriend. Trapped in a prison, some gothic domicile of fear, imagination, and hyperconsciousness, she wants release from the locked doors that separate her from her son, just as she craves escape from the sleeping husband next to her.

Of all Oates's elliptical, highly condensed stories concerning feminine consciousness, none are more imaginative, risky, or nightmarish than "Little Blood-Button" and "Nuclear Holocaust," both from *Raven's Wing*. In "Little Blood-Button," at three paragraphs and under two pages, and "Nuclear Holocaust," at five paragraphs and also shy of two pages, Oates composes two of her most audacious, risk-taking, and ambitious fictions about the destruction of feminine desire. These stories exist and are meant largely as performance pieces, almost as actor's exercises. They drift away on the fumes of the anguished, hard-luck woman's voice that gives them dissonant, atonal rhythms and thwarted imaginative life. Both stories inhabit the minds and verbal lies of two itinerant women at near bottom of the food chain. One voice, a blousy prostitute, confronts readers as if her only auditors were a male audience of pimps, johns, and potential customers, while the other speaker, a deranged, rambling mental patient, looking for Jesus and finding only anger in His place, offers her audience a theory of nuclear holocaust that combines the Book of Revelation with visions of Hiroshima and Nagasaki. In both instances, Oates, with amazing sympathy and startlingly poetic language, asks who or what has sucked these women dry and how can two such debased imaginations admit of the visionary? The most illuminating method for revealing Oates's technique and insights in these angry, arresting monologues is to juxtapose each story against the other. In "Little Blood-Button" the prostitute speaker, a fatal woman, caustically indicts all of the men she is speaking to as responsible for the venereal chancre that has appeared suddenly after sex and has quickly swollen into an ugly, deforming blemish that cannot be covered, effaced, or healed. In her description of a herpes cyst that quickly becomes a hideous scar, this prostitute accuses all men, all her customers, whose blunt physicality is an effort to wound and own each woman they abuse: "This thing growing on my lip, upper lip, right in the middle, little bud or pimple, hot black blood, scared me to touch it! From you kissing so hard. Kissing and pressing. Biting. Sucking" (274).

In "Nuclear Holocaust," Oates's typically deformed fatal woman becomes a rambling mental patient who sets fire to herself and in her immolation sees a vision of nuclear holocaust granted her by the male psychiatrist who questions her; by the institution, drugs, and shock treatments that restrain her; and by Jesus himself, whose love, like male domination, will come to bless and destroy her in a single blinding inferno.

Oates's crazed voices in both stories have overwhelming and frightening affinities: an incongruous obsession with their bodies, physicalities, and once good looks; a savage vengeance directed at a masculine world that quite literally burns and scalds them and then contorts their bodies to its own purpose and for its own ends; and above all, a sense that their own purification, redemption, or catharsis lies in continuing connection, anguish, and physicality with the brute male force that has destroyed their beauty or integrity in the first place. Both monologues end a few short paragraphs later with each woman's assertion that her salvation—physical or spiritual—can only come from the removal of the poisons and defacing that men or male institutions have inflicted on them. Yet terrifyingly, both women are dependent on their abusers for ending the plagues and curses under which they suffer. First, the narrator of "Little Blood-Button" wants the same man, or a different succession of men, to take away with more love, more pain, more sexuality, the blood button they have burned into her flesh.

Similarly, the apocalyptic mental patient desires her lover Jesus who has, blessedly, incarcerated her once more in this mental hospital to destroy the world in a wave of thermonuclear heat that will return sinners like herself to the love of God. Just as in the magazine photos she has seen of Hiroshima, some men and their violent shadows would be baked into the walls, and these men could no longer torment her: "Dear God, I say in my prayer, send the bomb to punish us at last in your mercy and bless us in the same instant, forever and ever. Amen" (255).

In a fascinating conceit, Oates's short story collection would even hypothesize that these little blood buttons become the blinding, terrifyingly beautiful nuclear sunrise over Hiroshima, advanced technology for predatory, rapacious men to destroy fatal women and fragile civilizations.

Oates truly writes contemporary Gothic horror stories. Her fatal women are libidinous vampires and succubi, and her monstrous, predatory men are sometimes satyrs or ghouls, even more often, cannibals. A graphic, hallucinatory naturalistic writer who believes men and women are controlled by a range of forces beyond their control, from biology and genes to weather and cultural nationality, Oates's gothic feminism in some of her shortest fiction is about the mutilation of the body, the desire to bridge the unknowable abyss across another's subjectivity with some viscerating act of physical violence, even if this act numbs, destroys, or brutalizes the other—women who are often, but not always, its object. In these five stories, Oates's narrators, be they femme fatales, young women with new stepfathers, or sexually possessive mothers, clearly say: If you wish to survive in American society, eat or be eaten by the male presence in the biological niche competitive with your own. The blood button that all her customers have given the vituperative whore in this story is a localized blister, a gothic, feminist synecdoche for the illegal or therapeutic lobotomies inflicted on the weaker by the stronger, the irrational, unconditional love of Jesus and evangelical religion visited upon the meek in heart, and the blinding blow of cataclysmic technology on fragile civilization. The terrifying speed, intensity, and conclusion of each of these tales of the nightmare of feminine consciousness lies in Oates's expert dramatization of the swift reflexivity of all sexual desire. Oates simply believes, and convincingly demonstrates in these five stories that until men and women can know each other beyond sexuality, they will quickly, inevitably devour one another.

References

Oates, Joyce Carol. *Haunted: Tales of the Grotesque*. New York: Penguin, 1995.
———. *Night-Side*. New York: Fawcett Crest, 1977.
———. *Raven's Wing*. New York: Dutton, 1987.
Shapard, Robert, and James Thomas. *Sudden Fictions: American Short-Short Stories*. Salt Lake City: Peregrine Smith, 1986.

Postmodernism in Women's Short Story Cycles: Lorrie Moore's *Anagrams*

Karen Weekes

pulling the tenets of a life together
with no mere will to mastery,
only care for the many-lived, unending
forms in which she finds herself
                    —Adrienne Rich, "Transcendental Etude"

The malleable genre of the cycle has been used by authors for a variety of thematic purposes, but in the past forty years, it has increasingly come to reflect a dramatic fracturing of the self. Individual tales in this mode can be linked in any number of ways, including setting, common characters, or structural frame; however, a unifying element often used in works by contemporary women is that of a single female protagonist in stories presenting various aspects of her character, family, culture, and role choices. These pieces depict formative vocational and relationship decisions that are rife with emotional implications. The main character feels herself torn in various directions by familial, social, and personal demands; her divisive conflicts are perfectly reflected by the disjunctive possibilities of the genre in which they are presented.

Despite material prosperity and relative political stability, life in the last half of the twentieth century seems restless and disjointed, at least as reflected in contemporary American literature. The dejection and cynicism of the moderns appears to have culminated in the fatalism and brokenness of the postmodern era: fragmentation, alienation, and inescapable isolation permeate the characters of fiction. Expanding opportunities brought about through technological and social changes have not necessarily caused a concurrent expansion of personal fulfillment or happiness. As early as 1941, Erich Fromm commented that the freedom to be more "independent, self-reliant, and critical" (104) also increases man's isolation and fear, since

modern man, freed from the bonds of pre-individualistic society, which simultaneously gave him security and limited him, has not gained freedom in the positive sense of the realization of his individual self; that is, the expression of his intellectual, emotional and sensuous potentialities. Freedom, though it has brought him independence and rationality, has made him isolated and, thereby, anxious and powerless. This isolation is unbearable and the alternatives he is confronted with are either to escape from the burden of this freedom into new dependencies and submission, or to advance to the full realization of positive freedom which is based upon the uniqueness and individuality of man. (vii)

It is all too tempting to try to evade this terrifying independence by choosing not to explore individual potential and diverse goals, thus avoiding the difficult task of creating an authentic and autonomous self. But choosing this route actually creates its own discord, as the drive toward maturation opposes fear-induced acquiescence. As Sandra Bartky explains, "Each of us is in pursuit of an inner integration and unity, a sense that the various aspects of the self form a harmonious whole. But when the parts of the self are at war with one another, a person may be said to suffer from self-estrangement" (51). This inner conflict "causes a rupture in the human person," a type of psychological oppression enforced by both self and society. Alienation splinters "human nature into a number of misbegotten parts" (31). Fragmentation of the self echoes that of the family and a lack of cohesiveness throughout society.

This broken identity is reflected in the short story cycle as utilized by quite a few women in the wake of the 1960s and the second wave of the women's rights movement.[1] Although this genre dates back to the *Decameron* and *The Canterbury Tales*, its use is especially appropriate for contemporary women authors as they sort through the roles now available to their female protagonists and try to piece together a unified sense of self for them. Lorrie Moore is one of a group of writers, including Jamaica Kincaid, Harriet Doerr, Denise Chávez, Ellen Gilchrist, and Sandra Cisneros, who have used the form in this way. Although the point of view varies, fictional narratives by these authors consistently feature one contemporary female's perspective, present a multiplicity of roles from which she must choose, and emphasize the intense emotional pressure surrounding these decisions. Just as the short story cycle is greater than the sum of its parts, these protagonists' lives are richer than is reflected in any of the tales taken individually. Each illuminates a specific aspect of the protagonist or another role that is available to her; she integrates these elements as she works to create an empowering, authentic existence. The structure of these cycles replicates the complex structure of women's identities: it reflects attempts to connect these fragments in a meaningful way, to create a fulfilling and unified self.

Both sexes encounter forces that pull in myriad directions, but the situation for women is exacerbated by outdated sociological imperatives that are rarely practical or even desirable in the 1960s and beyond. Females also experience the current dislocation of the self in certain gender-specific ways. Sue Llewelyn and Kate Osborne point out that

> for women to resolve the dilemmas that they face throughout their lives often entails seeking out complex and apparently no-win solutions in a society where women are still second-class citizens with limited access to economic, educational, and professional equality with men. Women often have to struggle with hidden agendas which augment the difficulties of decision-making, the classic case being that of motherhood. . . . In women's relationships with others there is always this complex interaction of patterns that develop during childhood, pressures which come from others to perpetuate these patterns, and social structures which encourage conformity to particular ways of living. (7–9)

The plethora of choices, with the resultant conflicts and guilt no matter what their decision, has become central to the lives of contemporary females. Many changes have directly affected them: a huge increase in the number and type of vocations available, a freedom from biological reproductive mandates and their dependencies, longer and healthier life spans, and, most important, a new respect for their potential and contributions. These conflicts help to shape current writing, as Rosalind Brackenbury explains: "The Women's Movement has had a profound effect upon literature throughout the world; and just as our actions and decisions create our literature, so in turn we are represented by that literature, given back a new reflection of ourselves in portraits of other women, united by what we perceive we have in common" (56). Writing thus acts reciprocally; as contemporary females expand the short story cycle to emphasize identity conflicts, their protagonists provide role models for other authors and for readers.

The short story has itself been hailed since the beginning of the twentieth century as the perfect form for representing the *Zeitgeist* (spirit of the times) of the age. The episodic nature of this mode perfectly complements a content of isolated incidents to be knit together in the search for meaning. And this impetus toward unity and coherence makes the short story *cycle* an even stronger exemplum of contemporary life. Especially in the case of individual protagonists, the short story cycle allows the author to emphasize different aspects of a central character's personality or present various formative experiences that gain resonance by their juxtaposition with each other, eventually presenting a three-dimensional portrait. Rita Felski points out the relevance of fluid texts such as these to "the fragmented and incoherent workings of the unconscious." She describes modernism in its "disruption of hierarchical syntax and of linear time and plot, its decentering of the knowing and rational subject, [and] its fascination with the aural and rhythmic qualities of language" (26). According to Felski, these traits are the basis of a feminine aesthetic, but they also typify the cycle genre; thus the use of this mode seems especially appropriate for female authors.

The use of these aesthetic and structural principles to create a fully realized identity in the short story cycle reflects expectations both of and for women. Differences in these processes for males and females give members of each sex a distinct concept of themselves and their position in the world. These differences manifest themselves in a fractured identity, as women try to balance an increasing number of demands while also attempting to avoid being engulfed by guilt and feelings of failure both in terms of gender and culture. Contemporary cycles reflect this fragmentation of self in representations of the myriad roles a common protagonist plays.

Recent short story cycles show women in conflict with themselves and various aspects of their culture. Each tale shows another aspect of the protagonist's life that is dissonant in some way, and each collection strives to bring together the pieces into a comprehensible, if not necessarily harmonious, whole. J. Gerald Kennedy proposes that this genre continues to proliferate "perhaps because the aggregation of disparate narratives obscurely resembles the multiplicity of modern culture itself" (24). In many cases, this "aggregation of disparate narratives" more specifically reflects the diversity of roles and fragments of self that women are trying desperately to unify, or at least to understand, at the end of the twentieth century.

Lorrie Moore's short story cycles express this quest; her two early sequences, *Self-Help* (1985) and *Anagrams* (1986), both feature a contemporary woman's perspective and present a multiplicity of roles facing women. *Anagrams* especially deals quite directly with the creation of the self; it manipulates the real and imaginary roles that the protagonist and other characters assume in each story as they search for cohesive identity. Its unique structure reflects the fractured self of its protagonist, Benna Carpenter, who is shown in a series of metamorphoses. The book is comprised of four short stories and a novella, and each section features three continuing characters: Benna Carpenter, Gerard Maines, and Eleanor. The essence of their continuity transcends the flux of their varying situations and relationships to each other: In the first story, "Escape from the Invasion of the Love-Killers," Benna is a widowed nightclub singer, Gerard is her neighbor, smitten with unrequited love for her, and Eleanor is a friend of Benna's who has a child. In the fourth story, "Water," Benna is a single art history professor, a respected scholar on Mary Cassatt; Gerard is her teaching assistant, juggling the responsibilities of a wife, daughter, and graduate school; and Eleanor is an absent friend to whom Benna writes long letters. In the novella "The Nun of That," Benna is a poetry teacher and the widowed mother of an imaginary six-year-old; Gerard is her friend, a musician and an aspiring opera singer; and Eleanor is another figment of Benna's imagination: an acerbic, overweight woman who teaches physical education between cigarette breaks.

Appropriately, one of the epigraphs for the novella is taken from Lewis Carroll's *Alice in Wonderland*: "'Things flow about so here!' she said at last in a plaintive tone, after she had spent a minute or so in vainly pursuing a large bright thing, that looked sometimes like a doll and sometimes like a workbox, and was always in the shelf next above the one she was looking at" (61). This "large bright thing," shifting from a childhood doll to the workbox of adulthood, is a perfect metaphor for the cyclical and fluid nature of female identity posited by Nancy Chodorow and Judith Gardiner. Gardiner "picture[s] female identity as typically less fixed, less unitary, and more flexible than male individuality" (183). Rather than a linear progress toward autonomy and independence, females' identities are continually re-formed, allowing women to fluctuate between stages of development in response to the demands of relationships and maternal nurturing.

The consistency in both *Alice in Wonderland* and *Anagrams*, though, is this quest: the ongoing struggle on the part of the protagonist to try to make sense of experience and her longing for meaningful, permanent connections with others. In each story, Benna's personality remains basically unchanged: she is frightened of intimacy; self-doubting; uncertain of what her future will be, can be, or even should be; searching for fulfillment in her work and her relationships; and fighting off existential despair and excruciating loneliness. As she says at the beginning of the novella, "You might one day wake up and find yourself . . . say[ing] things to your students like, There is only one valid theme in literature: Life will disappoint you" (63).

Another consistent theme is that of motherhood and Benna's evolving response to that role. Benna initially is "a woman who said she had no desire to have children" (6). ("Once you've seen a child born you realize a baby's not much more than a reconstituted ham and cheese sandwich. Just a little anagram of you and what you've been eating for nine months" [6–7]). In the second story, she is told by the nurse-practitioner whom she consults about a breast lump that if she "had a child, it might straighten out [her] internal machinery a bit. . . . A woman's body is so busy preparing to make babies that every year that goes by without one is another year of rejection that is harder and harder for it to recover from. Soon it could go completely crazy" (21). Later, she accidentally gets pregnant by her insensitive and philandering boyfriend (Gerard) and has an abortion. But in the culminating novella, Benna is devoted to her daughter, Georgianne, who is funny, loving, interesting, perfect—and imaginary.

Of all of Benna's possibilities, her most satisfying role is her imaginary motherhood, where she is able to love and be loved unstintingly; to be intimate, creative, and active. Benna's motherhood is ideal and idealized in several ways: first, it contributes to her sense of her own normalcy and sanity. Throughout the book, Benna anguishes over whether she is crazy or will go crazy; Moore begins the novella, "In the dictionary, *lumpy jaw* comes just before *lunacy*, but in life there are no such clues" (63). As the nurse cautions her, a childless female "could go completely crazy" (21). In one sense, then, Benna's creation of Georgianne allows her to adopt women's most traditionally acceptable role. The next peculiarity of Benna's imaginary motherhood is that, of course, Georgianne is always GOOD, and the ramifications of child-rearing mistakes are nonexistent. Thus, Benna can be a parent without suffering any consequences or inconveniences; Llewelyn and Osborne's "hidden agendas which augment the difficulties of decision-making, the classic case being that of motherhood" (7) are neatly sidestepped. She does not have to stop her career, make divisive choices—she does not even have to give birth. She escapes the pain and difficulties of motherhood but savors the intimacy with and dependence of her child.

In contrast, her two relationships with actual people in the novella, her friendship with Gerard and her affair with her student Darrel (whose name is a near anagram for "Gerard"), are fraught with fear and posturing on all sides. Benna's imagination allows her to escape from her dissatisfying and disappointing relationships and experience their alternatives. When she is rejected, she is able, through the roles she lives in the short stories, to be intimate enough to reveal vulnerability. She is also able to explore other possibilities, to see herself perceived in different ways by various groups and individuals, as well as to recognize how she perceives herself. Ultimately Benna finds connections and meaning in a false world, a solace for the aching loneliness of her life.

The role of imagination is central to an understanding of both Benna and the book. Near the end of the novella, Benna reveals that much of significance in her life has been make-believe and hints that the stories that have come before are alternate lives that Benna has imagined. Elsewhere, Moore has commented on the importance for a writer of imagining alternatives, of being able to live vicariously through a character's choices:

Writing makes writers' lives safer, internally and mentally and spiritually, because it is the thing that they do: they make stories. . . . It's not like you're really experimenting with your life. You're not saying, "I wonder what it would be like if I walked out on my marriage and my child." That is an experiment that would be dangerous to get into. So in art, you're experimenting harmlessly. (McQuade 402)

In the first four stories and in her flights of fancy in the novella, Benna creates alternative lives for herself in the same way that a writer creates fiction; thus the structure of *Anagrams* becomes a metafictive comment on the vicarious experiences available to author, reader, and Benna herself.

The point of view of the novella "The Nun of That" underscores Benna's fractured identity, but a shift in perspective also dramatizes the depth of her loss and isolation. First person is used for segments that tell of Benna's friendship with Gerard as well as for segments about her imaginary relationships with Georgianne and Eleanor. However, third person is used for segments that detail her life as a teacher; in fact, the perspective is so removed that it refers to Benna as "the teacher" rather than by name. Benna appears to be observing her actions in this role as performed by a completely different entity. When she learns of Gerard's death, the point of view shifts abruptly from first to third person, and Benna is referred to as "the teacher" even though she is not performing a teaching role at all at that moment; in fact, she has lost her teaching position altogether. Benna moves from the vulnerable, revelatory first person to the extremely objective (and relatively controlling) role of teacher, an escape marked by her retreat into third-person narration. The next thirteen pages continue this point of view, although they refer to Benna by name. She is described as "feeling that she'd been made, forever and for now, . . . stupid with loneliness, bereft of any truth or wisdom or flicker of poetry, possessed only of the wild glaze of a person who spends entire days making things up" (213). Ultimately, though, Benna is returned to the telling of her own story; in the last two pages, she returns to a life amalgamated of fantasy and reality, resurrecting Georgianne: "She is a gift I have given myself, a lozenge of pretend" (225). Carol Hill notes that *Anagrams* "is a powerful example of how imagination can save us with temporary pleasures," as Benna's life is filled with intimacy, fragments of poetry, and self-realization about the meaning of her need for fantasy (15). Matthew Gilbert calls this emphasis on her imagined life "the unity and the punchline of the novel: Benna is a broken woman for whom fiction and humor are preferable realities, solutions to the emptiness and mediocrity of her life" (30). Georgianne's malapropism, "sometimes . . . I feel like I'm right in the mist of things," is all too accurate ("Nun" 225). Georgianne is certainly central to Benna's sense of herself, and Benna's imaginary life gives her will and hope in the "midst" of a lonely reality.

Anagrams was marketed as a novel, which emphasizes the connections between chapters, themes, characters, motifs, and plots. There are consistencies in several elements of this work, but the inconsistencies prevent *Anagrams* from fitting the novelistic genre, and the cumulative effect of the five sections of the work prevent it from being classified as a short story collection. The setting of almost all the stories is Fitchville, and the restaurants and bars in each tale have the same name if not the same ambience. Paintings of the idealized maternal figure by Renoir and Cassatt appear prominently in three of the five selections; significantly, the Renoir print of *Madame Charpentier* is defaced in the last story, mirroring Benna's having to confess and temporarily dissolve her imagined world. Throughout the cycle, the names and oftentimes the personalities of the characters remain the same; however, the shifts in their occupations and emotional situations violate the traditional character development that a novel offers. These alterations require a reader's negative capability in order to suspend an immediate need for the pieces to cohere. The information about Benna, Eleanor, and Gerard mounts through each story, but only in the novella does the reason for the variations in the preceding tales become evident.

The novelistic classification also implies a narrative progression in *Anagrams* that does not take place; rather, the novella provides the missing piece that clarifies the links throughout the book. The final tale provides an explanation for the discrepancies among the preceding stories, a culmination of Benna's experiences. The volume is an example of the "open structure" delineated by Sharon Spencer in that it

> reflects a vast, diffuse, confusing, complex world. . . . It seems jagged, full of points and thrusts, poorly balanced, and it perhaps even conveys the notion that it is either in motion or is capable of motion. Since it demonstrates the deliberate violation of classical ideals of proportion among parts, of harmony of tone and diction, of balance, of unity, and of a sense of being finished or rounded off, the open-structured novel may be said to be an "antinovel." (2–3)

The unequal lengths of the stories, ranging from 4 to 164 pages, the shifts in perspective and point of view, and the inconsistency of the characters' roles exemplify Spencer's "violation of balance." However, even though the text is open-ended, the explanation that is provided in the novella *does* give the work "a sense of being finished or rounded off" and is one of the features that classifies *Anagrams* as a short story cycle. A cumulative understanding of Benna in all her many lived and imaginary roles is achieved only through a consideration of all the stories.

The rest of the book is changed, in retrospect, by the information given in the novella. One of the most puzzling features of the first four stories is the lack of awareness by any of the characters of the events that have transpired in another tale. This situation is clarified by Benna's explanation of the significance of imagination. The four lives that Benna experiences in the short stories thus become possible existences that she has fabricated, her "roads not taken," which hearkens back to the book's epigraph from Robert Frost ("I shall be telling this with a sigh"). However, the answer that each provides is no more conclusive or productive than the one she reaches in the novella when she returns to her life of make-believe.

The themes and motifs that resonate through the cycle are as bleak as Benna's life at the end of the book; each story, in fact, contributes another facet to the disappointment and despair that permeate her life in "The Nun of That." In the first tale, the juxtaposition of the words *Visitor* and *Home* on the baseball scoreboard near Gerard's apartment introduces the idea that one can feel displaced even in the midst of one's family and friends. In "Strings Too Short to Use," Benna experiences disappointment in nearly every aspect of her life, as she loses faith in her best friend, her lover, and her health. Her pregnancy catalyzes Gerard's betrayal rather than encouraging intimacy, kindness, and a new respect for this bond between them. Her self-imposed detachment of the previous tale gives way to an isolation not of her choosing, and this loneliness and sense of loss pervade the next story, "Yard Sale," as well. In the fourth story, Benna begins to wonder if "she drives men away. Perhaps, without even being able to help herself, she just puts men into her ill-tempered car and drives them off: to quarries, dumps, small anonymous bodies of water" (56). Thus, self-doubt and fear of relationships are the "answers" provided by these previous lives. No matter how cleverly and humorously articulated, the other roles are reinforcements of the same austere themes, rather than true alternatives in any sense aside from the most literal rendering of the characters' physical parameters.

Each story compounds the sense of Benna's need for communication, as she is frustrated in her attempts to connect with family, friends, and lovers. She is also revising her self-image through these stories, from her consideration of facial sanding, to her unhappiness with her accomplishments as an art historian, to her meditations on the flexibility and interchangeability of identity. In the second story, television documentaries help her to rationalize the uncontrollable factors in her life as part of a natural world, and she later turns to science once again to understand the malleability of self and her creation of an identity that is solid and inviolable. She applies the principles of Darwinism to her personal life, noting that

the ant-mimicking spider is avoided because it appears to have the fierce mandibles of an ant, though it's really only a dressed-up spider making pretend. The function of disguise is to convince the world you're not there, or that if you are, you should not be eaten. You camouflage yourself as imperious teacher, as imperious lover, as imperious bitch, simply to hang out and survive. (194)

These stories reflect different disguises Benna uses to avoid intimacy. Although in some tales she is inexplicably aloof and in others her detachment is amply justified by her unfortunate experiences with men, she is ultimately self-protective. The structure of the novel is epitomized in her comment "that's mostly what people remember—that effort to leave themselves" (163). Benna attempts to escape the unfulfilling life described in the novella through her imaginative forays in the preceding stories and through the creation of Georgianne, but ultimately her actual existence is the one thing that remains; Gerard is dead, her affair with her student is over, and all that she is left with is the bare bones of her life and the imagination to flesh them out.

Benna's multifaceted identity is thus portrayed through an evolving sequence of narratives. Margot Kelley remarks on the parallels between this formal method and "feminist psychoanalytic models," noting that the characters themselves in works such as these are simultaneously shoring "up their own fragmented identities" while the cyclical structure uses the same accretionary method to unite the fragments of stories into a meaningful whole. Only through this cumulative structure do

relatively coherent images of/for the characters emerge. By foregrounding the constructedness of the characters' identities, and by recapitulating the formal discontinuities at the level of characterization, novel-in-stories writers prompt us to think about the characters (and, by extension, the subjects more generally) as multiply identified, as entities for whom identity is relational and, equally significant, negotiated. (305)

These aspects of the self are especially relevant for late-twentieth-century women. As their demands and opportunities expand, not only do they feel increasing pressure to negotiate between cultural expectations and their own specific goals, but they are often torn between the two poles of their own desires, as is shown in Moore's description of the successful female academic who is distraught at the revelation that her male graduate student is married and rearing a daughter while the professor "misses everyone she's ever known" and makes midnight forays to the supermarket, "searching, almost panicked, for *something*" that will satiate her loneliness (57–58).

Although short story cycles have been written for centuries, their proliferation, especially in the mode of focusing on the development of a single character, is both the result and a symptom of shifts in modern consciousness. Both modern and postmodern artistic theories foreground the significance of fragmentation on the psyche. Modernism breaks this ground and focuses primarily on the fragmentation of society and humanity's resulting alienation, but postmodernism, in its obsession with identity, often focuses on the fragmentation of the self. Kelley and Hayden White explain that the "sociocultural context" must be appropriate for acceptance of both the genre and the content of a work (Kelley 302). The experimental and fractured forms of the twentieth century prepare a reading audience for works that increasingly reflect the episodic experiences of contemporary existence.

The short story cycle reflects prevailing ideologies, illustrating the conflicts inherent in developing or maintaining a unified and mentally healthy female identity. These interlinked stories, which require readers to identify unifying characteristics and assimilate the works into a meaningful whole, model the creation of postmodern identity from its many fractured parts and disparate influences. The short story cycle, as used by many contemporary women writers, is thus the ideal vehicle for representations of women's fractured sense of self.

Note

1. Social historians distinguish between the "first wave" of the American women's movement, occurring in the mid- to late nineteenth century, and the "second wave," which united and mobilized women almost a century later. The ideology of the first wave was crystallized in the "Declaration of Sentiments and Resolutions" produced primarily by Elizabeth Cady Stanton and adopted at the Seneca Falls Convention in 1848. The 1953 translation of Simone de Beauvoir's *The Second Sex* (1949) and the publication of Betty Friedan's *The Feminine Mystique* in 1963 catalyzed the second wave.

References

Bartky, Sandra Lee. *Femininity and Domination: Studies in the Phenomenology of Oppression*. New York: Routledge, 1990.

Brackenbury, Rosalind. "Women and Fiction: How We Present Ourselves and Others." *In Other Words: Writing as a Feminist*. Ed. Gail Chester and Sigrid Nielsen. London: Hutchinson, 1987. 56–61.

Chodorow, Nancy. *The Reproduction of Mothering*. Berkeley: U of California P, 1978.

Felski, Rita. *The Gender of Modernity*. Cambridge: Harvard UP, 1995.

Fromm, Erich. *Escape from Freedom*. New York: Rinehart, 1941.

Gardiner, Judith Kegan. "On Female Identity and Writing by Women." *Writing and Sexual Difference*. Ed. Elizabeth Abel. Chicago: U of Chicago P, 1982. 177–91.

Gilbert, Matthew. Rev. of *Anagrams*, by Lorrie Moore. *Boston Review* 11 (Dec. 1986): 30.

Gilligan, Carol. *In a Different Voice: Psychological Theory and Women's Development*. Cambridge: Harvard UP, 1982.

Hill, Carol. "Sestinas and Wisecracks." Rev. of *Anagrams*, by Lorrie Moore. *New York Times Book Review* 2 Nov. 1986: 15.

Kelley, Margot. "Gender and Genre: The Case of the Novel-in-Stories." *American Women Short Story Writers: A Collection of Critical Essays*. Ed. Julie Brown. New York: Garland, 1995. 295–310.

Kennedy, J. Gerald. "Toward a Poetics of the Short Story Cycle." *Journal of the Short Story in English* 11 (autumn 1988): 9–25.

Lee, Don. "About Lorrie Moore." *Ploughshares* 24.2/3 (1998): 224–29.

Llewelyn, Sue, and Kate Osborne. *Women's Lives*. London: Routledge, 1990.

McQuade, Molly. "The Booklist Interview: Lorrie Moore." *Booklist* 15 Oct.
    1998: 402–03.
Merritt, Stephanie. "Lorrie Moore: The Books Interview." *The Observer* (Lon-
    don) 8 Nov. 1998, review sec.: 13.
Moore, Lorrie. *Anagrams*. New York: Knopf, 1986.
Spencer, Sharon. *Space, Time, and Structure in the Modern Novel*. New York:
    New York UP, 1971.

CONTEMPORARY MEN AND THEIR STORIES

Along with a new group of women emerging as postmodern practitioners, the past decades have seen their share of a new breed of male writers claiming their own place in the literary circle: Barry Hannah, Thom Jones, Tom Paine, Denis Johnson, and Edmund White. In "Crippled by the Truth: Oracular Pronouncements, Titillating Titles, and the Postmodern Ethic," Richard E. Lee charts the theoretical implications of the concept of the "title" in contemporary short fiction, focusing on Barry Hannah as an exemplary practitioner. He discusses postmodern concepts and their relationships to titles. Lee argues that titles are "significant missiles." They allow for the handling of the text itself in shorthand at the same time that they both contain and constrain meaning. Titles are seductive, Lee says, in that they have the ability to collapse past, present, and future into a ceaseless now.

The essay "Male Paradigms in Thom Jones and Tom Paine" by Paul R. Lilly discusses two contemporary American short story writers who present contrasting images of maleness. Jones's boxer-warrior males tend to confront the moral dimension of their obsession with aggression, fascination with the violence of combat, and wariness of women, whereas Paine's aggressive male characters are often technocrats who are challenged by the male who is sensitive to the environment and who sees the female as redemptive.

J. Scott Farrin contends in his essay "Eloquence and Plot in Denis Johnson's *Jesus' Son*: The Merging of Premodern and Modernist Narrative" that Johnson's stories display a modernist rejection of narrative reasoning and portray a static character battered by accidents. His essay employs the concept of plot as developed in Rober L. Caserio's *Plot, Story, and the Novel*, which traces the development of narrative. Farrin also employs Kenneth Burke's notion of form, as he explains it in "Psychology and Form" in *Counter-Statement* as well as touching on Aristotle and the rise of modernism, using George Eliot as a transitional figure, then James Joyce, Ernest Hemingway, and William Faulkner.

"Skinned Alive" by Edmund White, published in *The Darker Proof*, a collection of short stories written in response to the AIDS epidemic, is the subject matter of Raymond-Jean Frontain's essay "Ardor with a Silent H: Submitting to the Ache of Love in Edmund White's 'Skinned Alive.'" Frontain maintains that the story's apparent lack of structure, the inconclusive ending, and an epiphany—the significance of which is never stated—all reflect both the indeterminateness of homosexual identity and a queering of love itself. The most that White's characters can do, Frontain argues, is to learn to submit to the ache of love, and—in a story fascinated by the limitations of language—to do so silently.

Peter Donahue states that Hemingway, in his now famous cycle *In Our Time*, was able to foster meaning at the same time he resisted it, thereby anticipating postmodern practices that writers such as Robert Coover and Donald Barthelme mastered a half century later. More precisely, Donahue's essay "The Genre Which Is Not One: Hemingway's *In Our Time*, Difference, and the Short Story Cycle" states that *In Our Time* embodies not only characteristics of modernist literature—emphasis on character psychology, themes of alienation, and a self-conscious literary style—but also many postmodernist practices such as destabilized character development, decentered organization, and a general distrust of literary representation.

Crippled by the Truth: Oracular Pronouncements, Titillating Titles, and the Postmodern Ethic

Richard E. Lee

If the label *postmodernism*—as opposed to the historical concept of *postmodernity*[1]—is so overused as to be essentially meaningless, then certainly yet another essay bemoaning the essential emptiness of the term is also of questionable value.[2] Its ubiquity notwithstanding, however, there does seem to be something beyond the mere cachet of the term to recommend it.[3] Bruce Robbins observes, commenting on the "calculated affront" and the "wit" of the title of the book in which his article, "Across the Ages," is published: "The wit, one sees, is in the play between postmodernism as a *period* (in the most common view it starts around 1945 and takes over from modernism) and postmodernism as a way of thinking valued precisely because, expanding aggressively 'across the ages,' it refuses the constraints of periodization" (qtd. in Readings and Schaber 238–39).[4] If one views the "postmodern" as a cache of tendencies, it is possible—desirable even—to evaluate that cache for its narrative systemic integrity. There is a "postmodern ethic." It values the fragment over the whole, the surface over the "depths," derivation over "originality"; indeed, whether our cultural paradigm is shifting, has shifted or not (à la Thomas Kuhn), it seems as though our version of Western culture is skeptical about everything save skepticism itself. This is one reason to value short fiction as the genre that speaks most directly to the parochial and local rather than the totalizing narratives of the novel. Short fiction is always and already "new historical" in its celebration of the ort. And what more appropriate structure to evaluate than the idea of the title of a work of short fiction: an interesting version of synechdoche—of the part standing for the whole? Titles are themselves simulacra and speak to a dehistoricized history in that they metaphorize the whole and represent it in the streaming narrative logic of sentences that refer to them. And no one writes more interesting titles than does Barry Hannah.

This essay will interrogate several issues: The timeless tendency of traditions to foster antitraditions, the (postmodern?) temptation to discuss authors/titles/texts by virtue of the fragment (the title, in this instance), and the work that the "titles" of Barry Hannah's short fiction perform as engines that are both substitutive (and therefore metaphoric) and combinatory (and therefore metonymic). Hannah himself has recently rejected any labeling of his work as "postmodern."[5] He has insisted that the rhythms of the oral and the oracular, and of certain sections of the King James Version of the Bible are "inescapable," and that their statements seem "carved out from the sky."[6] He thereby situates his work within a tradition that antedates the postmodern. But these statements presuppose that the postmodern and postmodernity are the same. Like the "idea" of *Postmodernism Across the Ages,* I begin with the supposition that one need not periodicize in order to investigate. This short essay takes its impetus from our need to label—the present book is, after all, one of several investigating postmodernism and Barry Hannah[7]—but also from this author's rejection of the simplicism of labeling itself: another type of "titling," perhaps. Ultimately, this essay is a conscious act of bricolage, and the act of accidental engineering—using whatever tools one finds handy—is preciously postmodern.

Titillating Titles

The idea of the title, "the name of a poem, essay, chapter, book, picture, statue, piece of music, etc." (*Webster's Third International Unabridged Dictionary* [*Webster's*]), is itself an idea with a history and a provenance. Of the ten nominative senses of the term listed by Webster's (the *Oxford English Dictionary* [*OED*] gives eleven), three refer to legal structures—by extension, the Adamic power of naming. The denotation that most closely links issues of ownership/legality with issues of naming states that a title is a "claim; a right"—as in the Shakespearean usage, "Make claim and title to the crown of France." The English word *title* comes from the Latin *titulus* (a title), especially the superscription on the cross of the crucified Christ (*OED*), a connection to which I shall return. *Titulus* is a second-declension noun—morphologically masculine—as was the naming power of the Genesis Adam. In the second declension, the genitive singular *tituli* (which shows ownership) and the nominative plural (used for plural syntactical subjects) are indistinguishable. One derives the root of the word by dropping the genitive singular/nominative plural ending (the long "i"). Thus, *titul-* functions as the ur-word, which makes one think of the adjectival form in English: *titular*—"existing in name only; nominal; having the title only" (*Webster's*). When academic critics discuss texts, they necessarily refer to the ort, the fragment which is title as carrying within its name all the tracks and passages of the "real" text. Yet titles are only titles, in the commonsensical understanding of the term. They contain nothing. They are oddly null, disappearing so that the text can reveal itself— make "sense" of the title. Whether they serve a semantic purpose in relation to the texts that follow them or not, our usage of them as handles for discussion is what matters at the moment. This conception of the title seems peculiarly and appropriately postmodern.

In my own title for this essay,[8] I refer to titillation. Except for *titlark* and *titivate* ("to dress up; to adorn"), *titillate* ("L. *titillare*, 'to tickle'") comes right before *title* in *Webster's*. One might think of all of these words, from titillate to title, as connected to a postmodern architecture of short story titles in general, and to Hannah's short stories in particular. Many commentators have mentioned the whimsical nature of Hannah's titles, often as examples of the lyricism of his syntactic structures in the stories themselves.[9] His titles are often more than mere subject, or nominative, references, often the norm for poems or stories. These "normative titles" titivate: they "adorn," they "spruce up," they "make to look smart" (*Webster's*) in the sense that they "finish" (in both its ambiguous senses) by beginning the work in question. And these "regular" titles, like "The Red Pony," "The Dead," "The Yellow Wallpaper," "The Cask of Amontillado," are larks: they fly above the work as a whole, certainly; they are also songbirds, announcing "with a very clear note" the subject, or fulcrum of the story to be begun. Inevitably, titles, even such as these, are larks of the other sort: only after the story is read can the potential playfulness of even serious titles—calling into question the pretense of linear reading in time, of beginnings and endings—be made apparent. Hannah has many of this type of title, ones that fulfill the normative need of superscription. They name, as phrases and clauses, that which the story purports to discuss. Titles such as "Water Liars," "Our Secret Home," Testimony of Pilot" (from *Airships*); "High Water Railers," "This Happy Breed," "Nicodemus Bluff" (from *Bats Out of Hell*); "A Creature in the Bay of St. Louis" and "Uncle High Lonesome" (from *High Lonesome*) perform this expected function. They do what we think titles should do, allowing a substitutive reference for discussion of the story. Beyond these, however,

Hannah's titles are often titillating, titivating titlarks of both sorts at once: teasing enunciators that clearly sound syntactic structures that tickle, yet adorn and presage as well. In a sense, all titles are titillating—they attract and entice. They are sexy, whether sex is overt or not. Perhaps that which we distinguish as literature—as opposed to the merely popular[10]—is that which avoids lurid jacket covers, approaching the condition of an absence. Think of a spectrum with flashy, splashy, graphics-laden book jackets on one end and the absence of anything save a title (and an author's name, another kind of thematic shorthand) on the other—this last being the staid, bound volume prized especially by those who commodify books either partly or entirely as things. Titles then take on the traces of the titillation one has "escaped" from in the popular, transforming the act of absence into an autoerotic act. If this seems overdetermined, consider the selfishness of reading—its isolation, its insularity, and its refusal of the social—in the light of autoeroticism.[11] One need not have overtly (or ambiguously) erotic titles like "Mother Mouth" or "Upstairs, Mona Bayed for a Dong" (from *Bats Out of Hell*) or "Get Some Young" (from *High Lonesome*) to consider sexuality as a component of titling. The goal of both masturbation and reading is the achievement of a desire.

Postmodern Titling

When I began writing about Barry Hannah's use of titles in his short fiction, I was in that zone of lost time, itself a type of masturbation, where I reveled in sexy thoughts about fragments, simulacra, synechdochic relationships, divisions of meanings, and other nifty things. After the initial thrill of first love, rationalization began—as it always does. I started doing a little research. I started on the Internet, the most perfectly postmodern of conceptualizations: the virtual copy of a thing on the 'Net is itself more "real" than any original, after all. Like Werner Heisenberg, I realized that the questions I would ask (of my search engines and web crawlers) would predetermine the kinds of answers I could potentially get. I input the word *title* in the "Title" search categories of *ArticleFirst* and the like—drawing phone-number-sized responses to my searches, including every "Title Page" in every database everywhere. Love (of subject) is still cool, but slightly tempered. I'm a postmodern Mr. Goodbar, looking for love in all the wrong places. There is a lot of scrounging around and the need to establish margins—"refine search" parameters—to limit the "titles of titles." Then I come across multiple book review entries that eventually lead me to Anne Ferry's fine book *The Title to the Poem*, which continues the spadework begun by John Hollander in his "Haddock's Eyes: A Note on the Theory of Titles."[12] The love affair is almost over as I discover that many have visited here/her before. My beloved has a past.

Ferry's introduction summarizes the work of prior title searchers: Gerard Genette, Jacques Derrida, Harry Levin, Hazard Adams, and other names whose identities—whose author function, if you will—have been the recipient of the death of the aura of the original discussed by Jean-François Lyotard et al. *paen ad infinitum* (painfully without end) since about 1972. The nature of infrastructural, technological, change—such as that discussed in Walter Benjamin's discussion of photography and the idea of the original in "The Work of Art in the Age of Mechanical Reproduction"—has meant the transference of the aura of the original to such virtual structures as the author, or the event. Finding that Derrida has dealt with an idea such as "titling" is not a good thing. I wilt. But wait: since there is no aura of originality, there can be *jouissance* (enjoyment)! I can sample the author aura at my leisure, play P. Diddy to Ferry, and—like e. e. cummings—"say never to was." The first flush is over, but, as Professor Harold Hill in *The Music Man* opines, "the sadder and wiser girl's for me." I can appropriate—claim title to—the concept and the conquest.

As Eleanor Shevlin has observed, there is often an overlap—she refers to it as a "metonymic relationship"—between the legal concept of one's title to a claim of property and the textual use of a title for a book-length narrative. Other critics and theorists have mined this issue deeply, though none speak particularly of the short story title.[13] The closest would be those who consider the idea of the subtitle as a category of rationalization of larger narratives. Gerard Gennette's work on *paratext* is particularly apt here.[14] Genette refers to the paratext as that set of assumptions that seem ancillary to the narrative, but are actually part of the conditional set of circumstances that accompany the narrative—and the reader's expectation of just what it is that narrative is supposed to do. Paul Fournel has written a visceral example of the categorical imperatives associated with our conception of a "complete" text in his Oulipo work *Suburbia*.[15] In this extended parody of just what elements make up a "real" novel, Fournel forces attention away from words and into readerly habits—away from passivity. Since there is no "text," one is forced back on the paratextual elements at work. More to the point of Derrida et al., having examined the idea of the title—of poems, of novels, of whatever—is the "'paradoxical and provocative' expression which the Oulipo uses to identify . . . authors who have previously used methods now seen as 'Oulipian'": I am an "anticipatory plagiarist" (Brotchie and Mathews 207). I have arrived at a theme that has a history—I have been historically co-opted—yet one of the precepts of the very theme of the study (postmodernism) speaks to the collapse of linear history: all is a timeless now, open for reification and continual reintegration of parts. Just as Lope de Vega and Pindar can be seen as anachronistic members of the Oulipo—Pindar's "Ode to Sigma" and the seventeenth-century Spaniard's five novels are all lipograms—terminal exhaustion of any thematic analysis likewise lies outside the bounds of postmodernism's embrace. Like the time-honored poetic form, the *cento*—a patchwork of other author's lines of verse crafted to create a new poem—academic analysis too can approach the condition of pastiche. What, after all, are many doctoral dissertations but prose cento?

The issue raised at the start of this essay by Bruce Robbins in his examination of the title of the book within which his work was published, *Postmodernism Across the Ages*, connects up pasts with present without enforcing a structure of presumptive influence on either.[16] Barry Hannah was both wrong and right about his status as a postmodern practitioner. He is right because he writes from his sense of what the world is in language that is now his. One critic has observed that "Hannah's plots are not conventional, they constitute a significant postmodern 'chaos' of mini-plots designed to appeal to the narrative desires of writer, hero, and reader to find meaning in the gap between dreams, lies, and confessions" (Weston 428). Unfortunately, identifying a mode of writing alone allows us to make Pindar a postmodernist, too. Hannah's right: That which covers too much ends by covering too little.

But he is also wrong: he is postmodern, not least because the titles of his short stories evince so much of the best of Hannah—the lyricism, the bon mots—and are metonymic oracles atop the stories themselves, even as they serve the metaphoric purpose of substitutive replacement that is the conventionalized role of an individual title in any discussion of the work atop which it sits.

Titles, Metaphor, Metonymy

This metonymic/metaphoric opposition derives from Roman Jakobson's famous essay on linguistic aphasia[17] and from subsequent work linking realistic prose narratives to dominantly metonymic patterns of expression, and expressivist (and modernist) prose and poetry to dominantly metaphoric tendencies. Jakobson (and structuralists in general) posit the twin operations of selection and combination, of metaphoric (paradigmatic) replacement and metonymic (syntagmatic) linear connectedness. Jakobson parses the linguistic sign into "two modes of arrangement." The first is

Combination. Any sign is made up of constituent signs and/or occurs only in combination with other signs. This means that any linguistic unit at one and the same time serves as a context for simpler units and/or finds its own context in a more complex linguistic unit. Hence any actual grouping of linguistic units binds them into a superior unit: combination and contexture are two faces of the same operation. (74)

Titles are inevitably connected to, and part of, the context of stories themselves. A given title functions as a discrete syntactic unit in its superscriptural role. Even titles that avoid the strictly nominative, subject function of what I have called "normative" titles operate as an apparatus of connection and context. Some of Hannah's short story titles—such as "Dragged Fighting from His Tomb," "Get Some Young," "Knowing He Was Not My Kind Yet I Followed," "Ride Westerly for Pusalina," and "Through Sunset into the Raccoon Night"—are actually predicate phrases or clauses. Some use the perfect tense and presuppose a closure prior to the actual reading of the story—a closure irrelevant to history but specific to the act of reading. Some use the progressive tense, speaking to a continuing event—thereby obviating history into an all-encompassing present; hortatory exhortations, demanding activity, also function in avoidance of past and present in the service of an indefinite future. These types seem like selections from the Book of Proverbs in their calls for activity in a formless temporal void. Like Proverbs, these titles bespeak a desire to instruct, to structure, to connect. They are evocative of the "Wisdom Tradition," or what Biblical scholar James G. Williams refers to as the binding perspective of the books of Proverbs, Ecclesiastes, Job, and the Song of Songs. This tradition is "dedicated to articulating a sense of order. The world is viewed as an order informed by a principle of retributive justice" (Williams 263). Such themes are inevitably grounded in a certitude our culture no longer embraces, but the pronouncements themselves can be seen as a pining for a past in which such certainty was a possibility.

Jakobson's second "arrangement" speaks not to syntagmatic connection but to paradigmatic substitution:

Selection. A selection between alternatives implies the possibility of substituting one for the other, equivalent to the former in one respect and different from it in another. Actually, selection and substitution are two faces of the same operation. (74)

When we speak or write a title, such as Hannah's "Coming Close to Donna" (from *Airships*), we are, quite obviously, using a referential shorthand, a conventional substitutive turn. Such titles are *metaphora* in its primary sense: an attempt to identify the unfamiliar using replacement terms. Yet to enclose words within " " is to create a break in the syntagmatic flow of information from writer to reader. This disconnection in the tumbling chain of signification, which is a sentence, is a lacuna, a gap, an Iserian moment of perfect indeterminacy. To insert " " into a chain of signification is to launch a metaphoric missile directly at the reader; to call attention to the metaphoric at the moment of "pure" reading is to call attention to the construction of meaning itself.[18] One could substitute gibberish for the "actual" title (and here the quotation marks signaling nonstandard usage presuppose a connection impossible to achieve between sender and receiver)—as in "lihjbyugu liuyo lkiun" for "Coming Close to Donna" and still achieve part of the substitutive title function. One assumes that titles stand in for—and therefore constrain and contain—whole stories, yet meaning itself is actually held in abeyance by the very act of referencing the title.

And this deferral at the moment of assumed connection is heightened when there is the potential for the title itself to be "meaningful." The irony of "Coming Close to Donna" can only become apparent (to a reader) upon reading the story and learning the ambiguity of the protagonist's "coming close"—both nearing her and sexually "spraying" her. Another type of ironic ambiguity connects this idea with the Bible in Hannah's "Quo Vadis, Smut" (also from *Airships*). The Israelite Wisdom tradition speaks to retribution, of having returned to you what you meted out. Although this essay is not the place for this thematic examination, its redolence in many of Hannah's stories is worth passing mention.

In fact, titles are ironic even when they have no desire to be so. According to the *OED* (and referenced earlier), the word *title* comes from the Latin *titulus*; its earliest recorded usages refer to the inscription on the cross on which Christ was crucified. The inscription on the plank read (according to Mark 15.26): "Jesus of Nazareth, King of the Jews" (foreshortened further by becoming the acronym "INRI" in Latin). The already ironic reference to the presumptive title Jesus' judges bestowed on him lends an ironic provenance to all titling in perpetuity.

Irony, calling attention to itself at the moment of referencing something else, conflates the metonymic and the metaphoric functions of language.[19] That which refers to something outside of itself cannot then substitute for the very thing which it purports to represent. Naturally, this is the signal for the structuralist or poststructuralist to recognize that the system of language is always/already the *real* subject of language. Another, pithy approach to the problem is that schematized by David Lodge in *Working with Structuralism*. He suggests that one way of categorizing the various guises in which prose narratives present themselves is connected to a movement away from realistic notions of understanding the world. Lodge locates the tradition of realism as a historically loaded tradition, interested in extrinsic analyses of what texts have to offer. In other words, Lodge states, "Antimodernist art . . . aspires to the condition of history. . . . It regards literature as the communication of a reality that exists prior to and independent of the act of communication" (6). Titles that perform a normative, referential function vis-à-vis the stories they cap might be viewed as antimodernist. Lodge offers a conventional view of modernist art, pointing out that *modernism* in his sense of the term refers to art—to texts—that prioritize form over content, thereby calling attention to themselves as constructions rather than mimetic copies of some external object or event. The expressivistic pronouncements of many of Hannah's most lyrical titles are modernist in this sense—they "aspire to the condition of music," as Lodge quotes Walter Pater (5).

Lodge also acknowledges Jakobson's dichotomization of metaphor and metonymy, even while he attempts to systematize postmodernism:

Jakobson's theory asserts that any discourse must connect its topics according to either similarity or contiguity, and will usually prefer one type of connection to the other. Postmodernist writing tries to defy this law by seeking some alternative principle of composition. To these alternatives I give the names: Contradiction, Permutation, Discontinuity, Randomness, Excess and the Short Circuit. (13)

I suggest that the title is always a permutation of some sort—even when there is a conscious attempt to refuse meaningfulness. The discontinuity between title and text seems apparent, existing as it does in a neither/either state: not text, not not-text. Randomness seems not only possible, but desirable: Hannah's "Through Sunset into the Raccoon Night" seems sufficiently random, disorientingly discontinuous, and wonderfully excessive to me. And I have suggested throughout that titles are a sort of short circuit in the wiring of the textual network: pitched, seductively, to readers by authors (yet editors surely change titles to suit the needs of the market?[20]), both inside yet not truly of the text. Like the tempos of ancient wisdom, they are "carved from the sky": there to be viewed, too obvious to ignore, yet surface merely, and gauzy beyond one's ability to hold securely. The ultimate virtual reality.

Conclusion

This essay recapitulates a major strand of philosophical inquiry during the twentieth century, one which is very much related to postmodernism. Often skating on surface alone, the essay moves from a sense of (pseudo) objectivity (I), to an interrogation of the subjective stance of the author (II), to a recognition of the confluence of theoretical and narrative issues evidenced in Hannah's titles as a location that is both metonym and metaphor (III). This movement echoes, "samples," the movement from early-twentieth-century structuralism to the reinsertion of the human subject that is the signature move of poststructuralist analysis. Structuralism's search for a ground, a baseline of commonality in its various investigations takes as its starting point the idea that meaning only exists within a system of relation, that meaning is not present in the thing itself. The signifying process which is language—in the present case the language of literary reference that makes of a title a part that is both a part of, and a replacement for, the whole—thus functions in the absolute absence of the human subject (the author) since individuals are carriers of codes. The scientism at the core of the structuralist tendency rejects what David Lodge has referred to as "antimodernism" in favor of what he calls "modernism." Language that calls attention to itself as a differential, arbitrary system still adheres to the Derridean notion of a transcendental signified: a ground for the system, a reference point to stop the bifurcation of signifier and signified. Lodge's postmodernism clarifies the twentieth century's embrace/rejection of certainty/uncertainty. "Postmodernism continues the modernist critique of traditional realism [what he refers to as antimodernism], but it tries to go beyond or around or underneath modernism, which for all its formal experiment and complexity held out to the reader the promise of meaning, if not of *a* meaning (Lodge 12).

Hannah's titles function as exemplary engines of all three of Lodge's trends, and thus of the great tendencies in literary theory over the past one hundred years. They can be antimodernist (realist, referential, nominative), modernist (playful, expressivist, predicative), or postmodernist (resistant to metonymic or metaphoric dichotomization, and thus beyond meaning except insofar as they are part of the paratext and its assumption by a readership). Often, too, they are oracular and aspire to the condition of the transcendental—looking back to the Bible and ahead to the rhythms of literary discourse at the base of human existence.

Notes

1. Terry Eagleton distinguishes between these two terms elegantly:

The word *postmodernism* generally refers to a form of contemporary culture, whereas the term *postmodernity* alludes to a specific historical period. Postmodernity is a style of thought which is suspicious of classical notions of truth, reason, identity, and objectivity, of the idea of universal progress or emancipation, of single frameworks, of grand narratives or ultimate grounds of explanation. . . Postmodernism is a style of culture which reflects something of this epochal change, in a depthless, decentred, ungrounded, self-reflexive, playful, derivative, eclectic, pluralistic art which blurs the boundaries between 'high' and 'popular' culture, as well as between art and everyday experience. (vii)

It is my contention that Hannah's work, indicative of a particular style of short fiction, links these two concepts.

2. Tim Cavanaugh, speaking of the overuse of the term *irony*—and its overreported demise in the wake of recent terrorist attacks, creates an apt analogy for the overuse of the term *postmodernism*: "The War on Irony never had a clear enemy. Any concept that describes the corporate froth of *Entertainment Weekly*, Swift's "Modest Proposal," and the deadpan satire of *The Onion* is already broad enough to be valueless" ("Ironic Engagement: The Hidden Agenda of the Anti-Ironists." *Reason Online*. Dec. 2001. 4 Dec. 2001. <http://www.reason.com/0112/co.tc.rant.shtml>.)

3. John McGowan makes a comment typical of those who deal with the subject: "Everyone begins the discussion of postmodernism by asking what the word could possibly mean" (ix). He then proceeds to acknowledge the slipperiness of the term (x) and the need to move "toward a definition of Postmodernism"—the title of his first chapter. The unavoidable nature of the term might well be seen in the spate of "readers" and exegetical texts on a subject which, ironically, suggests the subversion of exegetical closure. See, for example, Ray Linn.

4. Perhaps inevitably, Robbins problematizes this very statement immediately after he makes it. One of the central precepts of postmodern culture and criticism is precisely the relativistic tendency: the refusal of declaratory statements in favor of "interrogations" and interlocutory engagements.

5. Interview with Terry Gross on *All Things Considered*, National Public Radio, 31 July 2001.

7. Telephone interview 5 Jan. 2002.

8. Ruth Weston's *Barry Hannah, Postmodern Romantic* and Fred Hobson's *The Southern Writer in the Postmodern World* come immediately to mind.

9. The title of this essay on titling is written in a recognizable form. For example, there is the requisite colon separating suggestive subject from categorized structural preview. For a discussion of academic tendencies in titling, see Ann O'Neill's deftly named article "A (Very) Concise History of the Impact

of Electronic Journals on Graduate Students: The Title of Which is Almost as Long as the Actual Article: Continuing the Fine Ancient Tradition of Less Publishable Units by Faculty: And Contains Many Colons; That Shows the Importance of a Work Which Has Significant Titular Colonicity (and One Semi-Colon)" (*The Serial's Librarian* 26.1 [1995]: 13–16).

9. See, for example, John Updike, "From Dyna Domes to Turkey-Pressing," *New Yorker* 29.9 (9 Sept. 1972): 121–24; and Terrence Rafferty, "Gunsmoke and Voodoo," *Nation* 240.1 (1 June 1985): 677–79.

10. As I have already mentioned (see note 1), another of postmodernism's central tenets collapses the distinction between "high" and "low" art. However, the staying power of the perception of this dichotomy is impressive. One need only consider The Oprah Book Club in the light of some recent authors to see that snob appeal and the class affiliations with which it is associated run deep.

12. I am indebted to Ellen Damsky for this insight in particular, and for her sharp editing instincts in general during the draft stages of this essay.

13. Ferry comments that she, too, had begun her work—thinking and writing about titles and their implications—without realizing that a creditable body of work had preceded her. She states: "Although I did not read Hollander's essay until I had begun working on this history of titling practices, his expressed sense of the importance and interest of the subject and the need for a full exploration of it has been an encouragement" (8). It seems that one of the necessary moves that titling and its study requires is the creation of a liminal space—one that becomes existent by shouldering aside the physical existence of prior titles and the figurative remove of oneself into the position where your title, in the sense of a claim, has room to act as a doorway.

13. The history of criticism on titles and their various relationships to texts is a long one, well summarized by Shevlin in her endnotes (70); Ferry in *The Title to the Poem* (especially in the notes to the Introduction, 283–84); and Gerard Gennette in his thorough structuralist study, "Structure and Functions of the Title in Literature."

14. Gennette speaks for himself and is aptly summarized in Jane Lewin's translation of *Paratexts: Thresholds of Interpretation* (Cambridge: Cambridge UP, 1997).

15. *Banlieue* (translated by Harry Mathews and Iain White as *Suburbia* [*Oulipo Laboratory: Texts from the Bibliothèque Oulippiene* (London: Atlas, 1995), 21–36]) is an example of antitraditional literature from the *Ouvroir de Litterature Potentielle* (Workshop for Potential Literature). Founded in 1960, the stated aims of the group, which has included such authors as George Perec, Italo Calvin, and Raymond Queneau, include an intensely heightened attention to the restrictions of the various elements of literary creation. One proposes a "constraint"—such as the imposition of a mathematical form, or the restriction of working in any of a variety of palindromic forms—and then tests the restraint to destruction. In Fournel's case, he has created a lipogram—a text that excludes one or more letters—of the entire alphabet in his presentation of a supposedly complete novel. The novel has, in fact, most of what a published work "must" have to be seen as complete—introductions, a preface, a title page, a dedication,

copyright and publication information, a table of contents, an index, footnotes, a page of errata—it is merely missing the actual text of the novel. By calling attention to the conventional, culturally determined, and therefore variable elements of textuality, the Oulipo—and the many groups that have followed in their footsteps—force an attention on many of the same issues that postmodernism takes for granted (e.g., the modernist insistence on the created text itself as an object of study and not the "reality" that the text reflects).

16. Certainly one of Hannah's recurring themes is the redolence of the past in the events of the present, of our inability to unknow that which has gone before. See, for example, Richard Lee, "Barry Hannah," *The Dictionary of Literary Biography: American Short-Story Writers since World War II*, 3rd ser., ed. Patrick Meanor and Richard E. Lee (Detroit: Bruccoli Clark Layman, 2001) 105–16.

17. Jakobson's development of this schematic is most fully treated in Chapter 5 of Part 2 of *Fundamentals of Language*, "The Metaphoric and Metonymic Poles" (Jakobson and Halle 90–96). The second section, entitled "Two Aspects of Language and Two Types of Aphasic Disturbances" (67–96), also treats "the twofold nature of language" in Chapter 2 (72–77).

18. This disconnection from the presumed linearity of reading and the construction of syntagmatic sense is, of course, mirrored in the use of footnotes. One holds meaning in abeyance as one flits between text, comment, parenthetical aside, and so forth.

19. See note 2.

20. See, for example, Donald McGlathery. "Does Title Confusion Affect Magazine Audience Levels," *Journal of Advertising Research* 33.1: 24; and Sean French. "Book Titles Are the Very Devil to Get Right—Think of *Catch 18*—and Even the Definitive Title May Lose Its Edge as the Years Go By," *New Statesman* (8 Sept. 1995): 35.

References

Brotchie, Alistair, and Harry Mathews, eds. *Oulipo Compendium*. London: Atlas, 1998.

Cahoone, Lawrence, ed. *From Modernism to Postmodernism: An Anthology*. Oxford: Blackwell, 1996.

Derrida, Jacques. "Title (to be specified)." *Sub-stance* 31 (1981): 5–22.

Eagleton, Terry. *Illusions of Postmodernism*. Oxford: Blackwell, 1996.

Ferry, Anne. *The Title to the Poem*. Stanford: Stanford UP, 1996.

Fisher, John. "Entitling." *Critical Inquiry* 11 (1984): 286–92.

Genette, Gerard. "Structure and Function of the Title in Literature." *Critical Inquiry* 14 (1988): 692–721.

Hannah, Barry. *Airships*. New York: Knopf, 1978.

——. *Bats Out of Hell*. Boston: Houghton, 1993.

——. *High Lonesome*. New York: Grove, 1996.

Harvey, David. *The Condition of Postmodernity*. Oxford: Blackwell, 1989.

Hobson, Fred. *The Southern Writer in the Postmodern World*. Lamar Memorial Lectures, No. 33. Athens: U of Georgia P, 1991.

Jakobson, Roman, and Morris Halle. *Fundamentals of Language*. 1956. The Hague: Mouton, 1975.

Kellman, Steven G. "Dropping Names: The Poetics of Titles." *Criticism* 17 (1975): 152–67.

Lee, Richard. Telephone interview with Barry Hannah, 5 Jan. 2002.

Linn, Ray. *A Teacher's Introduction to Postmodernism*. NCTE Teacher's Introduction Series. Urbana, IL: National Council of Teachers of English, 1996.

Lodge, David. *Working with Structuralism*. London: Routledge, 1981.

Lyotard, Jean-François. *Toward the Postmodern: Philosophy and Literary Theory*. Ed. Hugh Silverman. Atlantic Highlands: Humanities, 1993.

McClatchy, J. D. "How To Begin?" *Partisan Review* 65.2 (1998): 326–29.

McGowan, John. *Postmodernism and Its Critics*. Ithaca: Cornell UP, 1991.

Motte, Warren F., Jr., ed. and trans. *Oulipo: A Primer of Potential Literature*. Lincoln: U of Nebraska P, 1986.

Readings, Bill, and Bennet Schaber, eds. *Postmodernism Across the Ages*. Syracuse: Syracuse UP, 1993.

Shevlin, Eleanor. "'To Reconcile Book and Title and Make 'em Kin to One Another': The Evolution of the Title's Contractual Functions." *Book History* 2.1 (1999): 42–77.

Weston, Ruth. *Barry Hannah, Postmodern Romantic*. Baton Rouge: Louisiana UP, 1998.

Williams, James G. "Proverbs and Ecclesiastes." *The Literary Guide to the Bible*. Ed. Robert Alter and Frank Kermode. Boston: Harvard UP, 1987. 263–82.

Male Paradigms in
Thom Jones and Tom Paine

Paul R. Lilly

As a writer of short stories, Thom Jones has reached a kind of star status that some critics have compared to the impact made by the young Hemingway in the early 1920s. Robert Stone, to cite just one example, called the stories in *The Pugilist at Rest* (1993) "an amazing blend of knowledge and skill, terror and release." Unlike Hemingway, Jones's first three books, *The Pugilist at Rest*, *Cold Snap* (1995), and *Sonny Liston Was a Friend of Mine* (1999) are all short story collections. Tom Paine's first book, *Scar Vegas* (2000), is a collection of ten stories, and if it did not have the impact of Jones's first book, *Scar Vegas* received excellent reviews and praise from writers like Rick Moody and Richard Bausch. One of the stories won an O. Henry Award ("Will You Say Something, Monsieur Eliot?") and two won Pushcart Prizes ("Scar Vegas" and "The Battle of Khafji").

Reading Payne's fiction, especially his efforts to dramatize a version of maleness, sometimes reminds me of Jones. Both use war as a definer of manhood (each has stories of Marines and Vietnam), and both portray males in conflict with an image of maleness they seem to want to emulate but cannot. Maleness exists as a dynamic; it is threatened by its antithesis, defined differently from story to story by each writer, but which usually involves the female—not always specific women characters, but a maleness perceived to be womanish, weak, "sensitive," a word both writers use. The males are always conscious of performing for other males.[1]

The image of maleness most familiar to readers of Thom Jones's fiction is the fighter, often a boxer or a combat soldier, such as the narrators in "The Pugilist at Rest," "Break on Through," and "Black Lights," the first three stories in *The Pugilist at Rest*. Sexual prowess is another dimension of maleness, found in stories like "Mosquitoes" in which the physician-narrator seduces his brother's wife, or "Wipeout" in which the narrator, wearing a $1,200 suit, shows off his techniques for seducing women: "You have to make them come to you and you just can't get emotionally involved" (89). In these stories women are trophies to be seized for the purpose of inspiring envy in other males. Another component of maleness is solitude, such as the narrator's state of mind in "Mosquitoes": he wishes he could "take a boat and my two German shepherds and go off to a tropical island" (111). The isolation of the psychiatrist in "Black Lights," Andrew Hawkins, is due to a missing nose; he "had been cut adrift from the human race," says the narrator (80). Perhaps the last component for Jones's warrior male is stoicism in the face of death, such as the Marine narrator in "Break on Through" who is facing his possible death in battle: "That was how you did it. You did not cry or whine. That was not permissible. You just had to take it, like in the cowboy movies" (47).

Against this macho image of maleness Jones places a counter-image, that is, the sensitive male, often the male as reader, such as Meldrich the janitor in "Silhouettes," who spends his time reading Spinoza and "investigating the riddle of existence" (143). Another is Jorgenson, the Marine in "The Pugilist at Rest" who dies creating a "stunning body count" of enemy soldiers (26); what Jorgenson really wanted to do is "have an artist's loft in the SoHo district of New York City, wear a beret," and listen to records of Edith Piaf (4). The narrator, Hollywood, is convinced that Jorgenson "had the sensibilities of an artist" (5). But Hollywood knows he himself is unlike Jorgenson: "There was a reservoir of malice, poison, and vicious sadism in my soul, and it poured forth freely in the jungles and rice paddies of Viet Nam" (20). Drawn to the image of the hard-bitten male warrior, Hollywood "committed unspeakable crimes and got medals for it" (20).

If aggressive males like Hollywood—and they abound in Jones's fiction—are drawn to males who are readers or artists, what then of Jones's images of the female, that is, of actual female characters? First of all, there aren't many of them—none in the first three stories of *The Pugilist at Rest*. When women appear, they seem to fall into two categories: older women and younger, sexual women. The older women are presumably beyond sexual desire or attraction, such as the narrator's grandmother in "Break on Through," who loved him as a boy. Another example is the mother-in-law of "I Want to Live!" who is consoled by the narrator as she dies of cancer: "She encouraged the son-in-law to clown and philosophize, and he flourished when she voiced a small dose of appreciation or barked out a laugh" (184).

The female characters for whom sex is by no means beyond them are mirrored versions of the strutting male and display an equal desire for life on the edge, love in extremis. Two of his stories are narrated by this kind of female. "Unchain My Heart" reveals a woman editor who risks her job with frequent flights to meet with a deep sea diver, Bocassio, who brings her to sexual ecstasy: "His pungent smell," she gushes, "lingers in the sheets with an opium effect and I float as if in clouds of heaven" (115). She becomes pregnant by Bocassio, but when she learns of his accidental death while diving, she aborts the fetus. Her primary thought during the operation is that the fetus cannot now grow into a boxer: "I put my feet in the stainless steel stirrups and the future heavy-weight champion of the world is tossed into a plastic offal bag without throwing a punch" (127). She is as danger defying as her dead lover; soon after his death she takes up with a Marine Corps fighter pilot who gives her a ride in his jet. "I've learned deep, now I want to learn speed" (128).

In "Rocketfire Red," a story in *Cold Snap*, the narrator, an Australian aborigine, dies her hair red, helps build a drag racer, and then drives it to various victories, each one risking the car's explosion: "Driving RocketFire Red at the Nationals I seen me birth, me whole life and me death in 4.9 seconds. I saw flamin' everything" (162). For this narrator—like Bocassio's lover—only risking death brings ecstasy, and ecstasy is all there is.

The most suitable sexual partner for the male boxer-warrior in Thom Jones's stories, it appears, is a woman equally aggressive. We think of the woman in "Wipeout" who has a deep voice, reads Wittgenstein and is, according to the narrator, tougher than nails: "When you go out with an alpha, they think they're screwing you; they think the guy is the piece of ass" (93). There is a logic here; if life is a battle that can only end in suffering and death—an assumption that runs through all of Jones's remarkable fiction—then both genders face the same problem and need to take on the same attitude: be tough, go down swinging, be the primal man, or in this case the primal woman like the aborigine drag racer who risks her life to see "flamin' everything."

Tom Paine, writing about the same time as Jones (Paine's "Will You Say Something, Monsieur Eliot?" appeared in the *New Yorker* in 1994), looks at the image of the male more critically in *Scar Vegas*. His fiction undermines the macho image by exposing it to a counterimage of maleness that we sense is the more genuine, that is, the sensitive male, often characterized by a feeling for nature. Paine's paradigm of the male is more politicized than Jones's; Paine sees the macho male as dangerous because—allied to technology—this kind of male can destroy the environment. One could say that for Paine the earth itself is the female, in danger of being raped by the techno-male, such as the construction engineer, Sherm Strickhauser, in "The Hotel on Monkey Forest Road." While Jones's natives of Africa are hapless bearers of pain and suffering in the form of exotic diseases, the natives of Paine's jungles come with an inner wisdom, like the Balinese holy man, the *pedenda*, who feels that the gods have to be propitiated before Strickhauser's native laborers can begin demolishing the pristine jungle to construct a luxury hotel. Strickhauser's friend Andrew, also an engineer for the same global construction firm, begins to lose his techno-male instincts in the company of a flower child, Victoria, who urges Strickhauser to expand his "sensitivities" (108). Strickhauser retorts, "Sensitivities didn't buy that Rolex watch, princess" (108). The crisis of the story occurs when Strickhauser, who has resisted all evidence that there is value other than the material in nature, the value sensed by Victoria, Andrew, and the native holy men, ends up being spooked by the evidence he holds in his hands, a clump of grass—two years old—that is as fresh as the day Andrew cut it.

Another story by Paine, "The Mayor of St. John," looks at this tension between the aggressive techno-male, and his female, earth-loving antithesis. Sebastian Vye, a native of the island and the illegitimate son of the black governor, is appointed by his father to be the mayor of the island, St. John, in the Virgin Islands. But Vye, a former substitute history teacher, has no talent for negotiating the claims of the native islanders against the powerful white landowners and developers. He is not man enough; his maleness is compromised by a nostalgic feeling for the old St. John and the simple life in harmony with nature once lived by its native inhabitants. He loves a young woman, Eustacia, and hopes some day to marry her and "live an old-fashioned, simple West Indian life" (150). Eustacia herself loves the donkeys that roam the island. But these very donkeys are opposed by the rich whites who live in "Chocolate Hole" because they eat their garden plants, which of course are not native plants but exotic imports. Outraged whites take Mayor Vye to see the damage, but he sees "the million-dollar villas that are slowly covering the island" (162). His island is being ruined by developers, and yacht-owning "liveaboards." Although Vye attempts to save the donkeys, he is defied by Lieutenant Jeffreys, a psychopathic black police officer who happily shoots several donkeys right in front of white tourists. In the end, Vye fails to save either the donkeys, his job, or Eustacia's love. The techno-male, in the form of Vye's brother Moses, who owns a construction company, triumphs over the sensitive male, Sebastian, who is left penniless, adrift in dreams of the island of his childhood when he used to walk into the rain forest alone to "listen to the orchestra of yellow-and-green tree frogs for hours barely breathing, for if he moved at all they stopped their ancient song" (163).

A more fearsome version of the techno-male dominates Paine's "The Battle of Khafji," set in the Gulf War. The first-person narrator is a member of an elite fighting unit, the Marine Recon (he was "sent" to this "best of the best" unit, unlike Jones's Marine narrator in "The Pugilist at Rest" who volunteers for Recon). Moreover, Paine's narrator seems somewhat skeptical of the warrior image his unit encourages; he says "we are supposed to be proud" of the ninety percent casualty rate such units normally incur. His commanding officer, Captain Beck, is a "poster" Marine with a "square jaw" and "ice-blue eyes"; but Beck is, the narrator confides, "seriously hung up on the high tech"(193). Beck delights in the laser device, the MULE, that guides a bomb to an Iraqi target. He sees war as just a video game. Beck's antagonist, Sergeant Parker, an overweight bus driver, refuses to press the button. Parker, it seems, is the true male, and asks of the narrator, "Is it still a war if nobody dies on one side?" To the narrator, Parker's question seems unmanly; Parker makes him think, and "in those days thinking made me feel like a faggot" (209).

Sergeant Parker is not a passive resistor to war; he leads his patrol through a minefield by himself when their guidance gadget malfunctions, then attempts to rescue an Iraqi woman he sees wandering through the minefield. He seems to have an uncanny ability to make technology go wrong. Some of the Marines believe that Parker generates a "weird effect on mechanicals" (206). When Parker unexpectedly sings *Silent Night*, the narrator is moved by Parker's voice: "[W]hen he sang[,] it was almost this female thing, all high and sweet" (207). Finally, to save the Iraqi woman from the minefield, Parker takes on a Marine Cobra helicopter about to shoot her, and fires at it with his sidearm. The Cobra shoots back, wounding Parker. But he has shown his mettle; bleeding, handcuffed for insubordination, Parker becomes the moral center of the story. He is the true male, opponent of technology and defender of the weak, especially the female, who in this case is not just the Iraqi woman but the desert and its natural inhabitants, from camels to desert tribes. Parker leaves the story for an undetermined fate at the hands of his Marine accusers, but the narrator suffers the effects of technology later on—he is poisoned by gas during Desert Storm, his hands turn to "claws" from arthritis, and his son is born with "veins outside his face" (215).

Paine's most compelling portrayal of the tension between the techno-male and the sensitive male takes place in "General Markham's Last Stand." Here a decorated Marine general, on the eve of his retirement dinner, steals a bra from the commissary and is caught shoplifting. It seems he has been wearing woman's underwear for years, ever since his wife, to whom he has remained faithful, sent him her own underwear at his post in Vietnam. Caressing her underwear consoled him in the midst of horrors there (he jumps on an enemy hand grenade to save his men, and is wounded). Markham's life has become a "microwave oven, cooking him," and lingerie somehow cools him "like parachuting out into a cloud bank" (20). The stolen bra reveals his secret to his commanding officer, General Bowles, who, enraged at the revelation that a decorated Marine general is not the macho male he is supposed to be, breaks Markham's nose, aims his pistol at his head, and threatens to shoot him. "You're a faggot, Markham. I kill faggots" (28). To save the Corps' reputation, Bowles plots an alternative version of Markham, namely the male icon of the Corps, as he phrases it, "a pussy-loving son of a bitch" (28). A prostitute is hired to confront Markham in public, creating the image that she is his lover. The retirement dinner follows, with his wife Beatrice sitting at his side. She is angry with him not for his seeming public infidelity but because she senses there is some truth he has not told her. Markham reveals this truth when he strips off his uniform at the party. To the horror of the Marine officers and wives, Markham is wearing panties. Everyone rushes from the room except his wife, who claps for him and for his performance, his last stand. She understands that he is not only faithful to her but a true male, braver than the warriors who have fled. Markham has acknowledged the feminine side of his nature and paid the price.

Paine's true males, then, Sergeant Parker and General Markham, are perhaps too easily recognized by the reader. They are brave in the traditional warrior ways first; we think of Markham and the grenade, Parker and the minefield. This public certification of bravery under fire legitimizes them as representatives of the sensitive side of the male. Both Parker and Markham are seen by the macho male as a serious threat, subject to expulsion from the elite warrior tribe that is the Marine Corps, but both win our approval for their resistance; their public disgrace is their moral triumph. Both stand out from their nearly two-dimensional antagonists, the psychopath "faggot" haters like General Bowles and Colonel Beck. The choices for the reader are clear enough, because Paine's sympathy for Markham and Parker is obvious.

For Jones, it is not as easy to identify the true male because his soldier-warriors, like the black Ondine, the baby-faced Gerber, Singh the

Indian who is adept at torturing prisoners for information, are accomplished killers of their North Vietnam antagonists, but they remain victims as well, and have our sympathy. Jones's Marine narrators, like Hollywood, who bashes in a fellow recruit's skull with his rifle butt, is also defending his own friend, the artist-soldier Jorgenson. Years later Hollywood expresses repugnance for the warrior image he once admired. He asks himself why he killed "my fellowmen in war without any feeling, remorse or regret? And when the war was over, why did I continue to drink and swagger around and get into fistfights? Why did I like to dish out pain, and why did I take positive delight in the suffering of others? Was I insane? Was it too much testosterone? Women don't do things like that" (22).

So in the end, at least for Jones's boxer-warriors, macho maleness fails precisely because its moral quality cannot meet the standard that women achieve, apparently, simply by being women. Paine's women function as moral beacons for their often misguided men; Victoria in "The Hotel in Monkey Forest Road," Eustacia in "The Mayor of St. John," and Beatrice—her name evokes an earlier moral focal point for a male adrift—in "General Markham's Last Stand," function to arouse in their male counterparts a realization of their own sensitivity, and they are willing to defend it. Jones's women are more of a passive force in his fiction. It is the knowledge of what women *won't* do that prompts a macho male like Hollywood to examine his conscience. Women in Paine's fiction are active presences. It is what they are and do that brings out the best in the male.

Note

1. For an interesting discussion of images of the male, see Chapter 1 of Kaja Silverman's *Male Subjectivity at the Margins* (New York: Routledge, 1992).

References

Jones, Thom. *Cold Snap*. Boston: Little, 1995.
———. *The Pugilist at Rest*. Boston: Little, 1993.
———. *Sonny Liston Was a Friend of Mine*. Boston: Little, 1999.
Paine, Tom. *Scar Vegas*. New York: Harcourt, 2000.

Eloquence and Plot in Denis Johnson's *Jesus' Son*: The Merging of Premodern and Modernist Narrative

J. Scott Farrin

Jesus' Son by Denis Johnson comprises eleven short stories following the life of its protagonist Fuckhead over an indeterminate number of years. Drug-addict, criminal, and American bottom-feeder, Fuckhead is, as Jack Miles observes, "disjointed and broken in speech . . . too anger-blinded for Aristotelian beginnings, middles, and ends" (121). In fact, the stories resemble modernist stories, containing only diffused conflict and sources of tension, a nonhierarchical chain of events, and a lack of resolution. For epiphany, Johnson's stories end in charged moments of uncertain meaning, hallucinatory articulations of an appetite for transcendence without any ability on Fuckhead's part to decipher those articulations. With no material resolution and with revelations that refute the efficacy of action, the stories appear static. But taken together, the stories track a more traditional plot with reversals and with resolution. Like the term *postmodern*, rooted in *modern* but hinting at more, *Jesus' Son* combines the modernist narrative with something else, premodern form, to create something greater than either tradition could provide.

To understand the structure of Johnson's stories, one must understand the structure of the modernist story. Before Modernism, fiction conformed to the Aristotelian plot, one that contained mounting tension, climax, and resolution: order disrupted and order restored. It is the basis of the traditional three-act drama. The modernists abandoned the Aristotelian plot in the early twentieth century, around the time of World War I, which was billed as "the war to end all wars," and, in fact, was a dispiriting event. Its combatants experienced not decisive battles but years of grueling trench warfare, mustard gas, and disease. Ten thousand more Americans died of disease or in accidents than from enemy gunfire (Croteau and Worcester 124). Afterward, disillusioned by the war and alienated by the inescapable presence of an industrialized society of the type satirized by Charlie Chaplain in *Modern Times*, writers rejected the idea of *will* creating *action* creating *change*. Robert Caserio describes them as believing "[p]lot, story, and narrative reason are fictions, elaborate evasions, artificial discourses only pretending to theorize definitively about the vital spiritual and material forces that may very well rule our lives because stories, plots, and narrative reasonings do not" (56). For the characters of the modern novel, life is done *to* them. The characters are passive; the story is how the characters intellectually and emotionally adapt to circumstance. George Orwell characterized and approved of a writer's reaction against narrative action in his review of Henry Miller's work:

The passive attitude will come back and it will be more consciously passive than before. Progress and reaction have both turned out to be swindles. Seemingly there is nothing left but quietism—robbing reality of its terrors by simply submitting. . . . Get inside the whale—or rather, admit you are inside. (Angus and Orwell 526)

No fictional character better embodies this passivity than Leopold Bloom in Joyce's *Ulysses*. Content finally to do nothing about his wife's infidelity after 604 pages of rumination, he lists as his reasons: "the futility of triumph or protest or vindication: the inanity of extolled virtue: the lethargy of nescient matter: the apathy of the stars" (604).

George Eliot, a premodern, prefigured the modernist aesthetic. Instead of rescue, Eliot's characters are often left with only enduring as resolution. The moderns embraced this idea of endurance. Of Dilsey, the most admirable character in *The Sound and the Fury*, Faulkner states in that novel's appendix, "They endured" (236). Leopold Bloom endures, as does Johnson's Fuckhead when, at the end of "Out on Bail," he states, "I am still alive" (42). The primacy placed on endurance arises from a view of event as arbitrary, apathetic if not hostile. It cannot be controlled by willed action; it cannot be planned. At the end of Eliot's *Middlemarch*, Dorothea tells Celia, "I could never do anything that I liked. . . . I have never carried out any plan yet" (795). And in that novel's afterword by Frank Kermode, he emphasizes the character Dorothea's inability to control event: "When she [Dorothea] acts positively, as in marrying Casaubon, she acts disastrously" (817). "In [George] Eliot, there is an arbitrary relation between what is done and narrative reasonings about what is done that always threatens to return action to the form of accident" (Caserio 105). The modern plot substitutes accident for action. Events do not build on each other. The historian Thomas Carlyle, in rejecting premodern narrative, believed that "what must go first and foremost is story understood as the chain of causal successions that incites memory, foresight, and relational coherence and that implies development and transformation" (Caserio 33).

All the elements that describe the modernist story also describe the stories in *Jesus' Son*. Johnson's stories, compared to early modernist stories, may go even further toward rendering event as accident. Narratively, the formula remains the same. The modern story ends with an epiphany such as the one found at the end of Joyce's "Araby": "Gazing up into the darkness I saw myself as a creature driven and derided by vanity; and my eyes burned with anguish and anger" (19). This is a revelation of nothingness, similar to the one at the end of Hemingway's *The Sun Also Rises*. Jake responds to Lady Brett Ashley's comment that they "would have had such a damned good time together" with "Isn't it pretty to think so" (247). It may be "pretty to think so," but the world does not allow for neat endings, no marriages as at the end of a Jane Austen novel. Johnson's Fuckhead wallows in nothingness and yearns for transcendence, but is unable to achieve it. Glimpses of transcendence reveal themselves as only a movie screen or a hailstorm, and if it were truly revealed, Fuckhead could not apprehend it. He may have a charged moment and a weighted line, but "those miraculous one-liners" don't turn into a "richer, more reasoned, calmed down, smoothed out, reliably and progressively self-explanatory inner monologue" (Miles 122). Fuckhead "may be overcome by what he has just said, but his awareness is so momentary that he doesn't know why he is overcome" (121). In the end—like modernist characters—Fuckhead never transcends the nothingness of his world. In individual stories, no plans are made, narrative reasoning is devalued, and actions lead nowhere.

Aristotle, conversely, stated, "Happiness and misery are realized in action . . . the goal of life is an action" (Caserio 78). In the premodern plot, therefore, the protagonist eventually effects his own rescue; he builds a pyramid of actions from which he leaps to safety, or—in tragedy—he commits mistakes that build and lead to his morally instructive downfall. His actions reveal character and the themes of the work. Life is not accident. "Because story and plot are the means whereby experience is understood as a relation, as a comprehensible or coherent sequence or chain of relations, they make the experience they tell 'tell'" (Caserio 6). The willed actions of the protagonist against his environment and antagonists, and toward his goals assume polarized

forces, and the struggle between the polarized forces, a motivated protagonist and plot elements opposing him, provides the tension and
conflict of a work of fiction. In the premodern plot, the give and take
between these polarized forces can be described as peripety or reversals. "Peripety or reversal is indispensable to story, since reversal
grounds the intelligibility of experience in an act of transformation and
in the significant differences created by transformation that I believe
are fundamental to thought" (Caserio 7). Caserio lauds Walter Scott as
an originator of the peripatetic plot, the plot that Charles Dickens bor-
rows, Eliot modifies, and the Moderns reject. Of Scott's use of reversal,
Caserio asserts, "One of Scott's principal uses of reversal lies in his
placement of the wavering figure at the center of his novels. . . . Of
course, the wavering of both the hero and plot is a form of constant
reversal: the plot fits the theme" (61).

At first, there seems to be little real peripety in *Jesus' Son*. Although
incidental actions and reactions exist—shallow reversals—they do not
result in anything. In each story, the protagonist exhibits that "radical
stasis of human character" consistent with Modernist fiction (Caserio
15). But the entire eleven stories present a more traditional plot. Over the
course of these stories, Fuckhead wavers and arrives at the collection's
end saved from the tyranny of circumstance. This "wavering" creates the
tension of a premodern novel, and it builds an audience's appetite for
resolution. In "Psychology and Form," Kenneth Burke states:

Form is the creation of an appetite in the mind of the auditor, and the adequate
satisfying of that appetite. This satisfaction—so complicated is the human
mechanism—at times involves a temporary set of frustrations, but in the end
these frustrations prove to be simply a more involved kind of satisfaction, and
furthermore serve to make the satisfaction of fulfillment more intense. (31)

The "wavering," the tease and frustration, the building of an audience's
appetite, happens in fiction through plot and eloquence.

This wavering, which Burke describes as "eloquence," does not
occur between embodied forces, a hero and villain struggling back and
forth from plot point to plot point, but between qualities: "the presence
of one quality calls forth the demand for another, rather than one tangible incident of plot awaking an interest in some other possible tangible incident of plot" (38). Thus, a feeling of despair would inspire in the
reader a desire for hope. Eloquence consists of this skillful manipulation of these qualities, an adroit representation of this type of wavering.

But this wavering of qualities, or "eloquence," though independent
of plot, is not opposed to it. Burke describes how an audience has its

appetite whetted for the ghost's arrival in the fourth scene of the first act of *Hamlet*, and how the audience's appetite is satisfied (29–30). The audience, with Hamlet, waits for the ghost and there is a blare of trumpets and expectations soar. But it is only Claudius coming home from drunken revels. At this time, Hamlet begins an even-toned and pedantic criticism of drinking, how it hurts the reputation of Danes abroad:

> But to my mind, though I am native here . . .
> This heavy-handed revel east and west
> Makes us traduc'd and tax'd of other nations.
> They clepe us drunkards. (*Hamlet* 1.4.14–19)

Suddenly and emotionally, the ghost arrives, and the tension developed between expectation and disappointment, then distraction and finally expectation's sudden satisfaction adds to the audience's pleasure. It is not only the lurch and cutback of event but of tone that develops the audiences appetite. Burke could not deny that the ghost's arrival plays an important role in the play's plot or that eloquence, in this instance, if not comprised of plot, serves plot by highlighting a scene crucial to the play's developing conflict. Conversely, wavering, when confined to an individual character as even in Walter Scott's novels, will have an internal aspect, often expressed through qualities. Certainly this is true in any first-person narrative. The qualities at war in *Jesus' Son* wage that war in Fuckhead's consciousness, and it is not his conclusions, of which he has little, but his perceptions that exhibit this struggle between qualities. In any story, these qualities may or may not lead to narrative action, depending on whether the story has a premodern or modern aesthetic.

In *Jesus' Son*, the qualities of healing, redemption, and Fuckhead's inarticulate yearning for such, war against the qualities of meaninglessness, fatedness; Fuckhead's addiction to drugs represents a grim destiny, proof against volition. Eloquence resides in the presentation of these warring qualities in each individual story. This eloquence serves, at most, to create at each story's end a charged moment as in a modernist story, although without definitive revelation or epiphany. But together, the stories lead, falteringly, to climax and to a resolution, a healing. In short, *Jesus' Son* contains stories that taken individually display the modernist rejection of narrative reasoning, portraying a static character battered by accidents, but which combined resemble a premodern plot in which a character wavers but then resolves all conflict to create resolution. As a whole, *Jesus' Son* forms a postmodern plot that encompasses premodern and modern traditions without slighting either.

Jesus' Son starts with a car crash in western Missouri. In "Car Crash While Hitchhiking," a family in an Oldsmobile gives Fuckhead a ride. They crash into another car on a two-lane bridge. Before this, Fuckhead tells us he had been riding with a salesman, both of them on amphetamines. But he felt alienated from the salesman when the salesman began speaking of love, his wife, kids, and mistress, his ties to others. In the Oldsmobile with this family, in his alien environment, the man driving, his wife, little girl, and their baby in back with him, Fuckhead feels fated: "[B]y the sweet voices of the family inside it [the Oldsmobile] I knew we'd have an accident in the storm" (4). Fuckhead's world and the world of this family meet and explode like matter meeting antimatter.

After the crash, Fuckhead leaves the car and every injured person inside it, carrying the baby in his arms. As the police arrive and question him, he becomes "the president of this tragedy" (10). At the end of the story, the man in the car the family's Oldsmobile has hit dies, and Fuckhead is sitting in the hospital, exhilarated by the cries of his widow. He says, "I've gone looking for that feeling everywhere" (11). Her cry of protest is for the loss of the happy ending, for her husband and for marriage, and for the death of the family, the idea of the family, the happy resolution. Fuckhead has only been the passive witness to tragedy, which does not surprise him, but he yearns for that other life, the one for which the grief-stricken widow also cries.

The line Fuckhead delivers upon the widow's outcry of grief, "I've gone looking for that feeling everywhere," gives the story "a sudden forward buck" (Miles 122). The last page of the story flashes forward to the book's end, with Fuckhead in detox in a Seattle hospital. The resolution is foreshadowed, as Burke says, "[i]n the opening lines [in which] we hear the promise of the close, and thus feel the emotional curve even more keenly than at first reading" (35). The end juxtaposes the promise of healing against the despair of the car crash. The baby lives, a symbol of the future and of hope, and is held in Fuckhead's arms as he stands on the side of the road, the wreckage that was the cars and their passengers smoldering before him. This story gives us eloquence and suspense. It hints at the resolution, but depicts a story in which our protagonist is totally passive, moved only by accidents instead of willed action.

The next story, "Two Men," is the collection's darkest. Fuckhead continues to feel alienated from those around him, as he was from the salesman in the previous story. He begins the story in the company of two friends (not the two men of the title) of whom he confesses, "Once again, I hated the two of them. The three of us had formed a group based on something erroneous, some basic misunderstanding that

hadn't yet come to light" (15). The three of them pick up a fourth, the
first of the "Two Men." They take the fourth man, a brute—deaf and
dumb—to various places, looking for somewhere that will take him in.
At one house, a woman tells Fuckhead, "If you don't take him off our
street I'm calling the police" (20). After the last house denies entrance
to the deaf man, Fuckhead looks at the people inside the house and
thinks "around these strange people I felt hungry" (25). Fuckhead too
craves entrance, is lost like this deaf man, and every time he stands
outside a house that has denied the deaf man—and himself—he is
"flooded with yearning" (20).

    Fuckhead and his friends ditch the deaf mute, leaving him stagger-
ing at a crossroads. Looking back, they see him "paused among the
fields in the starlight in the posture of somebody who had a pounding
hangover or was trying to fit his head back onto his neck. But it wasn't
just his head, it was all of him that had been cut off and thrown away"
(27). The deaf mute's plight underscores Fuckhead's; both are outcasts
yearning for entrance but without any way to express and effect such.

    The story ends when the three men chase a supposedly crooked
drug dealer to his home. The dealer escapes out a window, leaving behind his wife and children. The three men force an entry, hold the wife
at gunpoint, and, discovering the dealer gone, tell the wife, "You're
going to be sorry" (31). This makes a grim conclusion, leaving us with
the scene of Fuckhead standing over a crying woman with a gun, her
kids in the next room, intent on doing something, injuring the woman?
raping her? Taken alone, this story asserts nothingness, but in a way
that may "out-modern" the moderns. There is no tsk-tsking disappointment at a meaningless universe, but a violent and unreasoned
reaction to that universe.

    The third story, "Out on Bail," finds Fuckhead sitting at a bar with
Jack Hotel. Fuckhead imagines the bar, the Vine, as a home to lost souls.
It is either the occasion of Jack's sentencing on an armed robbery charge,
or of his acquittal; it's not clear to Fuckhead, who believes one thing then
realizes he's wrong. Fuckhead, explaining his confusion, states:

There were many moments in the Vine like that one—where you might think
today was yesterday, and yesterday was tomorrow, and so on. Because we all
believed we were tragic, and we drank. We had that helpless, destined feeling.
We would die with handcuffs on. We would be put a stop to, and it wouldn't be
our fault. So we imagined. And yet we were always being found innocent for
ridiculous reasons. (39)

    At the story's end, Fuckhead and Jack split a bag of heroin, both
overdose, Hotel dies—"he simply went under" (42). Fuckhead asserts,

however, in the last line, "I am still alive" (42). His survival is credited to chance, circumstances slightly different than Hotel's. But it is an affirmation of sorts. This affirmation alone, however, does not promise renewal or serve as moral instruction, but in the modernist tradition, is tempered and wary.

When Fuckhead visits Dundun, the title character of the fourth story, Dundun tells him, "McInnes isn't feelin too good today. I just shot him" (45). Inside the farmhouse, McInnes sits on the couch. The story does not tell us why Dundun shot him, there is no anger leftover from the shooting, and everyone else in the farmhouse seems either unable to deal with the situation, or unable to register it. They had attempted to take McInnes to the hospital, but drove the car into a barn and gave up. The reader is again presented with a world ruled by accident, the rescue attempt, the one narrative action, negated by accident. And Dundun stands as an agent of a capricious destiny, not to be evaded or even understood.

Fuckhead volunteers to take McInnes to the hospital, but McInnes dies on the way. Dundun cries, but then muses, "I wouldn't mind working as a hitman" (50). Fuckhead describes Dundun in the story's last paragraph: "Would you believe me when I tell you there was kindness in his heart? His left hand didn't know what his right hand was doing" (51). Dundun is not merely subject to a loss of volition and the tyranny of chance. Those elements are housed within him. And Fuckhead? He is both McInnes and Dundun, the harmed and the harmful. The story does not leave the reader with much hope for redemption. Dundun must pay for his crimes, and we are told he is in prison. As for Fuckhead, of his life and future, he says: "We'll never get off this road" (49).

In the next story, "Work," Fuckhead, nodding on heroin, encounters his friend Wayne at the Vine. He convinces Fuckhead to come with him "to make some money" (56). They go to an old house ruined by flood water and abandoned, and they strip the copper wiring from the walls with the intention of selling it for scrap. In the process, they work off the drugs and the sickness.

Wayne confesses that this abandoned house was once his. After helping salvage something from Wayne's past, Fuckhead decides "it was turning out to be one of the best days of my life" (62). He concludes:

All the really good times happened when Wayne was around. But this afternoon, somehow, was the best of all those times. We had money. We were grimy and tired. Usually we felt guilty and frightened, because there was something wrong with us, and we didn't know what it was; but today we had the feeling of men who had worked. (65–66)

In other words, they had taken action and accomplished something. Feelings of hope and renewal now serve as a counterbalance to feelings of helplessness.

The random world of "Emergency," the next story, mitigates the positive ending of "Work." Fuckhead and his friend Georgie work in an emergency room, taking drugs stolen from the medical cabinets. Fuckhead seems immune to the horrors surrounding him, but Georgie is more sensitive. When an injured man comes in, eventually it is Georgie who pulls the knife from his eye. After their shift is over, Georgie tells Fuckhead, "I'd like to go to church . . . I'd like to worship" (76). Instead, Fuckhead coerces him into visiting a county fair. When they run over a pregnant rabbit, Georgie c-sections it and removes the babies, intending to save them. Fuckhead, however, smothers them by accident. When they pick up a boy running from the draft, the boy asks Georgie, "What do you do for a job?" (88). Georgie replies in a way that Fuckhead tells us "suddenly and completely explained the difference between us" (86). Georgie says, "I save lives" (88). Georgie believes in the effects of narrative action as Fuckhead does not.

Throughout the story, visions of despair—Fuckhead and Georgie lost in a blinding snowstorm—war with images of renewal such as a brilliant, otherworldly sunrise. The setting of the hospital reminds us of the possibility of healing, but Fuckhead's actions there disappoint us. In a junkie's rhapsody, he states, "I could suddenly understand how a drowning man might suddenly feel a deep thirst being quenched. Or how the slave might become a friend to his master" (85). Or how an addict could come to love his addiction. This story, the one exactly in the middle, is the collection's most ambivalent.

"Crash," the first story, established setting, tone, and character, locating Fuckhead within an existential space. He is at the whim of chance and his addictions. Also in the first story, Fuckhead's time in detox in a Seattle hospital is foreshadowed. From "Crash," we descend into the world of "Two Men." Fuckhead yearns for redemption, for admittance, but reacts to his alienation by striking out at an innocent. "Out on Bail" offers hope in the form of Jack Hotel's acquittal, then in Fuckhead's survival contrasted with Jack's death. In "Dundun" Fuckhead is lost, if not as lost as Dundun. Fuckhead tastes, for a time, redemption in "Work," through work and his association with Wayne. But "Emergency" takes us back to a world of random tragedy, to a hospital. No healing takes place, and Fuckhead, unlike Georgie, distances himself from any narrative reasoning.

The seventh story, "Dirty Wedding," deals overtly with death. It begins with a paragraph describing Fuckhead's journey on an elevated train. It courses past the windows of buildings into which he gazes voyeuristically, captivated by the lives there (91). Then the train plunges into a tunnel. The journey descends into darkness as images of death overwhelm this story. Fuckhead has just taken his girlfriend to get an abortion. He makes a scene in the clinic and is thrown out, haunted by the "canceled life dreaming after me" (95). Fuckhead rides the train, ferried by a ghostly driver, follows a man he identifies as Christlike, and ends up at the Savoy Hotel, a dark underworld where he has come to buy heroin. At the story's end, he tells us that his girlfriend committed suicide sometime after they had separated, her new boyfriend dying soon after.

With the abortion, we have a death for which Fuckhead feels accountable, saying "I wasn't what the doctors did, it wasn't what the woman did. I was what the mother and father did together" (102). Fuckhead confronts death and responsibility to a greater degree than in "Dundun." This story marks Fuckhead's turning point.

"The Other Man" starts: "But I never finished telling you about the two men. I never even started describing the second one" (105). He refers back to the second story, to "Two Men." This story responds to "Two Men." In a scene in the earlier story, Fuckhead stands outside a house, denied entrance by a woman who lives there, yearning to get inside. This happens again in "The Other Man"; Fuckhead yells up at his friends' apartment, the landlady confronts him and denies him entrance. But this time, it is not for another, the mute in "Two Men," but for himself that he begs entrance. He admits to a desire to reconcile himself with those within and, symbolically, with the society from which he is outcast.

At the end of "Two Men," Fuckhead confronts a married woman, barges into her home—she is terrified—and does her some injury. In the end of "The Other Man," he meets in a bar a woman recently married. He dances with her, kisses her, and she wants to take him home. She accepts him. This event serves as a peripatetic answering to the event in "Two Men." And it is not only in the events, but in Fuckhead's perception and in the tone in which he relates events that establishes this as a forward swing in his interior "wavering." The married woman's behavior shocks him, but he finds something in it deeply moving, saying of the moment: "It was there. It was. The long walk down the hall. The door opening. The beautiful stranger. The torn moon mended. Our fingers touching away the tears. It was there" (113).

If the wistful yearning Fuckhead exhibits in the first eight stories denotes a certain volitionless dissatisfaction with his life, in the ninth story this yearning upgrades to a more *active* frustration. He wants an unattainable belly dancer and spends the story in fruitless search for her, gets in two arguments over money, and gets in conflicts with a bus driver and a man in a library. At this point, he believes he has been through it all, and asks the reader, "And what are you going to do to me now? With what, exactly, would you expect to frighten me?" (123).

We join Fuckhead, in the second to last story, at a hospital undergoing detox. "Steady Hands at Seattle General" consists only of the conversation between Fuckhead and his roommate Bill. Fuckhead's hands are steady, and it is he who is active, shaving Bill. The story contrasts the two of them. Unlike Fuckhead, Bill hates detox; his attitude is more pessimistic than Fuckhead's, more guarded. "You can take a couple more rides on this wheel and still get out with your arms and legs stuck on right. Not me," he tells Fuckhead (133). He describes his past as "wrecked cars" and inside: "people who are just meat now" (133). As Fuckhead shaves him, he asks Bill about the scars on his face. "I'm a writer," he says (130). Bill tells him he was shot by his wife in the face. When he was shot, he had a dream, but when pressed, he cannot describe the dream and will not try, saying "How could I tell you about it? It was a dream. It didn't make any fucking sense, man" (132).

But as a writer, Fuckhead intends to make sense of his world, thus he differs from Bill who sees nothing behind him but accidents and, we infer, nothing before him but more of the same. As someone with car wrecks behind him, with shootings and violence, his history parallels Fuckhead's. But unlike an earlier foil, Georgie in "Emergency," Bill serves to illustrate Fuckhead's hope and the possibility of his redemption. When Fuckhead tries to reassure Bill that he too will be fine, Bill asks him to talk into his bullethole and tell him he will be fine. The bullethole represents his only reality.

In the last story, "Beverly Home," a friend of Fuckhead asks the other participants of an AA meeting if they feel as he does, alone and "screwed up," looking at houses and imagining the happy people hidden behind the window curtains (151–52). The question hurts Fuckhead. Again: the issue of being outside normal society and craving entrance. He has himself been spying at night on a Mennonite couple, hoping to catch them doing something, having sex. At one point, trying to peer through a window, he says, "Two inches of crack at the curtain's edge, that's all I could have, all I could have, it seemed, in the whole world" (154). He feels the old yearnings of an outsider when he spies on them, and he wants to catch them doing something carnal to break the spell. But instead he witnesses an argument, an act of penance and of forgiveness when the husband apologizes to his wife by bathing her feet, an allusion to the biblical story of the fallen woman bathing Christ's feet, being accepted by him.

This story recounts Fuckhead's final healing. Early in the story, he describes a cactus flower as "one small orange flower . . . surrounded by a part of the world cast mainly in shades of brown" (141). Fuckhead becomes that: growing among the unredeemable. His girlfriend, he tells us, has had more boyfriends than anyone he has ever known: "Most of them had been given short lives" (158). They had met their deaths through mishap and misadventure, car wrecks and such, one was shanked in prison. Their ghosts, hovering around the two of them, exhilarated Fuckhead. He felt "sweet pity" for them, the kind only the living can give to the dead (159).

He works in a hospital for the aged and infirm. The residents are mad, disabled, or stricken with "impossible deformities" (138). He says of them, "they couldn't be allowed out on the street. . . . They made God look like a senseless maniac" (138–39). "You and I don't know about these diseases," he says, "until we get them, in which case we also will be put out of sight" (139). Like the dead boyfriends, these are the unredeemable, the final victims of chance, of accident. But Fuckhead struggles to make sense of his world; he acts and heals himself. The story ends with this: "But I was in a little better physical shape every day, I was getting my looks back, and my spirits were rising, and this was all in all a happy time for me. . . . All these weirdos, and me getting a little better every day right in the midst of them" (160).

In the seventh story, "Dirty Wedding," death invades Fuckhead's life in a way that he finally acknowledges. It motivates him. "The Other Man" responds to "Two Men," bringing positive qualities, acceptance and hope for redemption, to counterbalance the despair of the earlier story. Fuckhead exhibits an active dissatisfaction with his life in "Happy Hour," and in "Steady Hands," he compares favorably to his roommate in detox, Bill, an older junkie. The last story, "Beverly Home" witnesses Fuckhead's redemption, the active part he plays in achieving it.

It could be argued that the collection's unity of effect is accidental. All the stories of *Jesus' Son* were published separately. But their arrangement clearly testifies to an overriding plan. The stories that lead to "Beverly Home" give its resolution impact by developing the conflict and by building the readers appetite for resolution. The wavering of qualities and the events to which they are attached looks something like this:

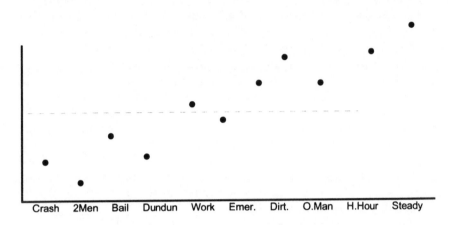

Crash 2Men Bail Dundun Work Emer. Dirt. O.Man H.Hour Steady

The climb of the line represents the increasing presence of positive qualities. The peak either occurs in "Steady Hands" where Fuckhead compares favorably with Bill in the Seattle detox unit, both men confronted by the chance to change their lives, or early in "Beverly Home" when Fuckhead's feelings of alienation wage their final war against the possibility of redemption, when he witnesses the Mennonites' argument. The collection ends in a clear dénouement, bringing together both premodern plotting and modernist movements.

Nevertheless, on the graph, the dots are not connected as they would be in a true premodern novel. For that to occur, we must see the transitions from one state to another, the character making the climb from point to point. We have instead a premodern plot seen through a kind of stop-motion photography. Such is the necessary method of this postmodern form and Johnson's artistic achievement. It lets him have it both ways: an overarching redemption and the compelling glimpses of nothingness that are evocative of our fractured moments and frustrated desires.

References

Angus, Ian, and Sonia Orwell, eds. *The Collected Essays, Journalism, and Letters of George Orwell*. London: Harcourt, 1968.

Burke, Kenneth. "Psychology and Form." *Counter-Statement*. Cambridge: Harvard UP, 1961. 29–44.

Caserio, Robert L. *Plot, Story, and the Novel*. Princeton: Princeton UP, 1979.

Croteau, Maureen, and Wayne Worcester. *The Essential Researcher*. New York: Harper, 1993.

Eliot, George. *Middlemarch*. New York: Signet, 1964.

Faulkner, William. *The Sound and the Fury*. Ed. David Mintor. New York: Norton, 1987.

Hemingway, Ernest. *The Sun Also Rises*. New York: Collier, 1986.

Johnson, Denis. *Jesus' Son*. New York: Harper, 1992.

Joyce, James. "Araby." *Dubliners*. New York: Dover, 1991. 15–19.

———. *Ulysses*. Ed. Hans Walter Gabler. New York: Vintage, 1986.

Kermode, Frank. Afterword. *Middlemarch*, by George Eliot. New York: Signet, 1964. 813–23.

Miles, Jack. "An Artist of American Violence." *Atlantic* (June 1993): 121–26.

Shakespeare, William. *Hamlet*. Ed. Harold Jenkins. New York: Routledge, 1982.

Ardor with a Silent H: Submitting to the Ache of Love in Edmund White's "Skinned Alive"

Raymond-Jean Frontain

"The French have such an attractive civilization, dedicated to calm pleasures and general tolerance, and their taste in every domain is so sharp, so sure, that the foreigner (especially someone from chaotic, confused America) is quickly seduced into believing that if he can only become a Parisian he will at last master the art of living," notes Edmund White in *The Flâneur*, his paean to his adopted home, Paris (50). Although White would no doubt resist being labeled a postmodernist,[1] this passage is a good example of his characteristically suggesting the possibility of some absolute value or achievable state of happiness only to undermine his own suggestion in the most subtle of ways. At first glance, the passage juxtaposes the sharpness and sureness of French taste "in *every* domain" with the chaos and confusion that supposedly characterize White's native America. Yet even as the gratification that comes of "master[ing] the art of living" appears to be coming within the hope-filled foreigner's reach, it must unfortunately be postponed to some unspecified future ("when . . . at last"). More problematically, this promised fulfillment depends on a conditional clause—"*if* he can only become a Parisian"—which, if the text does not state is impossible, the context suggests is unlikely to happen. White indirectly confirms the reader's growing suspicion that the very search for cultural preeminence is invariably inconclusive when he states that a person is "quickly seduced into believing" that such a transformation is possible, which reduces the promised gratification to be derived from cultural refashioning to a fantasy too quickly entered into by the naively hopeful foreigner. While the text does not identify the siren who seduced the cultural pilgrim into attempting to transform himself or herself, by the end of the sentence the possibility of such transformation and even the much vaunted "attractive[ness]" of Paris have been placed in doubt.

White, thus, erases with one hand the very possibility of happiness about which he writes with the other. The city perceived by foreigners as alluring may or may not represent possibilities unavailable in their own culture. Likewise, the foreigner's native culture may or may not actually be confused and chaotic, for it is unclear whether the speaker who dismisses American culture genuinely believes it to be worthless is only repeating what the French say stereotypically of Americans, or is enjoying quoting what insecure Americans think of themselves vis-à-vis the seemingly superior French. The sharpness and sureness of French culture—not to mention the cultural hegemony of Paris—have been reduced to a chimera that the narrator, with Proustian delicacy, not only never asserts outright is false, but also never makes clear whether the foreigner who has been seduced into pursuing the fantasy of happiness through cultural perfection is ever finally enlightened as to the nature of his or her delusion. (White intimates that some American expatriates may spend the rest of their lives in Paris awaiting a fulfillment that will never come.) Desire—that is, hope of gratification, whether from cultural refashioning or, as White dramatizes more frequently elsewhere in his canon, attained through romance and/or sex—is revealed to be the *illusion* of promised satisfaction, the movement toward a state that can never be achieved, yet the delusions surrounding which are never exposed or rejected. Desire, for White, is a suspended state in which a person is repelled by what appears to be chaotic and confused, yet in actuality suffers nothing but pain on behalf of the supposed source of gratification.

"Skinned Alive"—first published in *Granta* (1989) and reprinted as the title story in White's 1995 collection of his short fiction—is a narrative of unfulfilled desire set, not surprisingly, in Paris.[2] The unnamed narrator is an American whose only stated reason for living abroad is that so many friends at home have died of AIDS-related illnesses, yet who—like the archetypal foreigner of *The Flâneur*—is comforted to be living among a people whose taste seems "so sharp, so sure."[3] Far from making clear whether the narrator becomes a Parisian and masters the art of living (or, more importantly, discovers that he can never really become or do so), the story is inconclusive, leaving the reader uncertain as to the fate of either of the narrator's two relationships—that with a young Frenchman named Jean-Loup, the disintegration of which the story records; and that with Paul, a fellow American expatriate, with whom the narrator shares a trip through the south of

Morocco. Lacking any apparent structure, the story climaxes in the narrator's being beaten by the masochistic Paul during a night of love-making at a desert oasis, yet gives no hint of what the narrator learned during the epiphany that presumably occurs as a result of this beating. The apparent lack of structure, the inconclusive ending, and an epiphany the significance of which is neither stated nor implied, all reflect both the indeterminateness of homosexual identity and a queering of love itself. The most that White's characters can do is learn how to submit to the ache of love, and to do so silently.

Elusiveness of Character

Humans, says White, are "just a collection of random psychological states, predispositions, emotions, sentiments, and so on, not to mention bodily organs, more like a pile of objects than an actual unity of self" (qtd. in Christensen 73). This belief preempts his characters' displaying any consistent unity of being; they emerge, rather, as bundles of contradictions attempting to function amidst ambiguities that resist clarification. No matter how dramatic the events in which they find themselves caught up, the final impression that they make on the reader is of elusiveness: the reader acknowledges their identity, but finally has no purchase on them. No matter how seemingly provocative the details that White provides concerning his characters' relationships, his images invariably prove inconclusive.

Consider the opaqueness of the first-person narrator of "Skinned Alive." Certain concrete details emerge in the course of the story concerning his life and character: he is American, middle-age, a published novelist, and a homosexual who has lost many of his friends to AIDS-related illnesses. He is himself HIV-positive, but not sero-active. He enjoys hosting dinner parties for his "playpen" of French twenty-year-olds because he feels younger in their more animated company. He does not volunteer his name, however, and even though he is regularly addressed directly by other characters in the story, none of them use his name either, leaving him curiously unanchored in time and space.

A largely passive presence, the narrator's character emerges through his response to others. He is rarely seen initiating contact; his life seems spent, rather, meeting the demands of Jean-Loup and their joint friends. And when he does assert himself—as when, furious that Jean-Loup has left him for Regis, he tries to sway his friends' opinion against his former lover—other characters object to his misrepresentation of Jean-Loup's motive, leaving the reader to question the reliability of information delivered elsewhere in the story through the narrator's narrative soliloquy which, while available to the reader, is not open to his friends' corrections. While the reader feels at ease with the narrator, finding him a congenial presence, one finally knows little of the narrator's interior life, and may be surprised by what details do emerge. The reader, for example, learns about his having abstained from alcohol for ten years only when he mentions a bout of sex play during which good manners required that he allow Jean-Loup to pour half a bottle of Sancerre down his throat (64). And although multiple references to "hard" sex precede the climactic incident, the reader is nonetheless startled to understand the extent of the narrator's masochism when he seduces Paul into beating him during their Moroccan jaunt, focusing for the reader the passivity that is the most important component of his personality.

As White says in his interview with Richard Canning, "the first-person narrator is just this eye that travels over things, and if you come to know the parameters of his personality, it's partly because you learn where this eye goes. You see what he sees, and see what he's interested in looking at" (83). This holds true for "Skinned Alive," which is both driven and limited by its unidentified first-person narrator's perception.[4] Significantly, however, White never claims in his interview with Canning that the reader necessarily understands *why* the narrator is engaged by what his eye falls on; the reader of "Skinned Alive" is left to try to make sense, if there is any sense to be made, of the story's details. The narrator's acceptance of the chaos and confusion of his life leaves the reader with no choice but to accept the same conditions as holding for the story. For example, in the story's opening sentence, the reader is allowed to follow the narrator's gaze, but is not supplied with referents for either of the sentence's two pronouns. (Who is the narrator and what is he doing in Paris? Who is the "he" being observed by the narrator? And, in a related vein of questioning, who is giving the literary reading?) As in the episode when, checking into their oasis hotel, the narrator and Paul stop for a moment to stare into a shaded pool with glistening rocks that turn out to be tortoises, the reader is one step behind the narrator in processing the ambivalent information presented to the narrator's senses. Each strains to make sense of a chaotic and confusing world.

Other characters are similarly so ambivalent or contradictory as to elude the reader's grasp. Hélène considers the narrator her closest friend, yet, being French, is too discreet to ask him about his intimate life (56). Jean-Loup readily and repeatedly apologizes for his own "elusiveness" (59, 62, 63); because he is so unable to decide what profession he will enter, the narrator nicknames him "Monsieur Charnière (Mr. Hinge)" (60). Paul's accent is indeterminate (55), and his face both "open and unreadable" (71). Employed as the doorkeeper at a popular discotheque, Paul describes himself as a physiognomist. His very profession, thus, calls attention to how difficult it is to recognize someone whom one thinks one knows. Little wonder that the predominantly youthful audience gathered to hear the William Burroughs–type novelist read from his classic novel of gang rape, drug betrayals, and teenage murders is disappointed to meet a reformed drunk, serene in his optimism; and that Paul's mother prefers to think that his heterosexual brother, who died several years earlier of AIDS contracted from a shared needle, was gay, because she believed that to die for love is better than to die for drugs; or that Hélène advises the narrator that the correct answer to the question of faithfulness is always "yes." Identity, White emphasizes, is determined as much by what we see and what we need to see, by who we are and what we have become, as by how others need to see us. In a story that is itself the transformation of an Ovidian–Dantean metamorphosis (a point to which I will return), it is not surprising that Paul has been nicknamed Cerberus by the crowds who wait to gain admittance to his club: he guards the entrance to the underworld, peering beneath each applicant's veneer to see what his or her soul has become, and determining the arena in hell where the crowning transformation will take place.

It remains to note the extent to which the elusiveness of identity is compounded by what the narrator calls "the compromise . . . of speech" (72). Linguistic borders in the story initially seem strong and well-defended, the narrator impressed by the coloring suggested by certain French phrases and both Jean-Loup's and Paul's current French lover, Thierry, wincing when their American-born partners make mistakes in French grammar or pronunciation (compare 60–61 and 73). What are high compliments in France are clearly not so in America (58), certain cultural assumptions failing to travel across the great watery divide. But as the story progresses, language and national identity prove porous, one's identity shifting according to the language that one is speaking. The narrator, for example, notes that when Paul is speaking English he is sincere and when he is speaking French he seems to be amused (54), and Jean-Loup, while commending the narrator's unaccented French, hates the sounds that the narrator makes when speaking in his native American dialect (66). Jean-Loup likewise finds the narrator's attempt to write a love letter in French to be *mièvre* ("wimpy" or "wet") (67), undermining the narrator's presumption that French is a language more sharp and sure than English. And, thinking herself fluent in English, Hélène insists on speaking to the narrator in his native language, only to find herself easily lapsing into her native French (56). Language, far from signaling a firm border between discrete cultures or modes of perception, proves as elusive as personality. Characters' attempts to reveal themselves to others fail in large part because their language does not communicate what they intend it to.

The ultimate effect of the elusiveness of White's characters is the undermining of all forms of certainty. "Skinned Alive" presents a nebulous world in which the protagonist resists rethinking his opinions because the gap between his actions and his professed values is ultimately inconsequential. He is a "flâneur," as easily able to accept the delusory promise of gratification promised by union with either Jean-Loup or Paul, as to accept the failure of each (and, presumably, every) relationship. Whatever loss he feels is compensated for by the memory of sensual pleasures already enjoyed. His passivity is ultimately the sign of his willingness to live in a world that he knows is not sharp and sure, but whose illusion of being stable allows him, if for only the moment of desire, to believe himself on the verge of mastering the art of living and, more importantly, of loving.

Elusiveness of Gender Identity

The elusiveness of character in "Skinned Alive" results in part from postmodernism's rejection of art as an aesthetic completion, for a story cannot be sharp and sure if the author understands personality formation to be a weak and murky process, and vice versa. The greatest effect of the elusiveness of character in "Skinned Alive" is generated, however, by White's uncertainty concerning gender identity. "Skinned Alive" is a story not of shifting gender boundaries or orientations, as much as of the ultimate instability of any sexual classification.

White has commented on multiple occasions on the impossibility of successfully defining homosexuality. In the 1982 symposium at The New School, White suggested that the panel could not discuss "gay sensibility" with the same authority that its members might discuss "a French sensibility, a black sensibility, [or] a female sensibility," if only because "blacks have their color; the French have their language; [and] women have their identifying sex," whereas the only feature that marks men as gay is an invisible one—that is, "their sexual attraction to members of the same sex" (Bell 131). He elaborates this idea elsewhere when he observes that because probably only three percent of the population is gay, gay experience is ultimately unavailable to the majority of readers.

If you contrast the problem of gay literature with the problem of black literature, the truth is that once white readers got past the minor barrier of color,
they found themselves entire and intact in the black novel. That is, there are
mothers and fathers, children and divorce, adultery and breast cancer, and all
that stuff: church, sin, drinking, and wife-beating. There's a whole array of subjects they're interested in. It's all there, which isn't so in gay literature, unless
it's about straight people, which is the case of [David Leavitt's] *Family Dancing*
or [Stephen McCauley's] *The Object of My Affection* or Armistead Maupin's writing [*Tales of the City*]. (Canning 80)

White is not necessarily positioning homosexuality as the state in
which a minority is objectified by the majority (homosexuality as "not-
heterosexuality"). Rather, he is interested in the problem of writing
about "not-heterosexuality" for readers who are not homosexual, and
by the related problem of how one writes about homosexuality when
the only language readily available to use to describe interpersonal relationships is heterosexual-based. For decades American gays have de-
bated how to describe the same-sex object of one's affection. "Lover"
seems to overemphasize the sexual nature of the relationship; "partner" refers as easily to a business as to a personal relationship; and
"significant other," while most broadly inclusive and, thus, most politically correct, is so objective as to neuter the relationship entirely. Yet if
one uses the widely available language of socially sanctioned marriage
("husband," "wife," "spouse"), the argument goes, one is in danger of
subscribing to a model that one's sexuality by definition opposes. How,
White questions, can a gay writer assert a subjectivity that cannot be
known by the heterosexual majority, and for which gays themselves
have difficulty finding descriptive terms?[5]

Perhaps the queerest aspect of "Skinned Alive" is its taking for
granted the elusiveness of sexual categories. As casually as Jean-Loup
displays his penis in mixed company at the dinner table, he asks the
narrator—with whom he is still sexually involved—to help him find a
wife who is intelligent, distinguished looking, "a good sport and a slut
in bed" (58). Like Jean-Loup, the story makes no unwavering distinction between heterosexual and homosexual, or even between male and
female. Strategically, by setting "Skinned Alive" in Paris where questions of money or class are never discussed (unlike in America where
they are talked about openly and obsessively), White effectively throws
the American reader off balance, disarming his or her sense of the culturally familiar. The unnamed American narrator's experience of "the
unreality . . . of living in another language" (59) in which one might
"sooner ask about blowjobs than job prospects, cock size than the size
of a raise" (58–59), in part mimics that of the American reader whose

sexuality is typically not as fluid as Jean-Loup's and who is unsettled by the Frenchman's easy erasure of sexual orientation boundaries. The reader who enters the story supposedly secure in his or her orientation is quietly rendered, sexually, a stranger in a strange land. As the narrator observes of Paul's three former lovers, all were heterosexual "or fancied they were" (72).

This uncertainty regarding traditional sexual roles and orientations extends to homosexuals who have difficulty in the story finding words to describe their relationships. Jean-Loup experiments with introducing the narrator variously as his "husband" or his "patron" (63), and the narrator offers to accompany Paul to his upcoming high school reunion as his "spouse" (70). Not surprisingly, none of the gay couples in the story is certain how to fashion its relationship. Even as he blurts out to Paul "We should be lovers" (72), the narrator explains his struggle to announce his relationship with Jean-Loup who did not want the couple to appear domestic. After leaving the narrator for the wealthy Régis, however, Jean-Loup paradoxically begins wearing a wedding ring to publicly proclaim his new union (77), insisting that earlier he had been embarrassed by the narrator's "too evident" homosexuality, as opposed to Régis's, which he finds "very discreet" (78).[6] Similarly when Paul, tiring of the demands of his sadomasochistic relationship with Thierry, asks for some tenderness, Thierry would say, "'Oh-ho, like Mama and Papa now, is it?' and then leave the room" (73), thus rejecting the analogy of traditional marriage offered by heterosexuals, and exhibiting the corresponding uncertainty about what can be created in its place.

Gay ambivalence about how one man can fashion a satisfying love relationship with another man generates the appreciation in "Skinned Alive" of sexual orientation as performance. The narrator makes a number of references to how his friends dress, which collectively intimate that people costume themselves as though to perform their identity on stage. Hélène impresses men with her Japanese apparel and Paul dresses like a professional murderer. Clothing exists not to cover nakedness, but to provoke in the viewer an awareness of the body's sexual potential, the narrator happily indulging Jean-Loup's obsession with fashion because if he bought Jean Loup's clothes in the morning, he could undress him in the afternoon to expose his "priapic" body (57).

Such theatrical self-fashioning, however, proves as much the occasion to express a deeper personal reality as to disguise the absence of any secure center. Upon first seeing Paul, for example, the narrator could not be certain that the other man is homosexual. Similarly, when

attempting to understand his relationship with Jean-Loup, the narrator tries on various roles, all of them feminine, that he has absorbed
from the American cinema of his youth. When in the kitchen preparing
the next course while Jean-Loup remains in the living room entertaining their friends, the narrator smiles because he likes the idea of playing the wife while Jean-Loup plays the husband (65). When the
narrator, however, catches himself and acknowledges that "our marriage was just an invention of my fancy" (65), he reverts to another female role. Describing the experience of listening to Jean-Loup's
narrative of his summer holiday at a resort to which he himself was not
invited, the narrator likens himself to "a demimondaine" (66). Little
wonder that, discarded by Jean-Loup in a way that left no doubt that
he had been neither wife nor mistress, the narrator is uncertain what
part is assigned him in his initially unconsummated relationship with
Paul. Struggling to fit his relationship with Paul within familiar narratives, the narrator discovers only that they prove his sense of self to be
as "unstable" as his gender identification (76). Gender performance
may lead to self-discovery, but may just as easily mask the ultimate
instability of gender classifications.[7]

In a television interview, the narrator reports, he was once asked

"You are known as a homosexual, a writer, and an American. When did
you first realize you were an American?"
"When I moved to France," I said. (59)

One defines onself by antithesis, and becomes more aware of one's
own identity only by assuming another. Gay characters, experimenting
with words like *spouse* and *patron*, may try on heterosexual realities for
size, but inevitably reject them because they do not fit. Indeed, no sexual expectations logically hold in this story: Jean-Loup, for example,
can indulge himself more freely sexually with the narrator after shed-
ding him as a lover (62); and the need to keep their sex safe paradoxically makes it more "demented" (64). "Skinned Alive," however, does
not resolve the problem of how one expresses the subjective experience
of gay love. Like the *flâneur* or archetypal foreigner who is suspended
between the state that he rejects and that to which he aspires yet can
never achieve, the protagonist is caught between the desire to name his
experience and the frustration that the experience is so elusive that it
proves impossible to name accurately and satisfyingly. Little wonder
that the narrator himself is nameless.

It remains to be seen how in "Skinned Alive" the elusiveness of gay
relationships represents a queering of love itself.

Elusiveness of Love

The dynamic of imitation and consequent rejection of the model imitated that applies to identity formation in "Skinned Alive" apparently controls the narrator's choice of love object as well. For the uncertainty surrounding sexual orientation and the construction of homosexual relationships that leaves the first-person narrator nameless comments not only on how he defines himself as a gay man, but on how he learns to express love. The queerness of all love relationships is suggested by the Ovidian story of Apollo and Marsyas that is contained within the larger story of the relationships of the narrator with Jean-Loup and Paul.

Shortly after they begin their affair, Paul shares with the narrator a story he has written that the narrator describes as "Hellenistic . . . flirting with Pre-Raphaelite prose" (79). Like White's own story, Paul's poetic narrative "is slow to name its characters" (79) who are eventually discovered to be "a cheerful satyr" named Marsyas, who cleverly imitates people on a cursed flute that he has learned to play, and Apollo, the god of music whose own art is "pure and abstract" (80) and, thus, the antithesis of the comic, realistic efforts of the satyr. Paul's story follows the general lines of the most famous recension of the story, contained in Book 6 of Ovid's *Metamorphoses*. But whereas Ovid treats the music competition only in passing, Paul goes into explicit detail concerning the differing aesthetics of each performer, as well as the radically different affect that each song has on its audience. Conversely, whereas Ovid describes in explicit detail Apollo's flaying of the still living Marsyas (145), Paul's story concentrates on the "sacramental" (73) quality of Apollo's violence. The god ties the rope around the satyr's withers with "no tenderness but great solicitude," and "neatly," even ritualistically, slices into his belly and "peeled back the flesh and fat and hair" (81–82).

As Edith Wyss in Chapter 2 of *The Myth of Apollo and Marsyas in the Art of the Italian Renaissance* has demonstrated, the myth of Apollo's defeat of Marsyas has traditionally been interpreted to figure the difference between the Apollonian and Dionysian modes of artistic expression as represented by the universal harmony that emanated from the god's harp and the Bacchic frenzy associated with the satyr's wind instrument. In Paul's version of the myth, however, it is the classical Apollo who de-creates the world by playing his song backward, and Marsyas—who, says Wyss, could be used variously to suggest the humiliation of the human artist who aspires to perform the task of creation reserved to God (or the gods) alone, or the truth revealed by the artist when surface distractions are stripped away—who believes that he is "inspiring the very breath Apollo expired," thus reversing the poles of divine and human creation traditionally associated with the story.

The vignette's emphasis on the eye contact shared by the god and his victim, however, suggests that the story of Apollo and Marsyas is included in "Skinned Alive" as a comment on *"la baise harde"* (60)—that is, rough sex—that dominates the narrator's relationship with both Paul and Jean-Loup. Although moved to have Paul dedicate the piece to him, the narrator questions whether the story does not contain a message addressed to him by his new lover about the nature of their relation: "As I read his story I stupidly wondered which character Paul was—the Apollo he so resembled and whose abstract ideal of art appeared to be his own, or the satyr who embodies the vital principle of mimesis and who, after all, submitted to the god's cruel, concentrated attention" (82). Here is the dynamic of "Skinned Alive" distilled to its essence in terms of an elusive meaning that can be as accurately applied in either of two antithetical ways, neither of which, the reader suspects, is correct. Paul's vignette is a story about writing, about how and why mortals create art. But art, Paul's allegory suggests, is related to love, to *la baise harde*.

Apollo's flaying of Marsyas models both the sadomasochistic relationship, which Paul shares with Thierry, and the *baise harde* to which the narrator has introduced Jean-Loup. Significantly, however, the narrator's role changes in each pairing. In the earlier relationship Jean-Loup is the cheerful, boyishly priapic satyr of whom the narrator is jealous and to whom the narrator tries to make amends by writing the concluding prose poem in praise of Jean-Loup's ass (87–88).[8] In the later relationship with Paul, however, Paul's majestic size and golden beauty, which invite repeated comparisons with Hercules, make him the Apollo figure who brutalizes the narrator, Marsyas.[9] (The same image of "cambered marble" used to describe Apollo in Paul's story was previously employed by the narrator to describe Paul's neck.) The narrator volunteers to play the role of Paul's victim in presumably the same sex games as those into which he earlier introduced the boyish Jean-Loup.

These sex games, Paul's story of Apollo's flaying of Marsyas suggests, are but the beloved's way of seducing his lover into giving him his undivided attention; offering onself to be skinned alive is the satyr's way "of inspiring the very breath [that] Apollo expired." In a world where one can talk with one's partner about one's desires only after that partner has lost the ability to satisfy them (60)—where one understands the value of a relationship only after one has lost it (61)—and where "only men of refinement recognize the nobility of hopeless love" (86)—the unaspirated "h" of *harde* in French allows the word to be pronounced as the first syllable of "ardent" (60). One holds one's lover's attention by provoking him to "hard" or "ardent" acts, sacramentalizing the present through violence. One submits masochistically to the silent "h" or ache of love (65).[10]

Conclusion

If desire, for White, is a suspended state in which a person is repelled by what appears to be chaotic and confused, yet in actuality suffers nothing but pain and humiliation in the pursuit of beauty, then how does one read "Skinned Alive," which is the *written* or voiced record of the supposedly *silent* ache of love?

"Skinned Alive" opens with a telling scene, a reading by an unnamed American writer "whom everyone had supposed dead," yet who had come to Paris "to launch a new translation of his classic book, originally published twenty-five years earlier" (54). White's narrator observes how, during the reading, the author "was slowly, sweetly, suicidally disappointing the young members of his audience. They had come expecting to meet Satan, . . . but what they were meeting now was . . . not at all what the spiky-haired kids had had in mind" (54). As has already been noted, the incident is but the first of many in a narrative about anticipation's inevitable disappointment. That it should concern a reading audience's expectations of, and disappointment by, a fiction writer seems White's way of challenging the readers of his own short story to admit their exasperation at his own literary self-presentation.[11]

"Skinned Alive" is, at first glance, an unstructured story—a web of shifting relationships depicted without a frame or center, a series of contradictions that do not resolve themselves—rather than an organic whole. As White says of Proust, "Proust's explanations, his ceaseless authorial interventions, are necessary in order to impart his unique and radical point of view" (in Bell 132). Similarly, in "Skinned Alive" the narrator begins the story talking about the relationship with Paul that is initiated as his affair with Jean-Loup winds down, yet concludes with a sensual evocation of Jean-Loup's body but no explanation of what happens between the narrator and Paul after their sadomasochistic encounter in the desert. The final effect of the story's contradictions and paradoxes is the distillation within the narrator's voice of the experience of unknowing. Hélène challenges the narrator's seeming exploitation by Jean-Loup, yet the narrator claims that he is not being exploited; Jean-Loup insists that his attraction to Régis is not influenced by the older man's wealth, but the enormity of his wealth is the only detail about Régis that emerges in the story, leaving the reader to question Jean-Loup's motives even if the narrator does not. Paul has the body of a killer, yet has fashioned himself as a masochist. And the narrator reports that in Morocco, shortly after Paul tells the narrator that he would love and protect him, Paul pounds him "in the face with his fists, shouting . . . in a stuttering, broken explosion of French and English, the alternatively choked and released patois of scalding indignation" (86). Significantly, after this seeming proof of his affection for the narrator, Paul disappears from the story, leaving the narrator to offer Jean-Loup the belated gift of a description of the younger man's ass. The reader is asked, not to make sense of the characters and conclude who is truthful and who is self-delusory, but to accept self-delusion as the most elemental aspect of character.

Likewise, the story's extraordinary clarity of style only masks the fact that nothing in the story is clear. Just as the narrator does not know how to interpret Paul's parable of Apollo and Marsayas (82), the reader is, finally, uncertain how to interpret White's story. However concerned its characters are with the correctness of language, "Skinned Alive" is finally not "accurate" but opaque. It possesses a seeming objectivity—as in the concluding description of Jean-Loup's ass, which the narrator hopes does not "sound too wet" or *mièvre* (87)—but such objectivity also betrays no indication of why the story should end this way. How is it the logical conclusion to what has gone before? How does it answer the question of the fate of the narrator's relationship with Paul, after being beaten by him at the desert oasis? Will the narrator continue his relationship with Paul? Or, not satisfied by the beating that Paul administers, has the narrator abandoned hope of that affair progressing satisfactorily, and returned to mooning over Jean-Loup's imperfect but lovable *derrière*? As Peter Christensen has noted of White's epiphanies in general, "White leaves us to speculate on the actions that the epiphanies may generate" (75).

Rather, White's story operates like the "Leica lens, shut now but with many possible f-stops" to which the narrator compares Jean-Loup's anus: "An expensive aperture, but also a closed morning-glory bud" (88). The narrative offers as precise a view of what happens to the narrator, but from the same emotional distance that a camera allows a picture of a scene. It is not *mièvre* or emotionally sappy. Adapting to French society, the narrator learns to greet the most bizarre story with a shrug as though distanced from the absurdity by viewing it from the objectivity of a camera lens. How can the reader object to the narrator's being beaten by Paul when the narrator presents the incident as being "perfectly normal"?

What the reader is presented with, finally, is an oracle that cannot be interpreted, one that allows the possibility that it means everything or nothing at all.[12] In his concluding paean to Jean-Loup's ass, the narrator describes the younger man's penis as a "Daily Magic Baguette" (87), as the bread of life, and the adolescent Jean-Loup's maturing genitals as the grapes that will make for a great Bordeaux (88). Such description does not parody the Eucharist but invests Jean-Loup's body with the sacramental mystery of the Eucharist—the mysterious body and blood, flesh and fluid, that are capable of redeeming the narrator, but that finally elude him. The narrator who, like Marsayas, has incurred the wrath of the god whose favor he had been trying to win, is "skinned alive" by both Paul and Jean-Loup, and reduced (emotionally, not physically) to a pained, quivering mass of exposed nerve and muscle. Neither relationship offers the narrator complete "mastery of the art of living." Instead, each brings him within reach of a satisfaction that he can never finally enjoy. And just as the narrator must submit to the silent ache of love, the reader must submit to a story in which words prove inadequate or ineffective. Well may he or she, like the *flâneur*, hope to master the art of living through White's story, but ultimately the reader can only submit to being skinned alive.

Notes

1. Taking part in a roundtable discussion at New York City's The New School on November 29, 1982, White seemed to take pains to disassociate gay sensibility from what he termed the recent trend toward "starkness" in fiction writing, focusing instead on the "four elements of contemporary [American] affluent, white, gay male taste": "ornamentation, the oblique angle of vision, fantasy and theatricality, and finally, in terms of content, an interest in, and an identification with the underdog" or socially marginalized (Bell et al. 131). Likewise, in his interview with Richard Canning, he reveals that "[w]hen I read other kinds of criticism [than reader-response theory]—postmodernist or whatever—I think: 'Oh, that's true; that's interesting; why not?' But it never seems to reflect anything that would go on in my mind when I'm actually writing" (Canning 90). White is clearly postmodernist, however, in the challenge that he consistently offers to what Berlant and Warner term "the comfort of privilege and unself-consciousness" (347), and in terms of his "awareness of diverse culture boundaries" (345).

2. Indeed, in a passage discussing the sharpness and sureness of French manners that seems to echo *The Flâneur*, Jean-Loup compliments the narrator for having become a perfect Parisian: "*Plus parisien tu meurs*" (57). Yet, as the narrator notes, he himself thought that he would die if he did not become *more* Parisian (57).

   3. A narrative of frustrated or inconclusive desire set in Paris might seem an oft-told tale, White having been anticipated in this by Henry James's *The Ambassadors* and James Baldwin's *Giovanni's Room*. Both are narratives of naive and, to varying extents, sexually ambivalent Americans whose self-discovery in Paris is shaped both by the author's difficulty accepting his own homosexuality, and by his personal sense of liberation experienced upon leaving a sexually repressive and aesthetically stultifying America. White's postmodernism, however, is thrown into high relief when "Skinned Alive" is compared with James's and Baldwin's narratives of an American in Paris. Whereas his predecessors leave no doubt that their protagonists had something significant to learn by their experience, White is suspicious of claims of profundity; thus, there is no scene in "Skinned Alive" remotely similar to Lambert Strether's encouraging Little Bilham to "Live!" or Jacques's climactic speech to David encouraging him to love Giovanni.
   4. White may be indebted to the "I am a camera" style of narrative developed by Christopher Isherwood in The Berlin Stories, which similarly presents in shocking or unsettingly neutral terms behaviors that a first-person narrator would traditionally have been reluctant or embarrassed to relate.
   5. On the way that White's narratives "reveal the ways [that] socially and culturally imposed restraints on gay freedoms necessarily deny gay subjectivity and isolate in gay men an idea of a homosexual self as Other that they themselves conceive as being separate from their apparently essential selves," see Nicholas F. Radel (176). Radel in effect provides one reason for White's inability to believe in a unitary self.
   Annamarie Jagose's *Queer Theory* provides a helpful overview of conflicting languages of gay and lesbian self-identification, and of the conflicting views of sexual identity that inform each language. It is precisely because there is no clear sense of what homosexuality is or how orientation occurs that recent theorists and critics have attempted to create "queer" tests, provoking an "awareness of diverse culture boundaries" (Berlant and Warner 345).
   6. The suggestion of homosexual marriage is sustained by the narrator's twice describing Jean-Loup's buttocks as being the color of "wedding-gown satin" (57, 88).
   7. Paul's narrative of how he defuses potential violence at the club where he works by pretending not to be aware of the very real personal threat that he faces (75) models how performance works in the story on levels other than the sexual. Jean-Loup, for example, is initially frustrated that the narrator does not "perform" his sense of betrayal after being told that Jean-Loup is leaving him for Regis. Then, as though in a B movie, each provokes the other into saying hateful things. It is only by playing the roles of the unfaithful coquette and the jealous, abandoned lover that Jean-Loup and the narrator can bring their relationship to a conclusion, proving the depth of their love by the theatricality of their recriminations (77–78).

8. The narrator's prose poem in praise of Jean-Loup's ass is another modernization by White of a classical motif. On the callipygian poems so numerous in *The Greek Anthology*, see Raymond-Jean Frontain 99–102.

9. Classical myth plays an important role in this short story in which a friend is described as a "mythographer," as opposed to a liar (60). Paul's repeated association with Hercules raises a number of parallels between the classical hero's myth and the circumstances of "Skinned Alive." As Pierre Grimal notes, Hercules engaged in combat with Apollo when, frustrated at not receiving an answer from Apollo's oracle at Delphi, the hero ransacked the god's temple to establish an oracle of his own elsewhere (47–48). Hercules's death was inadvertently brought about by his wife who, jealous of his straying affections, prepared what she thought was a love potion by dipping his tunic in the blood of the slain centaur Nesses. The potion, however, proved a poison activated by Hercules's body heat when next worn (206–07). Hercules, thus, was "skinned alive" by a jealous lover who was, paradoxically, trying to preserve his affections.

10. Peter Christensen's brief reading of "Skinned Alive" is that for White "the pursuit of beauty justifies any humiliation" (81).

11. White's story, in postmodern fashion, is a fiction that purports to be something else. The narrator of "Skinned Alive" is not named, but like the actual Edmund White, he is a middle-age American male living in Paris in the 1980s. An author, he is, like White, famous for the style of his first two novels. A gay man, he is, like White, HIV-positive but not sero-active. And his relationship with Jean-Loup resembles in many ways that of White with Hubert Sorin, with whom White collaborated on *Our Paris* (1995), to which Sorin contributed whimsical drawings reminiscent of those which the narrator attributes to Jean-Loup in "Skinned Alive." (White further fictionalizes/documents his relationship with Sorin in his novel, *A Married Man*, 2000.) In daring the reader to consider "Skinned Alive" as barely veiled autobiography, White is again blurring the line between autobiography and fiction, as he does in his tetralogy of so-called autobiographical novels. Similarly, White's fellow Violet Quill writer Felice Picano published "a memoir in the form of a novel" (*Ambidextrous*, 1985), and in *Book of Lies* (1998) challenged the reader to approach the novel as a *roman à clef* even while mocking him or her for doing so.

12. "An Oracle," another story in the collection that includes "Skinned Alive," is equally "oracular." White does not make clear if the oracle in the title is something that the protagonist's dead lover once said to him, is the local boy with whom he connects while visiting a friend in Greece, or is the story itself. The story does not, like Robert Frost's "Secret," sit in the center of a circle, smiling knowingly as humans dance around it and try to decipher its mystery. Rather, White's stories deliver something almost understood that cannot be put into words because White himself is ambivalent about its significance. Richard Dellamora provides an intelligent reading of "An Oracle" as "apocalyptic utterance."

References

Bell, Arthur, et al. "Extended Sensibilities: The Impact of Homosexual Sensibilities on Contemporary Culture." *Discourses: Conversations in Postmodern Art and Culture*. Ed. Russell Ferguson et al. Cambridge: MIT P for The New Museum of Contemporary Art, 1999. 130–53.

Berlant, Lauren, and Michael Warner. "What Does Queer Theory Teach Us about X?" *PMLA* 110.3 (May 1995): 343–49.

Canning, Richard. [Interview with Edmund White]. *Gay Fiction Speaks: Conversations with Gay Novelists*. New York: Columbia UP, 2000. 75–112.

Christensen, Peter. "'A More Angular and Less Predictable Way': Epiphanies in Edmund White's *The Darker Proof*." *Review of Contemporary Fiction* 16.3 (fall 1996): 73–83.

Dellamora, Richard. "Apocalyptic Utterance in Edmund White's 'An Oracle.'" *Writing AIDS: Gay Literature, Language, and Analysis*. Ed. Timothy F. Murphy and Suzanne Poirier. New York: Columbia UP, 1993. 98–116.

Frontain, Raymond-Jean. "'An Affectionate Shepheard Sicke for Love': Barnfield's Homoerotic Appropriation of the Song of Solomon." *The Affectionate Shepherd: Celebrating Richard Barnfield*. Ed. Kenneth Borris and George Klawitter. Selinsgrove: Susquehanna UP, 2001. 99–114.

Grimal, Pierre. *The Dictionary of Classical Mythology*. Trans. A. R. Maxwell-Hyslop. London: Blackwell, 1986.

Jagose, Annamarie. *Queer Theory: An Introduction*. New York: New York UP, 1996.

Ovid. *Metamorphoses*. Trans. Mary M. Innes. Harmondsworth: Penguin, 1955.

Radel, Nicholas F. "Self as Other: The Politics of Identity in the Works of Edmund White." *Queer Words, Queer Images: Communication and the Construction of Homosexuality*. Ed. R. Jeffrey Ringer. New York: New York UP, 1994. 175–92.

White Edmund. *The Flâneur: A Stroll through the Paradoxes of Paris*. New York: Bloomsbury, 2001.

———. "Skinned Alive." *Skinned Alive: Stories*. New York: Knopf, 1995. 54–88.

Wyss, Edith. *The Myth of Apollo and Marsyas in the Art of the Italian Renaissance: An Inquiry into the Meaning of Images*. Newark: U of Delaware P, 1996.

The Genre Which Is Not One: Hemingway's *In Our Time*, Difference, and the Short Story Cycle

Peter Donahue

In their 1940 work *How to Read a Book*, Mortimer J. Adler and Charles Van Doren set forth their "General Rules for Reading Imaginative Literature." The first command the authors give is "1. You must classify a work of imaginative literature according to its kind" (209). Adler and Van Doren, following the classical model, proceed to distinguish between the lyric, the novel, and the play. Their facile proscription of literary categories, however, proves inadequate to readers of a work such as Ernest Hemingway's *In Our Time*, which is often cited as an early example of the twentieth-century short story cycle. While *In Our Time* has been recognized as different—neither novel nor traditional short story collection—from the time of its 1925 publication, critics have puzzled over how formally to classify the work and, from there, how to analyze the dynamics of its constituent parts.

In attempting to describe the ambiguous literary genre of the short story cycle, critics have routinely come to rely on figurative language. Forrest L. Ingram compares the genre to tapestries, wheels, and finally mobiles—"because the interconnected parts . . . seem to shift their positions with relation to the other parts" (13). Robert M. Luscher talks of bubbles within a "thematic current" (152). Such a use of figurative language to conceptualize the genre suggests its un-fixed nature, that it can be *like* something—like a novel, like a short story collection—but apparently not something definite unto itself. Further complicating efforts to define the genre is the plethora of terms used to identify it. The first two book-length studies of the genre, by Ingram and Susan Garland Mann, identify it as *short story cycle*. Luscher argues for the term *short story sequence.* Other terms include *short story composite, composite novel, rovelle,* and *integrated short-story collection* (Creighton; Hark; Lemmon; Reed). Luscher aptly points out that all these terms "suggest the static unity of combined independent parts" but fail to recognize the "more dynamic unity" of the genre (149). The problem remains, however, that all of these terms, including Luscher's own short story sequence, assume and emphasize a definite unity, static or otherwise, within the genre. This emphasis places the genre in the service of a modernist ideal rather than recognizing the destabilizing characteristics that mark the genre as a highly postmodernist practice. In Hemingway's *In Our Time*, as in perhaps no other example of the short story cycle, the tension between the modernist ideal of unity of form and the postmodernist practice of a dispersal of form becomes apparent. In this respect, *In Our Time* exhibits the genre's paradoxical nature of simultaneously promoting and frustrating a conclusive apprehension of its own form.

This Janus-faced nature of the short story cycle has led to the urge among critics to ascribe and argue for a single, all-purpose term for the genre. The urge also stems from a certain *unity imperative* that most critics bring to their discussion of the genre with near missionary zeal, as if the absence of final unity were a heresy against the truest of all literary values—and certainly, by high modernist notions of artistic hierarchies, it is. Only J. Gerald Kennedy, in recognizing the overdeterminability of the aforementioned terms for the genre, acknowledges that such "proliferation of terminology . . . points to the pervasive assumption that some unifying principle determines form" (13). The following analysis challenges the unity imperative—or "unifying principle," as Kennedy identifies it—that lurks within all these terms and the critical approach that they signal, especially in regard to Hemingway's *In Our Time*. Having adopted the term *short story cycle* simply because it has the widest circulation, this analysis argues for the deficiency of the unity imperative in examining *In Our Time* not only as a representative short story cycle but also as a short story cycle that enacts a postmodernist relationship to meaning (via form) at the height of the modernist era. This is to say that if the modernist purpose is, in T. S. Eliot's words, "a way of controlling, of ordering, of giving a shape and significance to the immense panorama of futility and anarchy which is the contemporary world" (qtd. in Brooker 6), then *In Our Time* serves equally, if not more so, the postmodernist purpose of upending control, order, shape, and significance to achieve its meaning.

This said, and despite the limitations of the many terms applied to the genre—that is, despite the unity imperative latent within each—*In*

Our Time, as a short story cycle, is a work not without unity. As the work evolved from its earlier incarnations as *Three Stories and Ten Poems* (1923) and then *In Our Time* (1924), Hemingway was conscious of putting together a collection of stories that was more than just a haphazard gathering of the pieces that he had available for publication. While most of the stories were written between 1923 and 1925 as separate, unconnected stories, the vignettes were mostly composed in 1923 when Hemingway was first experimenting with the pared-down style and use of repetition that he was learning from Gertrude Stein. When the time came to compile a fuller collection of stories, after the publisher Boni and Liveright expressed interest in publishing such a book, Hemingway began considering how best to arrange the work. According to Hemingway biographer Michael Reynolds,

> [Hemingway] studied carefully Joyce's *Dubliners* as his model. *Dubliners* was not merely a collection of unrelated stories, but a new form like Anderson's *Winesburg, Ohio*—a set of stories bound together by location, themes and characters. Looking over his ten stories, Hemingway saw that geography was not a possible unifier. . . . In fact, there was no real unity, for he had not written them to be a whole. But he saw how Joyce had used his massive story, "The Dead," to weld the *Dubliners'* themes together. Ernest needed such a story to end his book, a story bringing together everything he had learned. (202)

This recognition led Hemingway to write "Big Two-Hearted River," the final of the seven Nick Adams stories in the book. The fact remains, though, that *In Our Time* was not conceived of as a whole work, as Sherwood Anderson's *Winesburg, Ohio* was, and for this reason lacked "real unity." Nonetheless, Hemingway did seek to impart a sense of unity to the work, however loosely, through theme and character. According to Ingram's classifications of the short story cycle, *In Our Time* would qualify as a "completed cycle": begun as independent stories that the author starts to arrange as patterns of unity emerge with each subsequent story (19). It was neither a deliberate nor an accidental short story cycle. Rather, it was a work that became a short story cycle late in the composition process as Hemingway attempted to link the stories and at the same time began to recognize the degree to which the stories could not be welded into a comprehensive whole.

As Hemingway said in a letter to Edmund Wilson after the third and final incarnation of *In Our Time* appeared in October 1925, the work "has a pretty good unity" (*Selected Letters* 128). This statement, while often cited by critics as Hemingway's declaration that he had achieved his intended purpose of unifying *In Our Time* to the same degree as Joyce's *Dubliners* or Anderson's *Winesburg, Ohio*, seems not so much an assertion of unity for the work as a retrospective and self-reassuring comment on his decision to collect the stories and vignettes into a single book—a book which, as James R. Mellow notes, "was a more found structure than a rigidly ordained scheme" (266). Critics who play up the "pretty good unity" remark overlook the less-than-calculated manner in which the stories accrued into a single volume. When Hemingway says in the same letter to Wilson that the vignettes are intended "to give the picture of the whole between examining it in detail," it is as if he is aware of creating a kind of trompe l'oeil by which the reader will perceive unity even though it does not fully exist in the work (128). The critical arguments that tout the "pretty good unity" remark as evidence of Hemingway's intentions (and achievement) for *In Our Time* tend also to ignore the level to which the work resists, rather than enforces, unity on both a structural and a thematic level. This resistance results, in part, from the work's postmodernist flirtations with random composition—similar to the "field composition" experiments made decades later by postmodernist artists such as Charles Olson and John Cage—which are at least as important as the author's worried efforts to justify the book's organization.

In addressing the question of unity within the short story cycle, Luscher admits that "[t]he very looseness of the . . . form seems to undermine its status as 'strictly' or 'merely' anything," suggesting that he recognizes the possibilities for the genre beyond the unity imperative that most critics impose upon it (162). What Luscher views as the genre's looseness, Ingram sees as the "dynamic patterns" within the form (20). Despite the nonstatic possibilities offered by Ingram's phrase, ultimate unity of form remains its goal since these "dynamic patterns" lead, finally, to "recurrent development," which ultimately aims toward unity (20). Luscher, meanwhile, seeming to allow for an inherent degree of disunity in the genre, briefly shifts the unity imperative away from the genre itself and onto the reader, stating, "Our desire for unity and coherence is so great that we often use our literary competencies to integrate apparently unrelated material" (155). Although he is correct about the role of this readerly (and critical) impulse, Luscher, while allowing for variety, eventually reverts to the unity imperative in his definition of the genre: "There is no uniform model for the short story sequence . . . [yet] each one exhibits a distinctive unity and aesthetic integrity" (159).

Austin Wright's theory of "recalcitrance," although he did not apply it directly to the short story cycle, is useful in trying to account for the unrelatedness of the constituent parts within the genre. As

Wright says, "The notion of formal recalcitrance may rescue formal unity from some of its disadvantages" (115). One problem with how Wright presents this notion, however, is his obvious effort to formalize what appears to be an antiform concept, thereby establishing a rigid duality between "formal recalcitrance" and "formal unity." So while Wright's theory of recalcitrance may help us account for points of tension within the presumed unity of a short story cycle such as *In Our Time*, it cannot account for how the genre ultimately eludes even the closed and fairly static system of adherence versus recalcitrance, form versus antiform.

Rather than operating on such either/or formalism, the short story cycle engages a "process of difference" throughout the multiplicity of its thematic concerns and narrative strategies. Short story cycles typically include a grab bag of characters, settings, points of view, and themes. In Hemingway's *In Our Time*, there are at least twelve primary settings, ranging from Turkey in "On the Quai at Smyrna" to Oklahoma in "Soldier's Home." By comparison, his novel *The Sun Also Rises* has two: Spain and France. In addition to the many settings in *In Our Time*, and complicating the work even further, are the numerous thematic concerns and narrative strategies that the different stories and vignettes assume—all of which result in an across-the-board multiplicity that fosters further juxtapositions and further points of resistance to the work's overall unity. These juxtapositions heighten, in effect, the process of difference that the reader experiences between the work's respective elements, a process that continually counters the movement (whether initiated by Hemingway or by the reader) toward imposing formal unity onto the work. While postmodernist critical approaches recognize that all literary works at least implicitly undo (or erase) their own tendencies toward unity of form, the short story cycle, in part because of its wavering between novel and short story collection, frustrates these tendencies more than most genres. And within the twentieth century, *In Our Time* frustrates these tendencies even more than most other short story cycles.

In upending the emphasis on formal unity, the notion of difference through multiplicity first came to the fore in the modernist era in which *In Our Time* was written, even though it remained a notion to be countermanded by many modernist artists rather than exploited, as it would be in the postmodernist era half a century later. Within this historical context, it is important to recognize, as Peter Brooker does, the fission of modernism into reactionary and radical elements, the former represented by T. S. Eliot, W. B. Yeats, Sinclair Lewis, and Ezra Pound during the later stages of his career, and the latter by

Gertrude Stein, Louis Aragon, Samuel Beckett, and Ezra Pound during the earlier stages of his career: the former reacting with anxiety to the disruption to formal unity, the latter welcoming that disruption (6). Responding to the perceived crisis in traditionally stable forms of order, the reactionary modernist writers desperately experimented with assemblages of old forms in order to reestablish, in a nostalgia for lost cultural hierarchies, at least a semblance of order. As Malcolm Bradbury points out, "the shock, the violation of expected continuities, the element of de-creation and crisis, is a crucial element *of* the style" of these modernist writers (Bradbury and McFarlane 24). While the "violation of expected continuities" is endemic to both modernism and postmodernism—and is certainly present in *In Our Time* in its form and its themes of war, violence, and identity—it only becomes a true crisis of meaning for the more reactionary modernist writers. The violation of expected continuities leads Eliot (who was not a favorite of Hemingway) to respond with fear and classicism. Yet half a century later, in a postmodernist poet like Frank O'Hara, it invites playfulness and an appreciation for the quotidian—qualities that Hemingway recognized and appreciated in two of his most important mentors, Gertrude Stein and Sherwood Anderson.

In his lecture series at the University of Geneva between 1906 and 1911, Ferdinand de Saussure, the paterfamilias of postmodernist theory, violated the world's formal concept of language itself. According to Saussure, language is not merely representational; rather, it is comprised of linguistic signs that combine into "sets of relationships" that accrue meaning through difference with other signs (Cohan and Shires 12). Applying Saussure's concepts to written texts, Jacques Derrida, in *Writing and Difference*, speaks of a "system of differences" (280). When raised to the level of genre, this concept becomes particularly applicable to the short story cycle. *In Our Time* does more than simply fragment the novel, as D. H. Lawrence claimed it did (73). Instead the work takes advantage of a "system of differences" to foster meaning, while at the same time resisting formal unity. This process resembles (but does not quite duplicate) the narrative-deep structure that Kennedy finds in the short story cycle: "elemental narrative structures, resembling grammatical chains, which generate the individual stories and account for similarities and differences among them" (23). The process of difference in the short story cycle goes beyond Kennedy's explanation in that it destabilizes even the links in the chain. This effect becomes apparent—to focus on just one of many narrative elements in which the effect plays out—in the development of character in *In Our Time*.

For modernists as for postmodernists, the notion of "self" becomes as unstable as any other form of order. In the first decades of the twentieth century, modernists began to understand character, the representation of self in text, as being thoroughly implicated in language—and language itself, as Saussure demonstrated, was no longer stable. In the final 1925 version, *In Our Time* begins with "On the Quai at Smyrna," a story that presents a detached, imperial, and unquestioning narrator, a version of self already anachronistic in the post–World War I period. For this speaker—this "I"—narration remains "a most pleasant business," despite the carnage occurring about him (12). However, in the vignette immediately following "On the Quai at Smyrna," the first sentence reads: "Everybody was drunk," as if to signal that the old, assured version of self represented in "On the Quai at Smyrna" has been, now and forever, made less stable (13). To emphasize this new instability, which becomes a kind of lurching about in ontological uncertainty, the next sentence reads: "The whole battery was drunk going along the road in the dark" (13). To add to this uncertainty, in several vignettes the speaker is thoroughly indeterminate. Vignette 7, for instance, begins as a third-person narration with all the presumed reliability of such a narrative mode, yet halfway through the vignette the unexpected pronoun "we" intrudes, throwing into doubt our entire narrative orientation. Such a skewed use of point of view, especially in respect to its relation to character, was one of the lessons Hemingway was learning in the early 1920s from the coy and unsettling experiments with the sentence being made by Gertrude Stein, the playful materfamilias of postmodernist literature. According to Brooker's definition of postmodernism, "there can be no unified self, no narrative perspective" (18), and although these two items are not entirely missing from *In Our Time*, the ever-shifting nature of the stories and vignettes denies unified self and narrative perspective any opportunity to become established in the work.

Bradbury also points to the connection between language and self when he refers to modernism's "destruction of traditional notions of the wholeness of individual character, [and] the linguistic chaos that ensues when public notions of language have been discredited and when all realities have become subjective fictions" (Bradbury and McFarlane 27). In *In Our Time*, the main character is typically thought to be Nick Adams, yet since a postmodern subject never simply and unequivocally *is*, but instead, within the Derridian "system of differences," is always in the process of *becoming*, Nick can also be regarded as Krebs (in "Soldier's Home"), Elliot (in "Mr. and Mrs. Elliot"), Joe (in "My Old Man"), and any of the other characters who appear within the stories. This is not to say, as Harbour Winn argues, that Hemingway is "presenting in Krebs a carbon copy of Nick" (128). Rather, through juxtaposition with one, the other becomes known. Nick becomes as much a version of Krebs, as Krebs becomes a version of Nick. In Lacanian terms, Nick's subjectivity is perpetually contingent upon the Otherness of the characters in the non-Nick stories.

Debra A. Moddelmog is one of several critics who argues that Nick is the "unifying consciousness" of *In Our Time* (18). While this approach lends *In Our Time* a clear unity based on character, it is not sustainable across the entire work. The key to understanding character in *In Our Time* lies in Hemingway's use of various voices to create a plural subject. The vignettes alone include the following voices: a British naval officer, an American enlisted man, another British officer, an American tourist, an American bullfighting aficionado, a Spanish matador, and an American correspondent (Winn 130). It is the difference across these voices that creates the genuine character/subject of the work. Elizabeth D. Vaugn, in discussing *In Our Time* as "self-begetting fiction," argues a similar line:

These other voices contribute to the investigation conducted throughout *In Our Time* of the ramifications of language that create and comprise identity, the ways in which the linguistic reality of fictional characters engenders that of fiction and vice versa. (708–09)

Unfortunately, like Moddelmog, Vaugn locates all the voices as emanating from Nick. She sees them merely as contributions to Hemingway's "investigation" of how the work as a whole establishes Nick's identity, still placing the source of unity for the book squarely with Nick as its central character.

At best, if Nick is the central character (or consciousness) of the work, he is one whose subjectivity is forever being dispersed through the other characters, effectively dissolving his centrality as the work's protagonist. The character Nick Adams is developed not only in the stories in which he has a central role but also in the stories in which he never appears. As an aspect of the short story cycle genre in general and of *In Our Time* in particular, this inverted process of character development is part of the process of difference that occurs on two levels: at the level of each independent story and at the level of the entire cycle. The vignettes can be viewed as analogous to Saussure's "syntagm," the linguistic unit that "acquires its value only because it stands in opposition to everything that precedes or follows it, or to both" (qtd. in Cohan and Shires 14). As Earl Rovit and Gerry Brenner point out, the vignettes, which first appeared by themselves in the 1924 version of *in our time*, were meant to work in relation to one another "by repetition, juxtaposition, and muted contrast" (24). By adding the stories to the 1925 version of *In Our Time*, Hemingway further complicated this dynamic by inviting more prospective relations between the various parts. Through this proliferation of a "system of difference" in *In Our Time*, meaning accrues throughout the stories and vignettes as much through their differences as through their similarities.

Critics who seek an encompassing unity in *In Our Time* often argue that the final story, "Big Two-Hearted River," provides a culmination to the entire work. In his biography of Hemingway, Reynolds corroborates this view: "Ernest needed such a story [like Joyce's "The Dead"] to end his book. . . . Nick was there in the four stories [seven by final publication], and he would be there in this last one, holding the book together" (202). Having gone from a wide-eyed child in "Indian Camp" to a reluctant but responsible adult in "Cross Country Ski," Nick Adams reappears as a disillusioned young man in "Big Two-Hearted River," a story that in the standard reading of it caps his formative years by returning him to the landscape of his youth after, presumably, the trauma of World War I. This reading, however, does not take into account the many disruptions throughout *In Our Time* to the Nick Adams narrative. More likely, "Big Two-Hearted River" reveals—beyond representing the culmination of Nick's coming-of-age—an understanding that Nick is, ultimately, the sum of the "system of differences" from which his character emerges. The ritualized quality of Nick's actions that Carlos Baker sees as so reassuring in the story can be regarded, in a different light, as Hemingway's recognition of and response to the unsettling effects of the process of difference (126–27). This interpretation would account for why Hemingway so carefully represents Nick's experiences on such a basic physiological level and squarely within the moment: "It was getting hot, the sun hot on the back of his neck" (207), or "Nick was hungry" (187), and so on. To conjecture beyond such empirical information, to presume to know how Nick feels would require a degree of ontological certainty about the character's identity that is no longer available to Hemingway either as a writer in the modernist era or as a writer with an emergent postmodernist sensibility. Rather than attempt to represent a splintered psyche, Hemingway, in his narrative restraint, suggests a recognition that Nick is, finally, the sum of the sentences/actions by which he is depicted. Only momentary stability is available when language, and thereby character, is so processional. Hemingway's restraint, his penchant for parataxis over hypotaxis, testifies to his careful negotiation of narrative's slippery attempts to represent the world—a slipperiness that he both admired and questioned in Stein's prose. Throughout *In Our Time*, but nowhere more pointedly than in "Big Two-Hearted River," Hemingway nervously reckons with how difference simultaneously fosters and resists meaning within narrative—an insight that a contemporary postmodernist writer such as Robert Coover will happily indulge in a short story like "The Babysitter" several decades later.

In an interview in which he discusses Hemingway, the novelist E. L. Doctorow says of writing in general, "Every time you compose a book your composition of yourself is at risk. . . . Writing is a lifelong act of self-displacement" (61). Over the course of its evolution, Hemingway continued to make changes—omitting the poems or inserting the vignettes or adding another story—to the work that would become *In Our Time*. By 1925, the work had already been through two previous incarnations, *Three Stories and Ten Poems* (1923) and *in our time* (1924). Eventually, to extend the process of difference in his narrative world and commit the next "act of self-displacement," he left this work and moved onto the next—a leap that, with *The Sun Also Rises*, was to the traditionally more unity-dependent genre of the novel. It was perhaps only in his youth and in the charged creative atmosphere of Paris that Hemingway had enough creative temerity to engage difference to the degree that he does in *In Our Time*, an act that anticipates the postmodernist narratives a half century later.

If "Big Two-Hearted River" is indeed the culminating story to *In Our Time*, it serves this role not through Nick's character development and the attendant coming-of-age theme but through Hemingway's recognition of the role that difference plays in both making and unmaking meaning in the work as a whole. This recognition is most vividly represented by the image of the trout that keep "themselves steady in the current with wavering fins" and "changed their positions by quick angles," a movement that mirrors the narrative process of the work itself across its many narrative elements (177). The crosscurrents of difference keep the short story cycle steady rather than unified, at the same time ensuring that its form remains ever shifting, ever different, and ever meaningful.

Acknowledgment

I wish to thank Dr. Linda Leavell, of Oklahoma State University, and Dr. David Ullrich, of Birmingham-Southern College, for their thoughts and encouragement in the writing and revising of this essay.

References

Adler, Mortimer J., and Charles Van Doren. *How to Read a Book*. New York: Simon, 1940.

Baker, Carlos. *Hemingway: The Writer as Artist*. Princeton: Princeton UP, 1963.

Bradbury, Malcolm, and James McFarlane. "The Name and Nature of Modernism." *Modernism: A Guide to European Literature, 1890–1930*. Ed. Malcolm Bradbury and James McFarlane. New York: Penguin, 1976. 19–55.

Brooker, Peter. "Introduction: Reconstructions." *Modernism/Postmodernism*. Ed. Peter Brooker. Essex, UK: Longman, 1992. 1–33.

Cohan, Steven, and Linda M. Shires. *Telling Stories: A Theoretical Analysis of Narrative Fiction*. London: Routledge, 1988.

Creighton, Joanne V. "Dubliners and Go Down, Moses: The Short Story Composite." Diss. U of Michigan, 1969. DAI 31 (1970): 1792A–93A.

Derrida, Jacques. *Writing and Difference*. Trans. Alan Bass. Chicago: U of Chicago P, 1978.

Doctorow, E. L. Interview. *At Random* 2.3 (1993): 58–65.

Hark, Ina-Rae. "Unity in the Composite Novel: Triadic Patterning in Asimov's The Gods Themselves." *Science Fiction* 6 (1979). <http://www.depauw.edu/sfs/backissues/19/hark/19art.htm>.

Hemingway, Ernest. *Ernest Hemingway: Selected Letters, 1917–1961*. Ed. Carlos Baker. New York: Scribner, 1981.

———. *In Our Time*. New York: Scribner, 1925.

Ingram, Forrest L. *Representative Short Story Cycles of the Twentieth Century: Studies in a Literary Genre*. The Hague: Mouton, 1971.

Kennedy, J. Gerald. "Toward a Poetics of the Short Story." *Journal of the Short Story in English* 11 (1988): 9–25.

Lawrence, D. H. "In Our Time: A Review." *Hemingway: A Collection of Critical Essays*. Ed. Robert P. Weeks. Englewood Cliffs: Prentice, 1962. 93–94.

Lemmon, Dallas M. "The Rovelle, or Novel of Interrelated Stories: M. Lermontov, G. Keller, S. Anderson." Diss. Indiana U, 1970. DAI 31 (1971): 3510A.

Luscher, Robert. "The Short Story Sequence: An Open Book." *Short Story Theory at a Crossroads*. Ed. Susan Lohafer and Jo Ellyn Clarey. Baton Rouge: Louisiana State UP, 1989. 148–67.

Mann, Susan Garland. *The Short Story Cycle: A Genre Companion and Reference Guide*. Westport: Greenwood, 1989.

Mellow, James R. *Hemingway: A Life without Consequences*. New York: Houghton, 1992.

Moddelmog, Debra A. "The Unifying Consciousness of a Divided Conscience: Nick Adams as Author of *In Our Time*." *American Literature* 60.4 (1988): 591–610.

Reed, Pleasant Larus, III. "The Integrated Short-Story Collection: Studies of a Form of the Nineteenth- and Twentieth-Century." Diss. Indiana U, 1974. DAI 35 (1975): 6730A.

Reynolds, Michael. *Hemingway: The Paris Years*. New York: Blackwell, 1989.

Rovit, Earl, and Gerry Brenner. *Ernest Hemingway*. Boston: Hall, 1986.

Vaugn, Elizabeth D. *"In Our Time* as Self-Begetting Fiction." *Modern Fiction Studies* 35.4 (1989): 707–15.

Winn, Harbour. "Hemingway's *In Our Time*: 'Pretty Good Unity.'" *The Hemingway Review* 9.2 (1990): 124–41.

Wright, Austin M. "Recalcitrance in the Short Story." *Short Story Theory at a Crossroads*. Ed. Susan Lohafer and Jo Ellyn Clarey. Baton Rouge: Louisiana State UP, 1989. 115–29.

DEATH AS IMAGE AND
THEME IN SHORT FICTION

From James Joyce to Richard Ford, death casts its shadow across twentieth-century fiction in all its different forms. Larry D. Griffin explores death imagery and its transition from fiction to film in his essay "Short Stories to Film: Richard Ford's 'Great Falls' and 'Children' as *Bright Angel*." Griffin explains that Ford's "Great Falls" and "Children" provide the genesis for Michael Fields's 1991 film *Bright Angel* in which the protagonist, George, an alienated, postmodern character, seeks maturity in desolate Montana. He befriends Lucy, who serves as his "bright angel," and who ultimately sacrifices her own life, providing him with the illumination that violence can precipitate death, and which, Griffin ultimately argues, ushers George into the world of adulthood.

Brenda M. Palo's essay, "Melancholia and the Death Motif in Richard Brautigan's Short Fiction" employs the writing of Walter Benjamin and Julia Kristeva in order to explore the role of melancholia and death in Brautigan's work. Specifically, Palo claims that both Benjamin and Kristeva show that the deep sadness in response to death involves us in issues of time, language use and shortness. Brautigan's melancholic narrators, mired in their loss, speak from a type of hopelessness and use language to craft narratives that "always also focus on brief narratives from the past and are heavy with the conviction that the future is a future in name only." Palo goes on to state that, hoping against hope within this temporal dialectic, the melancholic narrators reveal the potential redemptive power of seemingly banal objects, which highlights the rich allegorical nature of Brautigan's short fiction.

Howard Lindholm writes in his essay "Perhaps She Had Not Told Him All the Story: The Disnarrated in James Joyce's *Dubliners*" that Joyce's historical collection "demonstrates the modern text as a convergence of diegetic and hypodiegetic voices, which questions and complicates the narrative relationship between a discourse and the events that it recounts." As a precursor to postmodernity, Modernist experimentation relies on the stylistic exaggeration of the partition between story and discourse. Lindholm contends that the extremity of this separation fragments and blurs the story, ultimately raising questions of narrative validity.

Short Stories to Film:
Richard Ford's "Great Falls"
and "Children" as *Bright Angel*

Larry D. Griffin

For the postmodern, the world often remains a desolate place inhabited by alienated people. When violence leads to death, the ultimate separation of the self from others, alienated characters in postmodern fiction find that language often has failed to provide connections that have the potential to overcome aloneness, loneliness, and alienation. The extremity of negative experience for the postmodern is violence, and the greatest extremity of that violence is death. Loneliness or aloneness may be overcome by making the connection of self to other, but for the postmodern such connections are often fragile and inadequate. The postmodern predicament remains, in part, that language may facilitate and maintain such connections, but if communication fails, then a self once again without the other may be more alone than ever before. Richard Ford's main characters in his short stories "Great Falls" and "Children" and the protagonist in his film *Bright Angel* represent such alienated individuals or postmodern characters.

Philip Orr has written that the stories in *Rock Springs* emphasize man's aloneness in the world—"man's emotional disconnectedness from his world and his attempts . . . to reconcile himself with his emotions" (143). In his introduction to his edition of *Perspectives on Richard Ford*, Huey Guagliardo notes that he and other Ford critics "all place Ford's texts within the framework of alienation" (xii), and the only defense against alienation is language's "power to redeem human loneliness" that Guagliardo considers "a central concern of his fiction" (xvii).

Such is the alienation of the young man, Jackie Russell, in Richard Ford's short story "Great Falls." Named George in "Children," he sees

his parents' marriage disintegrate in "Great Falls," and he must grieve
the loss of his family and replace it with connections to others, such as
Claude and Lucy in "Children." Ford elides his stories "Great Falls" and
"Children" from his collection of short stories *Rock Springs* (1987) to
provide the genesis for the Michael Fields film *Bright Angel*. At the end
of the film, the violence represented by George's friend Claude and the
sexuality represented by Lucy provide George with necessary experience. The mixture of sex and violence that precedes Lucy's death prepares George to take his place as a man in the world, one who can go
off by himself at age eighteen to the oilfields of Gillette. In their relationships the characters in the stories and the film use language to
accommodate themselves effectively to the others.

After he experiences the demise of his parents' marriage in "Great
Falls," Jackie Russell seeks maturity in desolate Montana. The title of
the story is both the setting and the allegory of the disintegration of
Jackie's family. The potential of male bonding between father and son
in the duck hunt in "Great Falls" diminishes in respect as to why Jack
Russell hunts ducks: "What my father did with the ducks he killed, and
the fish, too, was sell them" (31). Hunting for sale of the game remains
an illegal activity: "It was against the law then to sell wild game, and it
is against the law now" (31). Jack and his son return home to catch the
mother with another man; the mother leaves, and Jackie only sees her
several years later.

The great question the boy faces in his life is whether his parents
have always told him the truth. Until the night of his mother's infidelity,
Jackie did not know that his mother might have been married before.
The use of language to create the lie, remains, of course, the greatest violation of the ability of language to communicate between individuals.
The recognition of lies by an individual undercuts the power of language and has the potential to further alienate the communicators one
from another. Elinor Walker in her "Redeeming Loneliness in Richard
Ford's 'Great Falls' and *Wildlife*" writes that Ford's narrators discover
both "the frailty of human nature but also the frailty of language"
(121–22), and then she relates a discussion of Walker Percy's Delta Factor to Jackie's experience with language in "Great Falls." Walker provides the following description of Walker Percy's Delta Factor:

Under those circumstances, language is a slippery instrument. In its purest
use, language may function semiotically as a symbol connecting an object with
a word and, via the word, the person with the objects, just as the word "wind"
denotes that which is blowing, that Jackie hears as "wind," and also connotes
other meanings, associations of familiarity, security, knowledge of place. (129)

Walker then describes how Walker Percy adapted the ideas of Charles Pierce to place "this semiotic concept into a simple triangular diagram; the speaking person, the word, and the thing the word signifies each make up one point of the figure" (129). Walker then reminds readers that when another person is involved in the exchange of words, the situation becomes much more complicated because "then the word must signify the same thing to both speakers in order for communication to occur" (129). It is the loss of the meaning or the failure of signification that happens for Jackie in the yard when he learns from his mother's lover, Woody, that his mother may have been married before. At the end of "Great Falls," the boy's father, Jack Russell, is dead. The son still faces questions about the night his parents separated: "But I have never known the answer to these questions, have never asked anyone their answers" (49). Jackie suspects that it is the "helplessness that causes us to misunderstand" that finally leaves one "watchful, unforgiving, without patience or desire" (49).

Ford's male characters, when contrasted to his female characters, use language to try to overcome their alienation, but seldom are they successful in sustaining the connections with others for very long. Communication between men and women in Ford's world, while limited and short-lived, remains of enough intensity and duration that it allows his male characters brief respite from their alienation and afterward provides memories on which the male characters can rely when making choices about actions in their lives. Priscilla Leder in "General Relations in Richard Ford's *Rock Springs*" writes of Ford's men and women: "[W]omen seem mysteriously self-contained and serene, while men struggle to come to terms with their experience" (97). Because the masculine point of view of the narrators in the story, whether George's or Jackie's, shapes their understanding of communication, what is emphasized is their own individual struggles with connecting with others and the awe for the detachment they discover in the women they encounter.

In "Children," George, someone very much like Jack's son in "Great Falls"—the voices of the two stories appear the same—sets out on a supposed fishing trip from Sunburst, Montana, with his friend Claude and a young, transient girl named Lucy. These youths struggle toward maturity by experimenting with alcohol, flirting with minor violence, and teasing one another sexually. In "Children" first-person narrator George and his friend Claude take sixteen-year-old Lucy fishing; when she undresses for the boys, George is amazed at how young she is: "But it did not matter because she was already someone who could be by herself in the world" (94). George admires Lucy because he regards her ability to be alone as a sign of maturity. It remains an ability that neither George nor Claude yet have, but one to which George must aspire because now that he is without a family George must learn to be alone in the world. Inside one's self, a person can be safe, but George also knows that outside one's self, what a person often finds only is an "empty place": "Outside was a place that seemed not even to exist, an empty place you could stay in for a long time and never find a thing you admired or loved or hoped to keep" (98). Ford's two stories together demonstrate the theme of the movement from innocence to experience for its main characters, George and Jackie. Just as Ford combines the characters of George and Jackie from the stories into George of *Bright Angel*, the experience changes George, the protagonist in *Bright Angel*, when to the more innocent world of sex and violence in the stories, Ford adds the ultimate culmination with the death of Lucy.

Most Ford stories and novels explore alienation. Frank Bascombe in *The Sportswriter* notes the following about being by ourselves: "The stamp of our parents on us and of the past in general is, to my mind, overworked, since at some point we are whole and by ourselves upon the earth, and there is nothing that can change that for better or worse" (24). Guagliardo refers to Ford's *A Piece of My Heart* in his "The Marginal People in the Novels of Richard Ford" when he writes: "In Ford's own novels, discovery and growth are most likely to occur when the individual is pushed to the very brink of alienation and despair" (6).

Guagliardo writes that Frank Bascombe in *Independence Day* "expresses his faith in the power of language to console and to heal" (6). Frank as narrator in *The Sportswriter* simply says that some things cannot be explained—they just are they way they are: "Literature's consolations are always temporary, while life is quick to begin again" (223). After being sexually taunted by Claude, Lucy strips naked, and George looks at her and thinks "she was already someone who could be by herself in the world" (*Rock Springs* 94). George knows that he and Claude pale by comparison to Lucy: "And neither Claude nor I were anything like that" (94). George tries to make a subject of the object Lucy here, and Leder reminds us of Ford's heroes: "His male protagonists' experiences demonstrate how emotional need can shape one person's perceptions of another, and the language with which they describe those experiences reveals the limitations of their understanding" (120). Ford himself has spoken of the power of language to establish connections between people to overcome alienation: "I believe in my heart of hearts, that it's just those little moments of time, those little, almost invisible, certainly omittable, connections between people which save your life or don't, and that if your life has a habit of seizing those little moments, then, I think life can go on for you, have the possibility of being better"

(Bonetti 95–96). Of such affection Leder writes: "Though language may inevitably serve to distance us from others, may always fail, we continue to imagine that it might also help us to connect, to express affection" (110). Though communication that connects characters in fiction may ultimately fail, the postmodern must have hope for the possibility of overcoming alienation no matter how slim that hope remains.

In his "A Conversation with Richard Ford," Huey Guagliardo interviews Ford. Asked how his characters redeem themselves by affection, Ford indicates that his characters do so by giving value to their lives. All any of us can do, he says, "is to make our lives and the lives of others as liveable, as important, as charged as we possibly can" (182). Ford claims that such "*secular redemption* aims to make us, through the agency of affection, intimacy, closeness, complicity, feel like our time spent on earth is not wasted" (182–83). In "Children," the narrator says: "But I did not, as I waited, want to think about only myself" (96). George realizes that he has always been selfish: "I realized that was all I had ever really done, and that possibly it was all you could ever do, and that it would make you bitter and lonesome and useless" (96). Only by thinking of Lucy can George become a better, more selfless person: "So I tried to think instead about [her]" (96). Selfishness may be avoided, though with difficulty, and perhaps then only temporarily if the postmodern character remains selfless.

Although Ford told Guagliardo that *Bright Angel* "was not very good" (195), he did write the screenplay for *Bright Angel* in 1989. It was not made into a film until 1991. In Michael Fields's film, Dermot Mulroney stars as George. The cast of characters for *Bright Angel* also includes Lily Taylor as Lucy, Sam Shepard as Jack, Valerie Perrine as Aileen, Burt Young as Art Falcone, Bill Pullman as Bob, Benjamin Bratt as Claude, Alex Bucktail as Sherman, Delroy Lindo as Harley, Sheila McCarthy as Nina Bennet, Tyde Kierney as the detective, and Kevin Tighe as the man, or toolpusher.

After George experiences the demise of his parents' marriage in "Great Falls," Jackie Russell seeks maturity in desolate Montana in "Children," but in *Bright Angel* most of the action is set in Wyoming. *Bright Angel* provides an expansion of the themes of "Children" and "Great Falls" in that Ford expands on the innocence to experience theme and further explores the efficacy of language. In "Children" and "Great Falls," the narrators' mother's nurturing is gone, and in both stories and in the film, she is gone because of the nature of her sexuality. The question of Aileen's previous marriage looms even larger for George as Ford expands his themes of "Great Falls" and "Children" into his film *Bright Angel*. Jackie of "Great Falls" is George of "Children" and *Bright*

Angel. George has sex with Lucy in the story "Children." George, only seventeen—he's eighteen in the film—faces violence in the story, but there is more violence between males in the film *Bright Angel* than in the two short stories combined. From three stories in *Rock Springs*, Leder generalizes that Ford's "adolescent protagonists . . . confront the mystery of their mothers' sexuality and their fathers' potential for violence by striving for a detachment which will allow them to deal with what they have witnessed" and that "the protagonist tests the power of his detachment by trying to manipulate his world, and through encounters with women, learns the limitations of that power" (100). George's becoming an experienced individual relies in part on his coming to terms with the limits of the efficacy of language.

In *Bright Angel*, Ford combines "Great Falls" and "Children" to create the first part of his screenplay, but to the more naive world of sex and violence of the stories, Ford now adds the extremity of violence, death. Michael Fields opens his *Bright Angel* with George and Jack shooting forty-three ducks with a spotlight. Then after a break to bleak overview shots of Great Falls, the camera focuses on George walking with his back to the viewer. In the opening scenes, Ford as screenwriter and Fields as director provide the stark, lonely figure of George against the empty, alienating Montana landscape. Leaving his father, George goes with Claude, who is Sherman's son, to pick up Lucy from Sherman's motel room. Returning to town, Jack stops them and has George get out of the car:

> Jack: You don't know what I'm saving you from, son.
> Lucy: Yes he does.

On the way back to the house, Jack and George share a drink, and Jack tells George that his wife, and George's mother Aileen, once told him "Nobody dies of a broken heart."

Jack confronts Aileen while her lover, Woody, and George wait in the yard. Woody tells George that his mother Aileen had been married before. This same question haunts Jackie Russell in "Great Falls," and this haunting expands further in *Bright Angel*. "Do you think your parents ever lied to you?" George asks Lucy as she wades nude from the water after a bathing scene. Because in the film we cannot know what George thinks as we do in his narration of "Children," Ford provides us here with a substitute of the problem of the lie from the story "Great Falls." George and Lucy drive to Casper, Wyoming, and Claude accompanies them. After Claude threatens to kill Lucy, George drops him off at the next town, and he and Lucy continue to Casper. There, George looks for his mother, while Lucy attempts to get her brother out of jail.

By the time of George and Lucy's arrival in Casper, Aileen, Jack, and Claude have all disappeared from the film, and they will not reappear. Characters appear and then just disappear. At the motel in Casper, Lucy claims: "I'm where I'm goin'." To George who does not know where he is going, she says, "You can stay with me tonight until you figure it out." Allegorically, that night George enters Circe's bed, a crucial step in his quest for maturity and a preparatory one for his decent into the underworld of violence that he will experience the next day.

George visits his aunt Judy and his uncle Harley. Harley Reeves, an old wildcatter, resembles Les Snow's mother's boyfriend in Richard Ford's "Winterkill" in *Rock Springs*. Like Herb Wallagher in Ford's *The Sportswriter* and Troy Burnham in his "Winterkill," Harley is not a well-adjusted handicapped person.

In encountering the relationship between his aunt and uncle, George experiences only a dysfunctional marriage. Harley is an African American veteran and civil engineer who is relegated to a wheelchair because of an oil field accident, and George's mother's sister Judy remains only a woman too afraid to leave her abusive husband. Harley has armed his den, an enclosed garage, as if he were under siege from unknown enemies without. There, as Harley tells George, he can make a stand to keep off all those whom he imagines are against him. Harley remains a paranoid schizophrenic in a wheelchair who has settled in to protect himself against an imagined assault on his home by members of the Ku Klux Klan. Harley's delusions also include his having had an affair with Aileen, George's mother. While Judy and George both deny such a possibility, Harley's statement serves to remind George once again of his mother's infidelity to his father. This fragile marriage of his aunt and uncle further provides George with a comparison to his own parents' failed marriage.

When George starts to leave his aunt Judy, he tells her he is eighteen and has finished high school by going to summer school; in "Great Falls" he is only seventeen. Judy says to George after she walks him to his car, "I guess you're a man now, Georgie." She then admits her sadness over his having reached manhood, but she assures him that now he will have much to think about and that he will survive. While this scene reminds the viewer that it is time for him to become a man, George has not yet had the experiences both sexual and violent that he needs to make the complete transition to manhood.

Lucy and George visit Lucy's brother Johnny in jail. Like Quinn in *The Ultimate Good Luck* who goes to Mexico to get his girlfriend Rae's brother Sonny out of jail, George goes to Wyoming to assist Lucy in trying to get her brother Johnny out of jail. After visiting Johnny, the couple goes to a bar where George boxes and is defeated by a Native American.

In the stories and the film Ford associates most violence, short of death, with Native Americans, like Claude and the boxer whom George fights in the bar. This fight follows from the boxing discussions between Jack and George earlier in the film. It further establishes George's prowess as a boxer, which later allows George to whip Billy Adams in the fistfight at the end of the film. After the boxing match in the bar, George and Lucy return to the motel room, and George tells Lucy about the breakup of his parents' marriage, a topic he keeps returning to again and again. Grieving the loss of his parents' marriage, George reflects on his loss in the boxing match, and the following exchange occurs:

> George: You got to get use to losin'.
> Lucy: Tell me something I might not know.

Afterward Lucy and George may have only had sex, but at least they have had intimate exchanges. In attempting bribery of a witness who supposedly identified Lucy's brother in the oil theft, two criminals, Art Falcone and Nina Bennet, trick Lucy and George and take them against their will to an oil well site. There, Art Falcone informs the couple that there is no one to buy off because Johnny's crime was more than theft—murder was involved. Johnny had killed a pipefitter— stabbed him with a screwdriver—in the presence of several witnesses of whom Falcone is only one. Falcone takes Lucy's bribe money anyway, and he handcuffs George and the wounded Lucy—Falcone had earlier stuck her with the butt of his pistol-handled shotgun—to a christmastree, a control valve on an oil well head. Falcone and his girlfriend Nina then leave George and Lucy to either death or rescue that rainy night while they make their escape with part of Lucy's money.

While handcuffed to the pipes, George tells Lucy before she passes out, "I could marry you." Lucy's head wound and further exposure to inclement weather that night takes its deadly toll on her. When the tribal police arrive the next morning to rescue George, Lucy is already dead. George then spends an undisclosed amount of time in juvenile detention. Aunt Judy picks George up at the police station. George learns from her that his mother called her from Rock Springs to have some money wired to her. Aunt Judy advises George that he go home to Great Falls to his father or go see his mother in Rock Springs. George's family no longer exists as it once did. He faces the possibility of returning to either one of his parents, but not to both of them together.

At the bus station, George at first buys a ticket back to Great Falls, where his father lives. Then he encounters Billy Adams, the toolpusher whom he had met only briefly at the motel earlier in the film. Adams takes George into a back room and assaults him to determine if he is strong enough to take the hard work of the oil fields. Adams offers George $600 per week. George demands $800 and gets it.

Lucy becomes George's "bright" angel because she symbolizes the sexual attractiveness of the adult world and because, as she sacrifices her own life, Lucy also provides George with the illumination that violence can precipitate death. Rene Girard in his *Violence and the Sacred* explores how violence often remains a necessary component of the sacred experience. After his experiences with sex and violence with Lucy, George cannot and does not return to the Montana home of his childhood. When Billy Adams tests George's resilience to violence in a fistfight, he hires George to work in the oil fields of Gillette, Wyoming. As a result of his experiences with Lucy, George has become a man in the world.

Jeffrey J. Folks in his "Richard Ford's Postmodern Cowboys" characterizes Ford's drifter, outlaw, cowboy characters as "postmodern cowboys" who "are utterly out of place; they stumble through life, hoping at best to avoid being hurt or causing harm to others and aspiring only to understand and communicate their anxiety" (143). George in *Bright Angel* represents one of the postmodern cowboys. Folks writes, "Ford's narrative focuses on language as a way to admit and confront the emptiness of experience" (149). Folks reminds his readers that there is absence of social discourse in most of Ford's works (154). The same applies to George in Ford's film *Bright Angel*.

In conversation with Wolf Schneider, Ford says, "'The heart of it is the whole of it. . . . That's why literature, and I'm including film, has an essential value to our lives'" (51). In the stories "Great Falls" and "Children," the protagonists confront alienation with language to acquire and share affection with another. Ford enlarges the alienation of the protagonist to accommodate the large screen in *Bright Angel*. There Ford further amplifies the use of language to confront alienation, which finally permits George to move through his experiences from the innocence of his childhood with its dependency on his parents to the accountability of his own manhood.

References

Bonetti, Kay. "An Interview with Richard Ford." *Missouri Review* 10.2 (1987): 71–96.

Bright Angel. Screenplay by Richard Ford. Dir. Michael Fields. Perf. Dermot Mulroney and Lily Taylor. Hemdale, 1991.

Folks, Jeffrey J. "Richard Ford's Postmodern Cowboys." *Perspectives on Richard Ford*. Ed. Huey Guagliardo. Jackson: UP of Mississippi, 2000. 141–56.

Ford, Richard. Personal Interview. 6 June 1994.

———. *Rock Springs*. New York: Atlantic Monthly, 1987.

———. *The Sportswriter.* New York: Vintage, 1986.

———. *The Ultimate Good Luck*. New York: Vintage, 1981.

Girard, Rene. *Violence and the Sacred*. Trans. Patrick Gregory. Baltimore: Johns Hopkins UP, 1977.

Guagliardo, Huey. "A Conversation with Richard Ford." *Perspectives on Richard Ford*. Ed. Huey Guagliardo. Jackson: UP of Mississippi, 2000. 177–96.

———. Introduction. *Perspectives on Richard Ford*. Ed. Huey Guagliardo. Jackson: UP of Mississippi, 2000. xi–xvii.

———. "The Marginal People in the Novels of Richard Ford." *Perspectives on Richard Ford*. Ed. Huey Guagliardo. Jackson: UP of Mississippi, 2000. 3–32.

Leder, Priscilla. "General Relations in Richard Ford's *Rock Springs*." *Perspectives on Richard Ford*. Ed. Huey Guagliardo. Jackson: UP of Mississippi, 2000. 97–120.

Orr, Philip. "*Rock Springs*." *Northwest Review* 26.2 (1988): 143–47.

Schneider, Wolf. "*Bright Angel*: Richard Ford Ups the Ante." *American Film* 6.5 (May 1991): 50–51.

Walker, Elinor. "Redeeming Loneliness in Richard Ford's 'Great Falls' and *Wildlife*." *Perspectives on Richard Ford*. Ed. Huey Guagliardo. Jackson: UP of Mississippi, 2000. 121–39.

Melancholia and the Death Motif in Richard Brautigan's Short Fiction

Brenda M. Palo

Richard Brautigan is known for his genre play,[1] his tendency for brevity and simplicity, and his humor even within death imagery. Death motifs pepper his postmodern short story collection, wherein sixty-two stories of varying form present hundreds of variations on death, whether literal or figurative. Here is the shortest of his prose pieces:

The Scarlatti Tilt

"It's very hard to live in a studio apartment in San Jose with
a man who's learning to play the violin." That's what she told
the police when she handed them the empty revolver. (*Revenge* 50)

This poemlike, thirty-four-word narrative is a compact example from Brautigan's 1971 collection *Revenge of the Lawn: Stories 1962–1970*. Brautigan's humor is understated and wry—in a sense the man's violin playing both drives his roommate to harsh action and sounds a dirge for his impending funeral—and implies that a death has occurred. In the space of only four lines, Brautigan offers us two great Italian com- posers,[2] small urban living quarters, an earnest but novice musician, two mis-matched roommates, the stabilizing force of the law, and a probably smoking gun. In this literary wisp of California dreaming, music and death collide.

The brevity of this story, combined with the richness of the juxta- posed imagery in time and space, foregrounds Brautigan's ability to represent the intrigue of death within even the smallest, and perhaps incongruous, of spaces. The writer's hand is light here, as he embeds the weight of a potential homicide within a distanced description of its aftereffects. Brautigan juxtaposes three small, formal components—the story's title, the shooter's single-sentence "confession," and the narrator's contextualizing closure—that temporally frame a brutal act of "offstage" violence between a rich cultural and musical past and the seemingly calm resignation of a woman whose intolerance of discord results in her rather dim future.

In *Death and Representation*, editors Sarah Webster Goodwin and Elisabeth Bronfen assert:

Perhaps the most obvious thing about death is that it is always only represented. . . . Indeed, it is as antagonist that we most clearly figure death: it stands as a challenge to all our systems of meaning, order, governance, and civilization. Any given cultural construct . . . may be construed as a response to the disordering force of death. Culture itself would then be an attempt both to represent death and to contain it, to make it comprehensible and thereby to diffuse some of its power. (4)[3]

Their assertions inspire several questions about the death-filled short stories at hand. Is Brautigan's collection—this cultural construct, this gathering of stories that are themselves an attempt to make meaning with words—a response to death's pervasive presence in our individual and collective lives? Do these stories, containing hundreds of death motifs toward constructing that meaning, inscribe some sort of limit around death's force? Are short stories, Brautigan's being especially short, the most appropriate "container" for representing, and comprehending, death? And finally, do Brautigan's melancholy narrators manage to "diffuse" any of death's power by presenting it to us, over and over again, in a series of motifs whose frequency and variety might make death less threatening?

Engaging these questions about death motifs and the varied short story forms that contain them, I explore the presence of melancholia and death in Brautigan's short stories and employ the writings of Walter Benjamin (1892–1940) and Julia Kristeva (1941–). My work relies on the sections of their critical and theoretical studies that seem to speak to one another. In particular, both Benjamin and Kristeva address melancholia and death in relation to time as well as language use.

All of Brautigan's fiction, and his story collection is no exception, is delivered by melancholic narrators, narrators mired in a particular temporality determined by loss. While speaking from their present moment of narration, using language to tell their stories, they craft narratives that always also contain the past and are heavy with the conviction that the future is a future in name only. Both Benjamin and Kristeva are intrigued by writers and writing and both explore the relationships between time and language, melancholia and death. Benjamin asserts that a dialectical understanding might redeem the ruins, or fragments, of the past, and that melancholics focus on material, and necessarily allegorical objects, to reconnect them with a lost Messianic time. Kristeva views melancholics as hopeless prisoners of time who rely, though futilely, on the signifier both to defer their pain and to reconnect them with the lost maternal object.

In Brautigan's story collection, the melancholy narrators' focus on time reveals their hopeless position vis-à-vis experiencing—and representing—a meaningful life and foregrounds their reliance on language as an object that just might put them in touch with that lost meaning, just might reconnect them. These narrators persistently explore death via fragmentation, holding onto an unnameable, intangible certainty that a past, rich with oneness, wholeness, and meaning, is somehow to be found through the ruins that remain. For the melancholy narrator, playing with language that represents death is the only means toward overcoming hopelessness and loss. They focus briefly and repeatedly on small, banal objects—objects both embodied by the narrative forms comprised of words and reflected in the material objects as represented through words. Using few words to structure their allegories about death, the melancholy narrators spend their troubled time engaged with language and form, hoping against hope for a reconnection to a time and meaning that have been lost.

Revenge of the Lawn gives us dozens of stories that play with language and form while engaging death as an agent of exaggerated humor that might, paradoxically, provide the means to answering those quite serious questions about literature, life, and meaning. The stories range from the shockingly short, yet formally complex (as I have noted), "The Scarlatti Tilt" to the nearly seven-page "The Post Offices of Eastern Oregon." Within this length range, Brautigan crafts mostly one- and two-page stories that comprise a rich variety of forms.

I will examine two stories in greater detail, considering how their particular form impacts the melancholic representation of death, but outline here some additional representative examples of Brautigan's many challenges to form and genre lines, particularly his fragmenting of the stories with visual markers.

Brautigan's challenges to standard story forms implicate the allegorical nature of his postmodern writing. In Benjamin's view, allegory reflects a "godless condition in which name and thing have become separated, in which objects and their proper meanings no longer co-incide" (Wolin 68). Due to this separation from an originating whole-ness, allegory "signifies the necessarily fragmentary nature of that relation [of humans to the absolute] in a world that has itself been re-duced to fragments or ruins" (69). Indeed, in Brautigan's postmodern world, words are detached from their meanings and humans are de-tached from their godlike state and their god. Acutely aware of this de-tachment, the melancholic necessarily focuses on the only thing at hand, the ruins, the death-associated remainders and bits that might offer a trace of what once was.

The brevity or small size of these remainders is paramount in an allegorical understanding. If the melancholic remains aware of serial time, of the long, historical continuum that surrounds him day after day with crippling pain, his despair will do him in. In fact, his survival depends on his ability to concentrate on short or small entities, ob-jects isolated from their continuum. Benjamin terms these isolated fragments "chips of Messianic time" and insists upon "blast[ing] a specific era out of the homogeneous course of history," in order to break it free of the lengthy stream that imprisons it (*Illuminations* 263). Thus, the melancholic is best served by the fragmentary—the briefer and the shorter the better. Contemplation of the isolated object might enable an allegorical reconnection with lost time. However, for the melancholic to remain engaged with these fragments, Benjamin acknowledges that "the allegorical must constantly unfold in new and surprising ways" (*Origin* 183).

Fortunately, for his melancholic narrators, Brautigan's dedication to surprising forms and inventive genre defines his work. In his short stories, Brautigan sometimes begins with quoted material and then re-sponds to it with the subsequent story text, as in "The View from the Dog Tower" in *Revenge of the Lawn*. He begins his story of canine ca-tastrophe with a text fragment—this intriguing clause from a northern California newspaper: "three German shepherd puppies wandered away from their home up near the county line" (149). In the following text, the narrator then acknowledges having considered these words for months although it is but a small happening and does not compare to such grand horrors as starving by having too little food or being en-gaged in a never-ending war. Having made these comments, he begins to speculate on the dogs' fate.

This two-part structure sets up a dialogue between the distanced, "official" texts of our culture that newspapers represent and the personal musings that this narrator is compelled by. Struck by, and stuck on, a past narrative that apparently did not provide enough of something, the narrator hangs onto this past event. In response to his own melancholia, he creates a new story, writing out a version that incorporates and, more importantly, transforms the newspaper remainders into something more meaningful in his own life.[4] In the hands of this melancholy narrator, a fragment is allegorically transformed and unfolds, as Benjamin predicts, in new and surprising ways. Despite his manipulation of the old public story into a new personally driven form, the narrator finds no permanent exit from melancholia, for he concludes with the speculation that what happens to the lost dogs may adumbrate a future journey for all of us.

Additional stories continue the formal play, juxtaposing ideas from the larger, more public realm with those of the smaller, more personal realm, but do not provide the melancholic narrator a permanent solution. Although short enough to preclude much confusion if left whole, some of Brautigan's stories are pointedly broken up by numerals, letters, or symbols. A few are fragmented into numbered sections or chapters as if the short story's content held the complexity, detail, or temporal progression of a novel and required that genre's overt partitioning.[5] In fact, the intrigue of Brautigan's short pieces is often tied to their promise of something much larger, much more vast and important than a small entity might be expected to contain.

For example, the fragmented, multisectioned story "The Lost Chapters of *Trout Fishing in America*: 'Rembrandt Creek' and 'Carthage Sink,'" is a four-part presentation focused on retrieving something from the writer's lost past time. The narrator's introductory and concluding paragraphs frame two embedded short stories or "chapters" and explain that the stories were originally written as part of an earlier novel but lost in 1961. The narrator notes that the included stories, rewritten from partial memories in 1969, necessarily differ in form from the originals. He tries to assuage his melancholia about the lost writings, but admits that these chapters/stories have not succeeded. He had wanted to travel back in time to his twenty-six-year-old self who lived on Greenwich Street, and thus take himself back to a positive outlook on America.

Yet another multisectioned story that fails to satisfy melancholic desire, "Getting to Know Each Other" compares a male film director's many affairs with women resembling his daughter, with the structure of a Shakespearean sonnet. Brautigan twice inserts the schema "a b a b   c d c d   e f e f   g g," sliding it vertically down the left margin on the story's first and last pages and bracketing off the series with:

William Shakespeare
1564—1616

as might have been engraved on the bard's tombstone (*Revenge* 101, 104). The narrator invokes the grand, ancient ideas of Eros and Thanatos in juxtaposition with the very personal, sexual proclivities of an individual. He also displays the late Shakespeare's world-renowned creativity alongside an all-too-ordinary man's reverse-Oedipal preoccupations. Again, the contrast between the larger-than-life and the blatantly banal is striking and the futility of the director's transforming his lovers into his daughter in any permanent sense reveals that melancholia has not left the building.

In a slight shift on formal play, Brautigan toys with the expected relationship between a work's title and its contents. Some stories begin with titles that seem to promise more than a story's brief form could possibly deliver. They suggest exhaustive treatment of a subject, yet are followed by short narratives that might only tangentially relate to the title's topic. Consider the following stories from *Revenge of the Lawn*: "A Complete History of Germany and Japan," "A Long Time Ago People Decided to Live in America," or "A Study in California Flowers." Each could entitle a several-hundred-page book tracing national histories, suggesting motivations behind international emigration, or tabulating extensive and fascinating botanical variations, respectively. Instead, the narrators present stories of their very personal remembered pasts: of life in a motel next to a slaughterhouse during World War II; of an awkward exchange between a man and a woman that destroys any chance of a sexual encounter; and of a poor person's overhearing the coffeehouse conversation of a wealthy couple, respectively.

In these *über*-titled stories, as in the stories preceding them, it would seem that the grand ambitions of Brautigan's melancholic narrators are dashed. Yes, they had hoped to reconnect with lost meanings or to create something reflecting the vastness of grand, culturally sanctioned ideas, and have failed on that level. However, what these formal challenges reveal is that the vast, the important and huge, is in fact only accessible through the tiny scraps at hand. Because the melancholic knows that meaning is gone, that he does not have any chance of accessing it on a large scale, he can only try to find it through the small entities in his world—the very personal, the utterly banal. If there is to be any hope of escaping hopelessness, it must come through the fragmentary bits, the ruins that surround him. At the end of the day, or at the end of the story, however, the ruins will fail him. Death is, and will remain, ever-present, no matter how creative or original the structure that might carry the melancholic narrator, temporarily, away.

As this discussion of Brautigan's own overt manipulation of accepted or expected formal structures reveals, the melancholic's permanent position amid death and loss persists within the genre play. Death is an insistent and pervasive motif in Brautigan's writing. Motifs are defined as "recurrent images, words, phrases, or actions that tend to unify the work" (Holman and Harmon 302). Considering "unity" in connection with the short story necessitates a nod to Edgar Allen Poe. Poe insisted on unity as a requirement of effect when he judged a good "tale" and I assert that the motif can be very effective in unifying a short story and, especially in Brautigan's case, in unifying a collection of stories.

The motif and the short story serve each other very well. Both are, well, short-lived. The moment we begin reading a short story, we are cognizant that it will end, and soon.[6] Each word, each sentence of a short story brings us that much closer, that much faster, to the last sentence, the last word. Motifs, in their tidy form, add depth without unduly prolonging a story. In addition, the story's appropriately brief length serves the motif by providing a stage that is just the right size to prevent the motif's being lost among the other words and images. On Brautigan's 174-page series of story "stages," the death motif appears over three hundred times, starring in a variety of roles within three general categories. Brautigan gives us representations of literal death, those in which animate life ceases for people, animals, and plants. He also offers representations of figurative death, wherein something ends or is inexplicably lost, such as phases of life, eras of cultural history, and opportunities to attain a goal. Brautigan also explores the many events and images that have an inherent association with death, such as wars, holidays of remembrance, epitaphs, and fired guns. Moving from these broad categories to specific examples, Brautigan challenges us with stories containing dead grandfathers, dead pear trees, dead dogs, dead lions, dead seals, dead pigs, and dead enemy soldiers; his narrators ponder lost moments of youth, shadows from the time of Christ, amnesias and ghosts of bygone days; and his stories take place during World War I, World War II, funerals, divorces, and Halloween.

This brief overview of the death motifs that pepper Brautigan's stories underlines the variety and frequency of death within his collection. Death motifs are predominant. They are varied. They are consistent and insistent. Consistently, these motifs surface, again and again, in story after story, insisting that we notice and remain aware of death and its many forms. Taking it one step further, not only does Brautigan implant his collection with death motifs, he even permits his melancholy narrators to brag about their familiarity with death. One such narrator, the California resident in "Winter Rug," goes so far as to proclaim himself an expert on death and to outline his credentials, which depend largely on death-filled literature. He assures us that he has read *The Loved One*, *The American Way of Death*, *After Many a Summer Dies the Swan*, and, most intriguing within the context of late-capitalist postmodernity, *Wallets in Shrouds* (*Revenge* 56).

Returning to the shortest of Brautigan's short stories, "The Scarlatti Tilt," it is evident that Brautigan's death motifs are embedded in a time-dependent story wherein the melancholy narrator moves us from the seventeenth century to the twentieth, within seconds. Indeed, both Benjamin and Kristeva associate melancholia with a "past time/present time" composite. Here, the present time would be twentieth-century San Jose where a man practices his violin, poorly, effectively murdering potentially beautiful music. The past time would be the time of the Scarlattis, father and son, both seventeenth-century Italian opera composers, now dead.

As I have noted, Benjamin associates melancholia with allegory, history, and death. Events from the past, from cultural and individual history, including death, are material events, unique moments in time that, once experienced, are potentially lost to us forever. To save the historical moment, Benjamin insists on an allegorical understanding, which redeems that moment, as an image, by pulling it up from the historical continuum, the "then," rescuing it by recognizing it in a fleeting moment of the "now." This redemption of the ruins or fragments of the past depends on a dialectical understanding that anchors the melancholic, who is looking backward, in the present moment: "The dialectical image is a flashing image. Thus the image of the past . . . is to be held fast as an image that flashes in the Now of recognition. Redemption . . . is accomplished in this way and only in this way" (Wolin 126; c.f. Benjamin, *Reflections* 56). Ronald Schleifer explains that Benjamin calls for an allegorical understanding "in which different realms confront one another without reduction of one to the other" (320). Thus, a dialectical juxtaposition of the then and the now is not hierarchical, but validates both moments in a union that might lift the melancholic, temporarily, from a state of hopelessness.

In "The Scarlatti Tilt," Brautigan's melancholy narrator resembles most others from this collection, for he relates a story that features a present event in juxtaposition with a past one. Thus, the transporting beauty of a Scarlatti aria is called up from its seventeenth-century continuum, and, in a flash, joins with the twentieth-century violin practice in a very Benjaminian "Dialect at a Standstill" (Wolin 125). The beauty of the Scarlattis' music does not efface the irritating notes scraped out by the amateur violinist; rather, the image that this story presents, and *re*presents, is dialectical. Within this one image are two very different musical moments. Side by side they stand, in a nonhierarchical relationship: the exquisite to the ugly, masterwork to off-key squeaking. Both of these two time periods and both of the two musical realities are valid and powerful in their own right.

For Kristeva, who bases her discussions of melancholia largely on the writings of Melanie Klein and Sigmund Freud, melancholics are prisoners of time. Their melancholia is due to an intense connection to something from the past that has been lost, and they experience what Freudian theory calls "impossible mourning for the maternal object," the Freudian psychic object (*Black Sun* 9). Kristeva states that "melancholy people live within a skewed time sense. . . . Riveted to the past, [they] manifest a strange memory: everything has gone by, they seem to say, but I am faithful to those bygone days, I am nailed down to them, no revolution is possible, there is no future" (*Black Sun* 60). Time, for the Kristevan melancholic, does not move forward; the now is focused backward, on the then. Life is an eternal state of hopelessness for melancholics spend it missing something that is irretrievable and their present-tense emptiness is but a reminder of an aching absence.

Thus, the narrator of "The Scarlatti Tilt" skews time by moving from his present moment—needing to tell us a story that centers on a twentieth-century city event—to a lost, past moment—his personal vision of seventeenth-century Italy. He begins from his melancholy understanding of the woman's suffering and ultimate arrival at her breaking point, so intensely missing those "bygone" days when music could bring pleasure. Nonetheless, this narrator must acknowledge the tragedy of a hopeless situation—two people with very different desires are forced by the constraints of city life to share a small space and its sounds, no matter their qualities. To achieve a true representation of what had been lost and what had inspired the San Jose tragedy, Brautigan's melancholy narrator shifts his focus backward, aching in sympathy with this woman for an absent musical beauty, the rich ornamentation of the Italian Baroque.

Similarly, with regard to language use, Kristeva and Benjamin both foreground the primacy of language, as written object, in linking the present with a memory event from the past. Both insist that although melancholics operate from a position of hopelessness, they nonetheless use language to reach out toward a hope that they are certain cannot be found. Benjamin states: "With the joy of remembering, however, another is fused: that of possession in memory" (*Reflections* 57). As Brautigan's melancholic narrators recall and then relate their stories, the stories themselves—possessed by the narrators and then by the reader—become objects.

Thus Benjamin's melancholic, although hopeless, relies on language to renew the past within the present. Inherent to this Benjaminian view is the allegorical understanding of how objects serve the melancholic. Benjamin claims that "the only pleasure the melancholic permits himself, and it is a powerful one, is allegory" and states that the melancholic homes in on the fragments of daily life, writing of banal objects in order to construct these allegories (*Origin* 185).[7] While Brautigan's stories are themselves objects of contemplation, particularly as their brevity and fragmentation contribute to this identity, the banal objects of daily life featured within the stories are implicated in the narrators' melancholia as well. Benjamin appreciated Albrecht Dürer's engraving of the figure *Melencolia* wherein "the utensils of active life are lying around unused on the floor, as objects of contemplation" (*Origin* 140). The melancholic takes the time to focus on these ordinary objects because his condition includes a "deadening of the emotions, and the ebbing away of the waves of life which are the source of these emotions in the body" and since his life has lost its meaning he turns to "the most simple object [which] appears to be a symbol of some enigmatic wisdom" (*Origin* 140).

Indeed, Brautigan's narrators are experts on the simple and banal. In "The Scarlatti Tilt" the narrator focuses on a horrific, but expected, daily event: yet another murder in a big American city. An anonymous roommate struggles through his lessons, and the woman who fails to tolerate his mediocrity gives her incriminating police statement. Using few and selected details in this fragmentlike story, the narrator succeeds in delivering a larger message wherein his use and arrangement of language is primary. It is only after we read the two final, crucial words *empty revolver* that the plot line ends and, in its last second, the story presents its dialectical image. In a Benjaminian "flash" we suddenly understand that shots were fired by this woman, the man is probably dead, and we race back over the narrator's earlier language to connect with the missing part of the dialectic.

We join the last words *empty revolver* with the first words, the initially perplexing title with its off-kilter historical reference "The Scarlatti Tilt," and—flash—the image is complete. One concept, that a beautiful operatic aria filled listeners' hearts with expansive awe and transported them to the zenith of a human moment—bliss—faces another concept, the "tilted" notion that another listener could no longer endure the horrific, repetitive, wrong notes that filled her tiny living space and brought her to the nadir of human actions—murder.[8] On another level, *tilt* could be read in the Quixotic sense, where, instead of "tilting at windmills," the woman charges in on her practicing roommate, answering his aural challenge to a joust, and the gun outgores the bow, so to speak.[9] The revolver's five or six shots finish the violinist's phrase for him, punctuating the air as anathematical gong, sounding the end of his musical education.

That Benjamin's melancholic relies on language for a weak promise of redemption is, however, only half the story. For as soon as hope flashes up, it disappears. Benjamin laments the melancholic's state: "[T]he profound fascination of the sick man for the isolated and insignificant is succeeded by that disappointed abandonment of the exhausted emblem" (*Origin* 185). The banal object, the insignificant and small detail alternately fascinates and disappoints. It resurfaces and disappears, again and again, motiflike. The melancholic narrator realizes that the banal object is the only object he has, but in the end, it always disappoints. While the story continues, the narrator is occupied with language and his pain is deferred. However, the story cannot last forever. Thus, language, for Benjamin, "is in every case not only communication of the communicable but also, at the same time, a symbol of the noncommunicable" (*Reflections* 331).

At the end of "The Scarlatti Tilt" a man is dead. Has the narrator truly "communicated" death? Can he? We may see the allegorical flash in the last second of the story, but moments later, the story is over, and the narrator has already moved on to "The Wild Birds of Heaven," once again attempting, through story, to communicate the noncommunicable, death.

When Kristeva discusses the melancholic's loss of an absent and mourned time, she, too, emphasizes the primacy of language. The event that the melancholic remembers "belongs to lost time, in the manner of Proust," and this commitment to what is no longer present places the melancholic, with regard to language, in a dual position (*Black Sun* 61). In speaking or writing of bygone days, the melancholic creates a new object of focus, the spoken or written word, the story. This object, at the time of its writing, refers to an earlier time, for the melancholic is in a struggle within his present moment; he is always looking back. In fact, Kristeva commends the melancholic as especially tenacious in his fight for, although feeling bereft of, a future; the melancholic is "at the same time the most relentless in his struggle against the symbolic abdication that blankets him" (*Black Sun* 9).

Fighting against this weighty hopelessness, the melancholic necessarily turns to the signifier. Language is a demonstration of his faithfulness to what has left him, a link to that lost past, but it is also as a way to defer the sadness and pain of a present that holds no future promise. In "The Scarlatti Tilt," the narrator refers to an earlier, seemingly more beautiful time—that of Scarlatti—to defer the reality of a present-day homicide. Kristeva's melancholic mourns what was lost here, an irretrievable musical bliss, but she reminds us that "[signifying] bonds, language in particular, prove to be unable to insure, . . . a compensating way out of" the melancholic state (*Black Sun* 10).

In "The Scarlatti Tilt," Brautigan's narrator tries to secure his object, a representation of death, which might substitute for the lost maternal bond. Hope exists for a few seconds, as the object, the story, is told and defers his sadness. But in the end, language has not guaranteed the narrator's permanent departure from his melancholic state, the violinist still lies dead, and we, his readers, still do not "comprehend" death, and turn the page.

As we continue reading through Brautigan's other stories, the death imagery accumulates, the intellectual play with language stimulates, and the melancholy narrators intrigue. The narrators focus on banal objects while maneuvering within fragmentary structures and temporal juxtapositions. An examination of two other Brautigan stories demonstrates that, from the first to the last story in the collection, Brautigan's narrators continue to reach out toward a lost time, dwelling briefly on material objects, the only things that might reconnect them to what is missing. These objects, whether words or material entities within daily life, such as doors, animals, orchards, and shadows, provide the potential pathway of return, the allegorical means toward—maybe—reaccessing what is no longer accessible. Indeed, the task is impossible, but making the effort is the only way to continue living with any sense of hope. That hope is, of course, a false one, but it is all the melancholic has. Once hope is let go, all desire for meaning must be abandoned. It is only through continuing the search for meaning, continuing the experimentation with language, that a connection to that lost time—when objects and words *were* meaning—that the narrators can keep death at bay.

Brautigan's six-page title story "Revenge of the Lawn," delivers snippets of stories from the narrator's ancestors' lives in unremarkable paragraph form until it ends, five pages later, with this visual break:

★   ★   ★

These three stars visually acknowledge the melancholic narrator's pasttime/present-time struggle by representing the gap between the first and second parts of the story. The first part contains the narrator's attempt to re-create a narrative he has no access to, since it takes place between 1872 and 1936, before he was born and before he claims any concrete memories. The second part, two short paragraphs, admits the approximate date of his first recollection and interrogates the veracity of any family "history" revealed in the first section. In addition, this stellar pause reinforces the contrast between the melancholic's unfulfillable desire for access to meaning residing outside of his small, personal realm and his banal reality. However, he has only the personal, the intimate to concentrate on and it is only through the one personal memory he claims from 1936 or 1937 that he might hope to sense the larger-order truths of his American ancestors' stormy experiences.

Following the three stars, the closing fragment describes the narrator's first memory when his grandmother's boyfriend of thirty years, Jack, soaks a felled pear tree with kerosene and sets it on fire on her lawn. Jack attempts revenge on nature, which had exacted revenge on Jack for years, challenging him with bee stings, drunken defeathered geese, and a vengeful lawn. The shenanigans associated with Jack's and the grandmother's lives, while humorous and entertaining, provide the narrator a framework on which to travel back to an earlier time whose events are both significant and foreboding.

Embedded in this "cover" story of geese and bourbon is another, one that reveals the narrator's core fear for his own future and his fascination with time's role in it. The story-within-a-story, told completely on page 11, relates that the narrator's grandfather, whom he looks like, had the misfortune to see four years into the future and prophesize the exact date when World War I would start, a feat whose revelation hints at the narrator's melancholic position. This narrator looks only backward because it was the prophetic act of looking forward that doomed his grandfather. Shortly after his astonishing prediction, the grandfather was locked up in the Washington State insane asylum where time, effectively, stopped and for seventeen years he saw himself as a child waiting for chocolate cake. The narrator focuses on this ordinary object, the chocolate cake, and its seventeen years of baking, for its power to represent the grandfather's remaining alive but conceptually frozen inside his own past, until his death.[10]

Since the narrator resembles his relative, he is especially loath to replicate his actions, lest he, too, should mentally deteriorate and be exiled from the complexities of cognitive play and the awareness of progressive time. He cannot risk believing in a future for himself, and, as Kristeva asserts, is anchored to the past. Despite his intentions to avoid his grandfather's fate, his focus on his cover story's banal objects—the grandmother's whiskey still, the sheriff's supportive morning phone call, ripened pears, afternoon naps, and trips to the grocery store—reveals that he has failed. Just like his grandfather, the melancholy narrator is frozen in an era that has passed. Although his temporal frame goes beyond one afternoon's baking, he relies on his grandmother, who "shines like a beacon down the stormy American past," to light a path, through Jack's presence, to the grandfather's central position in the narrator's sense of identity (*Revenge* 9). It is by manipulating language, using this outer story and its characters to steer him toward revealing his core fear, that the narrator defers his own descent into madness.

A central object within this manipulation, as the story's title suggests, is the lawn—and Jack's relationship to it. Taking the grandfather's place in the grandmother's life, Jack allows this once-beautiful lawn, which had been the grandfather's pride and joy and the source of his mystic powers, to deteriorate, fearing that the lawn "was against him" (*Revenge* 10). Jack's car must share the lawn with the pear tree since the day he declared, in Italian, that "it was all wrong for a car to have a house" (*Revenge* 12). Jack's own relationship to language is revelatory and entwined with the series of events that demonstrates the melancholic narrator's Benjaminian relationship with time.

Speculating that Jack's "no garage" idea originates in "the Old Country," the narrator states that although Jack spoke English at all other times, he spoke only Italian for the garage (*Revenge* 13). The narrator sees that language connects Jack to his past, for when Jack sees a garage, something in that domestic object transports him back to an earlier moment in his historical continuum. As Benjamin suggests, when the past time and the present time collide, the now and the then coexist in a flash. When Jack sees the material garage in the English-speaking country of his middle years, the idea of "garage" from his Italian-speaking youth is pulled up from historical time and both garages crash together, side by side. In the moment that Jack *refers to* the building while standing on the lawn in Washington State, he literally speaks both *of* and *through* the garage of his Italian youth. "Garage" signifies both image and material entity and provides Jack (flash!) with access to lost time, to some lost but indescribable and in fact, indeterminable, "oneness" that is, for Benjamin, from Messianic time, when word and God were one, and for Kristeva, of the semiotic realm, when the universe, mother, and pre-mirror-stage infant were not yet perceived as separated or bordered.

The narrator uses language to construct Jack as his agent of melancholic deferral. As long as the cover story wanders along, the narrator is occupied on an imaginary level, shaping paragraph after paragraph of Jack's possible exploits. Kristeva states that "allegory is inscribed in the very logic of the imagination . . . in which the speaking subject first discovers the shelter of an ideal but above all the opportunity to play it again in illusions and disillusion" (*Black Sun* 102). After reflecting for a while on images of Jack's preposterous bad luck, the narrator reaches the painful story of his grandfather's pathetic outcome. The narrator's deferral tactics serve to entertain the reader, and himself, with illusions about Jack, the lawn, and his grandmother's bootlegging business, but the narrator finally disillusions himself by inserting the formal fragment at story's end.

Once the reader realizes that the earlier narrative is constructed from something besides the narrator's legitimate memories, his "story" becomes suspect. Kristeva cautions that "the imaginary constitutes a miracle, but it is at the same time its shattering: a self-illusion, nothing but dreams and words, words, words. . . . It affirms the almightiness of temporary subjectivity—the one that knows enough to speak until death comes" (*Black Sun* 103). Brautigan's narrator does just that. Rather than dwell on the disturbing thought that madness lurks in his future as it did for his grandfather, the narrator keeps that madness, and the death of intellectual rigor and self-sufficiency that institutionalization signifies, at bay. It may be just outside his reach, just beyond the tip of his pen, but this melancholy narrator must rely on that pen, on its ordinary utility for writing down this imagined story, to save him. Thus, it is through confounding Jack's remembered and legendary actions that the narrator shapes this seeming "man versus nature" story that instead *and* in addition tells the (temporarily) victorious story of "the narrator versus his own melancholy nature."

As we arrive at the collection's final story, we see that nothing much, in fact, has changed for the melancholic narrator. This narrator, like those who came before him, looks only backward, telling of a past embedded in the present, and concentrating on material objects for possible access to a missing realm. Kristeva describes this missing "something" as "the secret and unreachable horizon of our loves and desires, [which] assumes, for the imagination, the consistency of an archaic mother, which, however, no precise image manages to encompass" (*Black Sun* 145). Brautigan's last narrator, like his first, holds on to the belief that some greater meaning exists, at some secret horizon, and that using language as object and to represent objects might put him in contact with a link to that meaning. In this story, yet another male narrator contemplates how he might engage different images to wrest meaning from the death of a man in his family, his father-in-law.

In "The World War I Los Angeles Airplane" the melancholy narrator uses language meticulously as he shapes his narrative into a three-part story.[11] Structurally, the story begins with an introductory paragraph that sets the scene from ten years ago, then reproduces the dialogue that he had with his wife, and finishes with a four-page, numbered list of thirty-three items describing selected events from the father-in-law's lived history.[12] In his opening, the narrator recalls that moment, ten years previous, when he learned of his father-in-law's dying alone in Los Angeles and had to tell his wife the news. He brings several small, ordinary details to the surface: the wife was out buying ice cream, the phone rang, the brother-in-law was calling, and the dead man was seventy. The narrator admits his difficulty in representing the truth of death to his wife, and calls our attention to the temporary usefulness of language in deferring sadness by stating how he tried to camouflage her father's death with words, but failed miserably because the end product is always death (*Revenge* 170). As both Benjamin and Kristeva predict, the melancholic knows he must engage with language but will be left disappointed every time.

This narrative structure again sets up the contrast between vast, higher-order concerns with what *life*, *truth*, or *death* might mean, and the more personal, daily snippets of errands, dessert, and banal conversations. As Brautigan's entire collection hands us small stories embedded with death motifs while struggling with important human questions about love, loss, and the need to connect with something outside of the individual, so too does his final narrator give us a listing of small, death-associated events from the father-in-law's life as he tries to connect with . . . something. The narrator, in his present moment, travels back ten years to a remembered conversation and realizes that the representation of death that he offered his wife was not then, and is not now, enough to satisfy him.

Hoping to decipher the meaning of death, he examines thirty-three fragments from the father-in-law's historical continuum. These Benjaminian "chips" of time are isolated remainders from a seventy-year series of lived moments and many months or years are absent between them. By pulling them out of serial time, where they lay frozen and forgotten, the narrator resurrects each tiny snippet of ordinary life, hoping for an allegorical connection to that meaning he seeks. The list highlights such remnants of loss as a failed marriage, a deadly automobile accident, several moves around the United States, and many abandoned careers, including banking successes and failures, sheep ranching escapades, bookkeeping efforts, and an embarrassing janitorial position. Within these items the death motif surfaces again and again, in the form of dead or lost marriages, friends, sheep, investments, dreams, and pride, leaving the father-in-law a careful but sweet wine alcoholic during his Los Angeles retirement years (*Revenge* 174).

Although each of the numbered fragments is worthy of contemplation, the narrator's repetition of one of them in two distant places on his list—as items #5 and #32—signals its importance. Item #5, in fact, is the longest entry on the list; most contain only one or two sentences, but this "chip" comprises three paragraphs. The first paragraph relates the father-in-law's intense desire to become a pilot despite discouragement; the second, his dropping bombs on railroad stations and being shot at by the Germans as he flies over France during World War I; and the third, a contrasting, nonviolent moment when he was flying over France and a rainbow appeared following every turn the plane made (*Revenge* 172). When the narrator repeats the father-in-law's World War I experience in #32, however, he blasts an even smaller "chip" out of item #5, rephrasing a small part of the third paragraph only and emphasizing the fact that his plane was carrying guns and bombs (*Revenge* 174).

By tightening his focus to the "followed by a rainbow" moment, the melancholy narrator both provides the flash of the Benjaminian "Dialectic at a Standstill" and decides that of all the father-in-law's past moments it must be this one image that reappears to him as he dies. This suggestion is evident upon recalling the story's title: "The World War I *Los Angeles* Airplane" (emphasis added). While in item #5 the father-in-law was flying over *France*, in item #32, the airplane is a *Los Angeles* airplane because as he dies he falls to the floor of his Los Angeles apartment, making that rainbow-guarded flight one last time—figuratively and imaginatively as the memory flashes up—before dying. A final quote from Benjamin is revelatory:

It is, however, characteristic that not only a man's knowledge or wisdom, but above all his real life—and this is the stuff that stories are made of—first assumes transmissible form at the moment of his death . . . as his life comes to an end . . . the unforgettable emerges and imparts to everything that concerned him that authority which even the poorest wretch in dying possesses for the living around him. This authority is at the very source of the story. (*Illuminations* 94)

This story ends with item #33, which pulls us out of the dialectical moment that reveals the beauty and authority of the father-in-law's "real life" and brings us one step closer to the present as the narrator quotes himself speaking ten years ago, "Your father died this afternoon" (*Revenge* 174). These words carry all back to the evening when the phone call came and the narrator faced his impossible task: communicating the noncommunicable fact of death. As the narrator closes his quote, and as we finish reading the story—and the collection—his own melancholy declaration, "always at the end of the words, someone is dead," proves true.

Brautigan's melancholy narrators surround us with images of death. They use language to unite moments of the present, the now with those of the past, the then, momentarily deferring the pain that their present moment holds. Their melancholy condition requires their concentration on the small, banal objects of ordinary life, whether a chocolate cake, a newspaper clipping, a brief confession to the police, or a few seconds of bomb-free flight. These tiny, death-associated objects—material, aural, and imagined—represented through language, are the melancholic's raison d'être. Without them, the hopeless hope for a connection to some greater meaning, to a reason for "being," would evaporate.

At the end of the day, then, having read Brautigan's collection of short and short-short stories, can we determine that the melancholic narrators have succeeded, through repeated and varied death motifs, in responding to death by containing it in many brief representations that enable us to transform death, to limit its power, and thus to comprehend it? Certainly Brautigan's beautiful, childlike ways with simple language enable his narrators to enrobe death in a softer context. While these gentle representations might transform death through bittersweet humor or absurd images of drunken, featherless, resurrected geese, and thus seemingly limit its powers, what do we "comprehend" that we did not comprehend before our reading?

Perhaps it is both through the death motifs *and* despite them that we might catch a glimpse of something more. While immersed, for a few moments, in a melancholic Brautigan story, perhaps we live more fully because of the distanced deaths we encounter. As we bob along, between the story sections, past the borrowed quotes and tiny "chapters," and over the dividing spaces and stars, the melancholy narrators guide us in sensing a vast, Kristevan "something" that the simple, banal details of life both mask and embody. We, and the narrators, still do not "know" death, but we believe, through the details of life, that there is something lurking behind them.

Brautigan's melancholy narrators remind us that the objects, the words, and the stories that we live among are significant for what they are, as funny, useful, or beautiful *material* entities within serial time, but that their significance extends beyond their material borders, if we isolate them from their context. It is through the gaze of the melancholic, living, but just barely, so close to the edge of death, that we can sense, allegorically, what we already believe: that there is something else, something we have long ago lost and are aware of without being able to articulate it. For Benjamin's melancholic, it is lost Messianic time. For Kristeva's, it is the lost maternal object. For Brautigan's melancholy narrators, speaking from a secular, postmodern position, it is something else. Although we cannot speak it and cannot touch it, these narrators help us get close enough to *almost* sense it. We can read their stories and hope with them—against hope—that our engagement with and immersion through language might temporarily connect "all of us" to something greater, something more vast—a promise of inarticulable meaning, if we can just . . . stop . . . *briefly* enough to read it.

Notes

1. Genre lines are consistently blurred within Brautigan's works. Some of his poems are longer than his stories (see the poems "Crow Maiden" or "Famous People and Their Friends" in *Loading Mercury with a Pitchfork* versus the short stories "The Scarlatti Tilt" or "Lint" in *Revenge of the Lawn*) and many of his stories in this collection could also be termed prose poems. Some of his poems are numbered and grouped within sections of a poetry collection, mimicking perhaps an artist's grouping of paintings or drawings centered on a theme, a collection of plastic arts such as might be isolated within one exhibition room as necessary components of a whole (see, for example, "The Galilee Hitch-Hiker," a nine-part grouping representing Charles-Pierre Baudelaire in nine mid-twentieth-century contexts in *The Pill versus the Springhill Mine Disaster*, or "Group Portrait without the Lions: Available Light," a fourteen-part series of poems, each a verbal portrait of an individual, in *Loading Mercury with a Pitchfork*). Brautigan's novels are often comprised of very short chapters that resemble prose poems or short stories themselves, some being only a paragraph long (see the single-sentence chapter "Margaret Again, Again, Again" in *In Watermelon Sugar* or the two-sentence chapter "Mr. Morgan, Requiescat in Pace" in *The Hawkline Monster*). Some of his novels could be considered short story cycles (such as *Trout Fishing in America* or *The Tokyo–Montana Express*, as I have asserted elsewhere). Indeed, our expectation that a poem or story would contain both a title and a text is even challenged by Brautigan's several titled stories or poems that, in fact, contain no subsequent content, presenting instead a blank page where the words would be (see "8 Millimeter (mm)" or "1891–1944" in *Rommel Drives on Deep into Egypt*) or that contain, surprisingly, a text of numerals rather than one of letters (see "Nine Crows: Two Out of Sequence" in *Loading Mercury with a Pitchfork*).
2. The name "Scarlatti," although it appears to refer to a single individual, might represent two Italian composers, a father and son, both born in the seventeenth century and rather long-lived for their era. The father, Alessandro (1660–1725), was both a composer and a writer of operas, and the son, Domenico (1685–1757), was likewise a composer and an opera writer as well as a harpsichordist and an organist particularly famed for his keyboard sonatas. The ambiguity of reference inherent to the two Scarlattis' living over roughly the same time period allows for a reading of Brautigan's title as a reference to two composers.

3. In their original text, Goodwin and Bronfen end the sentence with an endnote that states, "This is a point developed specifically by Berger (3–28), though it comes up repeatedly in the literature on death." The reference cited is to Peter L. Berger's, *The Sacred Canopy: Elements of a Sociological Theory of Religion* (Garden City: Doubleday, 1967).

4. I use the masculine possessive pronoun here, and masculine pronouns in general for Brautigan's narrators. Most stories in this collection are narrated in the first person, most often by a neutral or clearly male narrator and only occasionally by a possibly female narrator.

5. The two stories "The Literary Life in California/1964" and "Fame in California/1964" each total fewer than three pages and each is split into two numbered, chapterlike sections: "1" and "2." These stories are not consecutive, however, being separated by another that takes place in 1964, "Banners of My Own Choosing." In the two "/1964" stories, the narrator ponders both the vicissitudes of fame as a "minor poet" and the irony of his attaining renown via other artists' novels and photographs. The interim story's narrator considers that although no one erects statues of him nor presents him with flower bouquets upon his return to his writing task, he might have to settle for the possibility that "[p]erhaps the words [that he has typed] remember [him]" (*Revenge* 130). Temporal circularity and an emphasis on the past and on the writer's work are highlighted by the narrator's pondering that he "[returns] to this story as one who has been away but one who was always destined to return and perhaps that's for the best" (*Revenge* 130). Thus, formally, these three stories could be considered as three temporally linked chapters of a longer work, such as a short story cycle or novel.

6. A more thorough exploration of the importance of temporality and endings—and story readers' awareness of an immanent ending—in short fiction is undertaken in several excellent works, including Susan Lohafer's *Coming to Terms with the Short Story* and her coedited (with Jo Ellen Clarey) collection *Short Story Theory at a Crossroads*, and Michael Trussler's "Suspended Narratives: The Short Story and Temporality."

7. Benjamin himself is known for collecting written objects in the form of quotations and aphorisms that he would copy down and rearrange, mosaic-like, hoping to resurrect their power through fresh juxtaposition (Pensky 14).

8. The name "Scarlatti" resembles *scarlatto*, the Italian word for scarlet, a deep red that could be associated with passion, blood, and murder. In the story's final moments, the words *empty revolver* could also connect with *Scarlatti/scarlet*, evoking a dialectical image of tilted and bloody passion.

9. This reading is not unlikely, since Brautigan's postmodern settings are frequently visited by medieval imagery that incorporates princesses, knights, castles, and dragons. In addition, Brautigan's literature is rife with cultural and literary allusions, including nods to dozens of varied writers such as Emily Dickenson, Franz Kafka, Rudyard Kipling, Basho and Issa (seventeenth-century Japanese haiku poets), William Shakespeare, Dashiell Hammett, John Donne, and Dr. William Carlos Williams.

10. The idea of "chocolate cake" is featured both within the title story and on the collection's cover. In the cover photograph a broadly smiling young woman sits in a wooden chair pulled up to the edge of a table that holds a large chocolate-frosted cake. Benjamin acknowledges the allegorical power of both emblems—figural representations such as the dog or the sphere in Albrecht Dürer's engraving *Melencolia*—and words (*Origin* 151–55). An initial view of the book's cover "emblem" is striking. While the remarkable image is perhaps funny or odd, its allegorical promise parallels that of the described chocolate cake for the "Revenge of the Lawn" narrator. Although the cover image is in full view, the idea of the chocolate cake is hidden inside the story of the grandfather's downfall, which is inside the story of Jack's defeat by the lawn. Just as the melancholy narrator had to tell his framing story to arrive at his more significant story of the never fully baked cake so to mourn his grandfather's never fully lived life, both suspended in a time that does not move forward, so too does the cover image offer us first a bright green outer frame, then the central, smiling face, and finally this baked and even frosted cake. In the written allegory, the narrator eventually reveals that it is his *first* memory of an ordinary day in the life of "Jack against nature" that enables him to imagine his family's past and reveal his devastating fear for his own impossible future, en route to insanity. Thus, he remains mired in contemplation of an object—the story he tells—as a means toward (impossible) reconnection with his own lost past when there was no ability to imagine how time might carry inescapable doom, when there were no boundaries between himself, his mother, his grandfather, nature, and time. Likewise, it is the reader's *first* encounter with a death motif—the cover image—that enables us to sense the allegorical promise of Brautigan's collection. We can "read" that the anonymous young woman will never rise to get a knife and slice that cake, will never celebrate another birthday or holiday, will never age toward death. She, like Brautigan's melancholy narrators, is suspended in time; there is no future. As Benjamin and Kristeva might assert, she seems hopeful amid the hopelessness of her story. Tragically, she can forever have her cake and *not* eat it, too.

11. This story received the award for Best Short Story of 1969.

12. While I acknowledge the potential connections between the thirty-three items listed to represent the father-in-law's life and the thirty-three years in Jesus Christ's life, I defer further interpretation to a later study. The intrigue is fascinating, however, considering the narrator's attempts to somehow "resurrect" his father-in-law's life and breathe new life into what was, supposedly, buried ten years previous, and to invoke a collective audience as he searches for a way toward "what his death means to all of us" (*Revenge* 171).

References

"Alessandro Scarlatti." *Classical Music Pages*. Ed. Matt Boynick. 10 Oct. 2000. 25 Nov. 2001. <http://w3.rz-berlin.mpg.de/cmp/scarlatti_a.html>.

Benjamin, Walter. *Illuminations*. Trans. Harry Zohn. New York: Schocken, 1968.

————. *The Origin of German Tragic Drama.* 1963. Trans. John Osborne. London: NLB, 1977.

————. *Reflections: Essays, Aphorisms, Autobiographical Writings.* Trans. Edmund Jephcott. New York: Harcourt, 1978.

Brautigan, Richard. *In Watermelon Sugar.* New York: Delta, 1968.

————. *Loading Mercury with a Pitchfork.* New York: Simon, 1971.

————. *The Pill versus the Springhill Mine Disaster.* New York: Delta, 1968.

————. *Revenge of the Lawn: Stories 1962–1970.* New York: Simon, 1971.

————. *Rommel Drives on Deep into Egypt.* New York: Delacorte, 1970.

————. *So the Wind Won't Blow It All Away.* New York: Delacorte/Seymour, 1982.

————. *The Tokyo–Montana Express.* New York: Delacorte/Seymour, 1980.

————. *Trout Fishing in America.* New York: Dell, 1967

"Domenico Scarlatti." *Classical Music Pages.* Ed. Matt Boynick. 10 Oct. 2000. 25 Nov. 2001. <http://w3.rz-berlin.mpg.de/cmp/scarlatti_d.html>.

Goodwin, Sarah Webster, and Elisabeth Bronfen, eds. *Death and Representation.* Baltimore: Johns Hopkins UP, 1993.

Holman, C. Hugh, and William Harmon, eds. *A Handbook to Literature.* 6th ed. New York: Macmillan, 1992.

Iftekharrudin, Farhat. "The Aesthetics in Brautigan's *Revenge of the Lawn: Stories 1962–1970.*" *Creative and Critical Approaches to the Short Story.* Ed. Noel H Kaylor, Jr. Lewiston, NY: Mellen, 1987.

Kristeva, Julia. *Black Sun: Depression and Melancholia.* Trans. Leon S. Roudiez. New York: Columbia UP, 1989. Trans. of *Soleil Noir: Dépression et mélancholie.* 1987.

————. *Powers of Horror: An Essay on Abjection.* Trans. Leon S. Roudiez. New York: Columbia UP, 1982. Trans. of *Pouvoirs de l'horreur.* 1980.

Lohafer, Susan. *Coming to Terms with the Short Story.* Baton Rouge: Louisiana State UP, 1983.

Lohafer, Susan, and Jo Ellyn Clarey, eds. *Short Story Theory at a Crossroads.* Baton Rouge: Louisiana State UP, 1989.

May, Charles E., ed. *The New Short Story Theories.* Athens: Ohio UP, 1994.

Pensky, Max Andrew. *The Politics of Melancholia: Walter Benjamin and the Play of Mourning.* Amherst: U of Massachusetts P, 1993.

Poe, Edgar. "Nathaniel Hawthorne" (Three reviews concerning genre/the tale, from *Graham's Magazine*, April 1842, May 1842, and from *Godey's Lady's Book*, November 1847). *Edgar Allan Poe: Essays and Reviews.* New York: Library of Americas, 1984. 568–88.

Schleifer, Ronald. "Afterword: Walter Benjamin and the Crisis of Representation: Multiplicity, Meaning and Athematic Death." *Death and Representation.* Eds. Sarah Webster Goodwin and Elisabeth Bronfen. Baltimore: Johns Hopkins UP, 1993. 312–33.

Trussler, Michael. "Suspended Narratives: The Short Story and Temporality." *Short Story Theory.* Spec. issue of *Studies in Short Fiction* 33 (1996): 557–77.

Wolin, Richard. *Walter Benjamin: An Aesthetic of Redemption.* New York: Columbia UP, 1982.

Perhaps She Had Not Told Him All the Story: The Disnarrated in James Joyce's *Dubliners*

Howard Lindholm

The early part of the twentieth century sees a strong correspondence between the Russian Formalist concept of *ostranenie* or defamiliariza-tion and the narrative experimentation of the Western Modernists. In his 1925 *Theory of Prose*, Viktor Shklovsky proposes "making strange" literature to awaken literary critics from their passivity. Ezra Pound follows suit declaring the artist must "make it new" and "seek the unfamiliar" to revitalize the arts. In his discussion of Pound's famous demand for renewal, Frank Lentricchia suggests modernist experi-mentation emerges as a self-emancipation from the Harold Bloomsian "anxiety of influence" of traditional narrative modes. To break from the stale literary tradition, the modernist pledges himself to an exercise in Emersonian self-creation: "In order to kill himself off as an expression of history and simultaneously re-birth himself as the first man living utterly in the present, a man must 'go into solitude.' . . . The 'I' must therefore be emptied of everything, including its literary company" (Lentricchia 201).

James Joyce's *Dubliners*, in the tone of the Russian Formalists, marks the author's first attempts to defamiliarize the ordinary so that subjects commonly viewed as dull transform into the narratively inter-esting. In a letter to his publisher Grant Richards, Joyce writes that he "dares to alter in the presentment, still more to deform, whatever he has seen and heard" (*Letters* 134). Joyce's technique of deforming the familiar represents a primary objective of modernism and prepares our subsequent approaches to the postmodern texts that follow Joyce. Nar-rative deformations in the modernist work involve

a progressive fading of that realism which has long been associated with the
novel; language ceases to be what we see through and becomes what we see.
The novel hangs on that border between the mimetic and the autotelic species
of literature, between an art made by imitating things outside itself, and an art
that is an internally coherent making. (Fletcher and Bradbury 401)

For Joyce and the modernists, language itself is deformed, remade to
call attention to its strangeness. In the transformation previously familiar subject matter is reanimated, retold through a stylistically experimental lens. Thus, the crucial themes of a Modernist text "are
likely to lie not in anything which is explicitly affirmed, but in signifi-
cances generated by the way in which the story is told" (Miller 176).
    As a navigational precursor to postmodern's futher experimenta-
tion, the modernist text defamiliarizes and disorients the reader
through its use of semiopaque alternative windows of possibility, or
what Gerald Prince calls the disnarrated, which contains

alethic expressions of impossibility or unrealized possibility, deontic expressions of observed prohibition, epistemic expressions of ignorance, ontologic
expressions of non-existence, purely imagined worlds, desired worlds, or intended worlds, unfulfilled expectations, unwarranted beliefs, failed attempts,
crushed hopes, suppositions and false calculations, errors and lies, and so
forth. ("Disnarrated" 2–3)

Clearly, if an alternative narrative lies outside the "main" narrational
world, its view remains inevitably less familiar, less visually accessible
than that which lies within the diegetic frame of the text. Despite its appearance in any given text, the disnarrated enjoys a distinctive preva-
lence in modernism, highlighted by the movement's fragmented views
and voices which give way to multiple narrative possibilities. Modernist narrative, more so than any other genre, insists on our con-
fronting and defining the problematic relationship between what is
said and what is left unsaid.[1]
    With the disnarrated the reader is invited to apply the fragmented
"hints" of possibility concealed behind the veil of the main diegesis to
the incomplete narratives of characters and events. The disnarrated allows its readers to delve into the hopes, possible directions, dreams,
and fears of the focalized character. Joyce's "Little Cloud" opens with
Chandler preoccupied by thoughts of his meeting with Gallaher, yet the
reader is not enlightened as to what these thoughts encompass. We are
left to wait for Gallaher's arrival and in the meantime conjecture as to
what Chandler's thoughts mean. The disnarrated gaps in "Little Cloud"
demonstrate how "every narrative function opens an alternative, a set

of possible directions, and every narrative progresses by following certain directions as opposed to others: the disnarrated or choices not made, roads not taken, possibilities not actualized, goals not reached" (Prince, "Disnarrated" 5). As an outgrowth of narrative fragmentation, the disnarrated enriches the text, complicating it by allowing its narratives to venture beyond its diegetic parameters. Perhaps it is this quality of illuminating possible paths that makes a modernist text far more realistic than its nineteenth-century counterpart. The multiple possibilities of modernism represents a new realism to be inherited by postmodernism, one that no longer pretends to omnisciently capture the world, but rather discovers its reality in the collective experience of its narrative trails. The singular perspective of traditional realism's omniscience has proved to be an inadequate frame of all the narrative possibilities of any given "truth."

Prince's observation that "narrative accommodates the real as well as the fictional, lying and error as well as truth" seems particularly fitting to Joyce's work ("Narratology" 545). Frequently, Joyce either truncates or omits altogether the unnarratable so that it actually transforms into the disnarrated. With the subtle suggestion or omission of certain events, dialogues, and character names, Joyce in effect highlights and defamiliarizes these sideline narratives, bringing them to diegetic attention while refusing to satisfy our narrative expectations. What distinguishes the Joycean narrative is its insistence "upon the ability to conceive and manipulate hypothetical worlds . . . and the freedom to reject various . . . conventions or codes for world- and fiction-making" (Prince, "Disnarrated" 6). Prince's description of the deforming actions "conceive" and "manipulate" pinpoints the stylistic and theoretical approach that sets Joyce and subsequent modernisms apart from realist convention. The Joycean text derives its narrative complexity from its rejecting the full development of these suggested worlds into diegeses of their own. Joyce *chooses* not to name characters, delve into their thoughts, or describe their actions, and while this choice may stem partially from a desire for publishable brevity, it also indicates a decisive move toward the defamiliarization of the Russian Formalists and Ezra Pound.

Typographically, *Dubliners* does not proclaim itself "strange" the way the visual texts of *As I Lay Dying* (Faulkner), *Ulysses* (Joyce), *In Our Time* (Hemingway), or *Cane* (Jean Toomer) do, and still it subverts the diegetic tradition by more subtle means. As a loose unity of stories, the collection paradoxically refuses to be partitioned into freestanding texts, or counterwise to be fully unified as a whole.[2] As with *Tender Buttons* (Stein), *Winesburg, Ohio* (Anderson), *Cane, In Our Time*, and *Go*

Down, Moses (Faulkner), *Dubliners* suggests a genre incongruent with the traditional categories of short story, novel, or poetry. It is a "synergistic fiction," composed of simultaneous and somewhat independent fictions, which, unified under the frame of a title, work together (while retaining their autonomy) to provide a greater effect than the sum of their individual actions. Joyce's loosely linked fictions, each bordered by the frame of a chapter, create a partitioned and fragmented Dublin. The collection resembles a multiperspective Cubist portrait, incomplete and yet multidimensional, whose narrative windows threaten to open into territory outside the borders of the title *Dubliners*.

The disnarrated often surfaces in what might be called *Dubliners'* silent "death acts"—specifically those hypodiegetic narratives of characters' literal death that surface only in fragmented forms and remain partially stifled by the main diegesis. Joyce repeatedly creates disjointed secondary narratives deprived of the main narrative's access to suspense, climax, and the dramatic questions familiar to the classic narrative. There is, as Gerald Doherty puts it, "a paralyzing appropriation" of hypodiegetic narratives by the diegesis that disallows their full utterance (39). With this marked distancing, if not defamiliarizing, of the actual act of dying, death is displaced from its familiar function as the culmination of plot—an ironic stylistic twist considering death constitutes a predominant theme throughout the collection.[3] To achieve the distancing and obscuring of a death scene, Joyce plants the kernel of death as a spoken act (i.e., He *told* me she died) rather than a literal depiction of the scene.

Death in *Dubliners* occurs "offstage," spatially and temporally removed from the mourners who must "write" its narrative. In spite of any narrative expectations established by the literary tradition, Joyce's deaths remain curiously out of view of the narrative eye. The impact of death comes through its narrative absence as opposed to its traditional depiction as a climatic kernel. Since the mourner (along with the reader) is never present at the death act, he or she must rely on secondhand narrative "distortions" of the given event. Often we hear of characters' deaths only in passing, either through an obituary or by word-of-mouth as if their hypodiegetic narratives emerge by mere accident.

Although we can safely assume that the offstage deaths do occur since the deceased fail to reappear, we can never be sure of the circumstances behind the death act since the main diegesis defamiliarizes the death through its disallowing of both its own characters and the reader to bear witness to these seemingly key events.[4] This is not to say death is not important in Joyce. On the contrary, the absence of the death act as a narrative kernel intensifies the significance of death as the Joycean story explores how characters construct subjective, if not inaccurate, narratives to frame the inaccessible losses they mourn. The devaluing of death acts causes what Richard Terdiman calls "a lack of solidity that in our ordinary understanding makes an event the fact it is" (138). Mourners and readers alike cannot easily dismiss the uncertain narrative of death because Joyce complicates its absence by planting contradictory disnarrative hints that encourage our curiosity and speculation.

The opening line of "The Sisters," the first line of *Dubliners*, sets an atmosphere of death as Joyce introduces the living Father Flynn as there being "no hope for him this time: it was the third stroke" (1). Flynn dies at some undisclosed point before, during, or after the boy's study of "the lighted square of window," which leads the boy to the disnarrated speculation, "*If* he was dead," that dominates the rest of the story (emphasis added). The secondary narrative of Flynn's death opens the collection, then is quickly resubmerged and upstaged by the main and "living" diegesis of the nameless boy, paralyzed by that death. The ghost of Flynn, however, continues the act of "dying," hovering in the background and pitting the untold fragments of his hypodiegetic narrative against the living's own narrative of Flynn's life and death. Certainly Flynn's recurring haunting of the boy suggests a disnarrated story wanting to be told: "It murmured; and I understood that it desired to confess something" (3). In a similar moment from "An Encounter," the boy narratee to the old man's monologue thinks to himself that something "seemed to plead with me that I should understand him" (18). Both narratees within and outside the text sit as frustrated listeners, left to speculate from the fragmented evidence of its existence as to what the speaker's confession might be. Hence, the disnarrated surfaces as the narrative stimulation to hypothesize.

In the larger modernist paradigm Flynn's ghost represents the partially tangible disnarrated standing between presence and absence, affirmation and denial. The modernist disnarrated hinges on the simultaneous juxtaposition of being and not being, effectively negating the spatial, temporal, and verbal stability needed to fully confirm or reject the suggested possible worlds of its narrative. The in-between world of the disnarrated, like "the reflection of candles on the darkened blind" of a window, both invites and resists our penetrating its interior so that we recognize Flynn's constant presence only to perceive the narrative absence of his story. Aware of Flynn's paradoxical presence/absence, his mourners do not speak as they gaze "at the empty fireplace," a disnarrated void that frames the unspeakable significance of their mourning. The "silence [takes] possession of the little room" as Eliza stops "suddenly as if to listen" to Flynn's disnarrated confession. Flynn's confession, however, is wordless, unreachable through the frames of verbal representation. There is "no sound in the house" despite narrative prompts that Flynn's mourners should "extract meaning from his unfinished sentences." Old Cotter, along with the others, can only respond to Flynn's disnarrated through speculation fragmented by wordless ellipses: "'I have my own theory about it,' he said. 'I think it was one of those . . . peculiar cases . . . But it's hard to say'" (2).

In choosing October 6, 1902, the anniversary of Charles Parnell's death, as the setting for "Ivy Day in the Committee Room," Joyce splits his narrative into two conflicting voices: that of the present and living against the continuous interruption of the past. Although the idea of Parnell governs the entire scene, dominating the men's conversation, cynicism, and mutual distrust, the dead leader's narrative appears only in fragments. The scene is unpleasantly dim aside from the dwindling presence of fire (fireplace, cigarettes), flickering with the past glory of the increasingly obscure Parnell. The hypodiegetic narrative of Parnell surfaces for brief moments, literally illuminating the story, for instance, when Mr. O'Connor's cigarette throws light on the ivy leaf in his lapel. Like the ghost of Flynn, the wake of Parnell is unspoken, incomplete, inadequately voiced by the disnarrative patchwork of the sycophantic Hynes and O'Connor. The living's insufficient containment of Parnell, who is now disnarratively "united with Erin's heroes of the past," evokes Friedrich Nietzsche's point that the "religion of the historical power . . . over and over again turns into a naked admiration of success, and leads to idolatry of the actual" (263).

As narrated, the gathered Dubliners listen to Mr. Hynes's ode to the dead Parnell, which is a "fine piece of writing." As fine as it may be, it is still a piece of writing, a constructed narrative that reflects its author's virtual narrative of the absent Parnell rather than the hypodiegetic reality of his life and death. Hynes's ode describes the fallen leader in disnarrated terms, Parnell's principal actions being the narratively incomplete verb forms *would have*, *dreamed*, and *strove*. The "truth" of Parnell has "faded into impalpability through death, through absence," and the story's irony rests in the mourner's contradictory attempts to account for the indefinable space between Parnell's presence and absence (*Dubliners* 118).

Even characters such as Henchy and Lyons who choose to disregard Parnell cannot refrain from filling in Parnell's fragmented narrative. In a struggle between the living and the dead, the diegetic and the hypodiegetic, Mr. Henchy refuses to allow Parnell's spirit into the room: he "snuffed vigorously" and "spat so copiously that he nearly put out the fire which uttered a hissing protest" (109). And if at times the main narrative appears on the brink of yielding to the demands of the hypodiegetic narrative, it is only temporary as the former is quick to reassert its dominance: "'Parnell,' said Mr. Henchy, 'is dead'" (116). In place of what we might call Parnell's "confession," his living adversaries write alternate disnarratives, less flattering than the equally "written" nostalgic memories of his supporters. His opponents' narratives, which emphasize his adultery, are perhaps as fabricated as any positive narrative that monumentalizes him. As with the case of Flynn, the secondhand memories of Parnell, whose death act remains distant from those framing his narrative, make a poor substitute for the dead leader's inaccessible revelation.

In "A Painful Case" Duffy is haunted and unmasked by Mrs. Sinico's suicide four years after their acquaintance. Once again the death act occurs far removed in time and space from its retelling. As Mrs. Sinico's death is revealed through an obituary far removed from the actual event, Joyce denies both Duffy and the reader direct access to the pivotal death scene though it is key to our full understanding of the story's kernels. The dispassionate news article well cites the necessary "death evidence" we as narratees require to believe the event has transpired (Lowe-Evans 396). However, the specific circumstances behind the event occur outside the narrative eye of the story, thereby producing the purely imagined worlds of conjecture.[5] In a similar scene from "The Sisters," an unemotional card pinned to the drapery door "persuades" the boy that Flynn is dead, thus prompting him to speculate through the rest of the story. In each case Joyce proves that even the "just the facts" straightforwardness of reportage treads the narrow pane of the disnarrative window and remains subject to conjecture.

After reading the obituary Duffy gazes out the window, a framed view of the disnarrated, and his memory begins "to wander" as "the light failed." Asking himself, "Why had he withheld life from her," he confirms the subordinate relationship between the main diegesis and the secondary narrative. Mrs. Sinico's death narrative falls silent, paraphrased and truncated in the shadow of Duffy's main diegesis. As Flynn's mourners sit in a silent room, Duffy waits "for some minutes listening . . . and [can] hear nothing" (102). Since Duffy does not have access to Mrs. Sinico's hypodiegetic narrative, he can only speculate as to the reasons behind her death based on his role as narratee to the secondary account of the event. As Duffy evokes "alternately the two images in which he now conceived her," his guilt stems not from the true event—for the cunning Joyce refuses to do more than crack open that narrative window—but from his own disnarrated version, which in turn egotistically rules her death a suicide.[6]

Joyce carefully points out that Duffy "began to doubt the reality of what memory told him." Later in "The Dead" Gretta also writes her own perceived reasons behind Michael Furey's death ("I think he died for me"), a death reported to her after the fact, and her choice of the unsure verb *think* mirrors Duffy's self-doubt in speculation. Duffy watches a train disappear as its engine reiterates "the syllables of her name." In a similar passage from "Araby," the young boy hears the "syllables of the word *Araby*," which cast a disnarrated "Eastern enchantment" over their listener, reminding us of the boy's dream in "The Sisters" in which he travels "very far away, in some land where the customs were strange—in Persia" (5). The disnarrated meaning of the bazaar remains distanced from the boy, leaving him "burned with anguish and anger" akin to Duffy's final lament that "he was alone." The disnarrated fragments of Mrs. Sinico's death or the inaccessible Araby entice their listener to speculate and fill in the "perfectly silent" narratives these hypodiegetics evoke.

Gabriel's speech in the "The Dead," much like the obituaries and odes in the earlier stories, summons a fragmented resurrection of the dead in its romantic comparison of the dead present with a living but virtual past. The hypodiegetic narratives of Michael Furey, Gabriel's mother, and the two Patrick Morkans, as well as others all rise from the dead to challenge the story's diegetic frame. As the mythologized monuments of the dead they represent, ghosts illuminate an unresolved past and the paralytic attempts of the living to narratively retrieve that history. Throughout "The Dead" and the collection as a whole, the living blur the line between memory and obsession in their inevitable re-creation rather than recollection of the deceased. The living summon the dead through the speculative stories and fragmented songs that dominate the Day of the Epiphany. In the previous stories the epiphanies suggested by Flynn, the Araby, Mrs. Sinico, and Parnell all remain narratively inaccessible to their narratees. Here the epiphanic meaning of the dead haunts the Morkan home and demands center stage as the story's title dictates. The epiphany lurks as a similar present absence, its meaning narratively validated and yet unattainable beyond disnarrated speculation. Once re-created, the dead become disnarrated entities, framed outside the diegesis, separate from both past and present. They reside in the purely imagined as fusions of fact and fiction, memory and creation.

As the story develops, we recognize that despite his resurrecting speech, Gabriel ironically denies the memory of the dead. Like Henchy in "Ivy Day" who wards off the rising hypodiegetic of Parnell, Gabriel refuses to relinquish the narrative floor to the dead that haunt the room: "Our path through life is strewn with many such sad memories: and were we to brood upon them always we could not find the heart to go on. . . . Therefore, I will not linger on the past" (184). When Gabriel enters the Morkan house, he vigorously scrapes the snow from his shoes as if to distance himself from the dead's snowy narrative, which will dominate the story's conclusion.

As a book reviewer, Gabriel critiques stories rather than writes them, a further indication of his distancing himself from the disnarrated stories of the dead. He is confined to the realm of language, which my dissertation on Virginia Woolf demonstrates as inaccessible to the purely imagined worlds of the disnarrated. His "restless eyes" avert the disnarrated behind the "cab windows rattling" in contrast to the "slow eyes" of Julia Morkan and Mary Jane. Unlike the speech-giving Gabriel, the two women reside in a disnarrated realm of music, which encompasses the dead in both its evocation of past singers and its uncontainable fluidity. The deadlike Julia Morkan and the inarticulate Mary Jane remain silent throughout much of the story, their voices heard only when they perform a prosopopeic singing of the dead's "old songs." At times when the diegesis of dialogue is silenced by "distant music" or stories, the hypodiegetic dead seem on the verge of overcoming the main diegesis. And yet Gabriel, the son of a Morkan sister who "had no musical talent," cannot listen while Mary Jane plays "to the hushed drawing-room." Unwilling to relinquish diegetic space to the music of the dead, he waits for the end of the piece with "resentment . . . in his heart," and still his eyes and thoughts begin to "wander," surfacing disnarrated memories of his dead mother and his engagement to Gretta (167–68).

Gretta's character contrasts significantly with Gabriel as she willingly rekindles her past. Despite Gabriel's warning her to wear galoshes because of the weather, Gretta insists on walking in the snow without them, a feat impossible for her husband. Her fragmented memory of Michael Furey, evoked through D'Arcy's song, sculpts a mythic figure or virtual reality of her lost love. As Gretta embraces the disnarrated of her dead lover, Gabriel stands "in a dark part of the hall gazing up the staircase." He does not recognize the woman "standing near the top of the first flight, in the shadow also" (189). As a disnarrated window with a partial view, D'Arcy's song "The Lass of Aughrim" paraphrases Gretta's relationship with Michael. The narrative, however, is incomplete, fragmented into three lines as Gretta cannot remember the title and D'Arcy forgets the words. In a similar scene from "Clay," Maria sings the disnarratively titled "I Dreamt that I Dwelt." Midway through her performance of "one of the old songs," she inadvertently sings the first verse twice. Analogous to D'Arcy's song, Maria's musical narrative is fragmented by both her inability to sing or "write" the second verse and its disnarrative dream of possibility.

What we learn of Michael Furey depends on Gretta's distant account of his narrative. In *Ulysses* we listen as Molly gets the details of her courtship with Bloom wrong: "how he kissed me under the Moorish wall" (933). Here the "truth" of Michael's hypodiegetic narrative is lost, rendered inactive and silent by the dominant, living, and fictionalized narrative of Gretta. His fragmented story is deprived of Gretta's narrative access to suspense and climax so that her narrative of Michael is just that—hers—a narrative based on what she merely "hears" from Michael's people. Both Gabriel and the reader subsequently listen to the circumstances behind Michael's death act through narrative filters tainted by time, distance, and subjectivity. Along with Gabriel, we must wonder "perhaps she had not told him all the story" (201). Although Joyce does not provide concrete evidence either supporting or refuting Gretta's story, our estimate of its accuracy hinges on her inconclusive *thinking* Michael dies for her. We must remember that even the story's title conceals the circumstances behind Michael's death act, focusing our attention on the ambiguous dead as opposed to the specific event of his dying.

Although this narrative filtering is not necessarily a modernist invention, the modern text relies on its development and manipulation as a defamiliarizing tool that brings to light the disnarrated possibilities of a story. It allows the fragmented juxtaposition of multiple perspectives, highlighting some views while concealing others. As a crucial precursor to modernism, Joseph Conrad uses multiple narrative layers to distance and disorientate his narratees from events key to the text. In the final scene of his narrative in *Heart of Darkness*, Marlow delivers his infamous lie to Kurtz's Intended:

> "The last word he pronounced was—your name."
> I heard a light sigh . . . "I knew it—I was sure!" . . . She knew. She was sure . . . But I couldn't. I could not tell her. (75–76)

Conrad demonstrates how easily a narratee is misled by the disnarrated of the dead. By sparing her the truth, Marlow literally changes the truth. But we must remember that as narratees removed from the actual event we too may be subject to narrative inaccuracies. Perhaps Marlow is unable to tell the truth even if he wanted to, considering he himself struggles to grasp Kurtz's message. Kurtz's final utterance of

"The horror! The horror!" frames the unspecified, dark and abstract contents of his epiphany. Its viewer senses its presence but cannot concretely define its meaning. Twice removed from Kurtz's narrative, the Intended now has the death evidence for her own disnarrative of the silent Kurtz. It is not difficult to imagine Gretta in a similar scene during which she would be spared "the horror" of Michael Furey's demise.

By the time Michael's story reaches Gabriel and he recognizes the snowscape outside the window, Gabriel senses a meaning behind it, but he is unable to discern exactly what it is:

Other forms were near. His soul had approached that region where dwell the vast hosts of the dead. He was conscious of, but could not apprehend, their wayward and flickering existence. His own identity was fading out into a grey impalpable world: the solid world itself, which these dead had one time reared and lived in, was dissolving and dwindling. (202)

The disnarrated behind the dead surfaces in indecipherable "forms," as Michael's narrative "dissolves and dwindles" with each subsequent narrative filter. The metaphor of Michael's death act has been so far distanced and defamiliarized that its meaning is filtered out. Unable to understand or accept Gretta's resurrection of the dead, Gabriel longs to be "master of her strange mood" (196). He remains disconnected from the meaning of Gretta's confession, watching her sleep "as though he and she had never lived together as man and wife" (201). Like Bloom and Molly, they lie together in bed, yet remain apart. The snow has not unified the couple; rather it has further alienated one narrative filter from another. The living's history of the dead proves to be a fragmented and fabricated disnarrative bridge, a reframing of truth subject to the inaccurate focalization of memory.

Notes

1. Certainly postmodernism's more radical experiments further partition narrative into conflicting diegetic and hypodiegetic voices. I have, however, omitted these experiments as they represent secondary developments based on the narrative lessons learned from modernist experimentation. Without an understanding of the modernist narrative, we lack the framework to understand the subsequent narratives of Samuel Beckett, Harold Pinter, Franz Kafka, and others.

2. Of course the stories were first serialized separately. They are also often anthologized individually, but together within the frame of a title, their intertextuality form a more cohesive, albeit fragmented, frame of Dublin.

3. John Mepham's "Mourning and Modernism" examines the absence of death (or of death serving as a work's closing action), in contrast to the distinct presence of mourning in Virginia Woolf. His essay equally applies to Woolf's Modernist contemporaries, especially Joyce.

4. Though Joyce's offstage death characterizes a Modernist strategy of de-familiarization, it is not necessarily a new device. Shakespeare's conspicuous refusal to "show" Ophelia's death suggests an equal disnarrative quality. As is often the case in Shakespeare, the "truth" of characters' deaths in Joyce may only be established through their narrative absence. All other circumstances surrounding their deaths remains speculative.

5. Suzanne Katz Hyman proposes that the news report is written in eu-phemistic and vague code phrases as a way of saying sotto voce that which cannot be uttered aloud. "The language of the newspaper," she writes, "seems, like all of the language in the story, inadequate to the job it has to do" (117).

6. *Ulysses* subsequently provides us with death evidence contrary to that of Duffy, thereby complicating and further obscuring the truth. Bloom asks if Stephen knew Mrs. Sinico who was "accidentally" killed at Sydney Parade station (815).

References

Conrad, Joseph. *Heart of Darkness: An Authoritative Text, Backgrounds and Sources, Criticism*. Ed. Robert Kimbrough. New York: Norton, 1988.

Doherty, Gerald. "Undercover Stories: Hypodiegetic Narration in James Joyce's *Dubliners*." *Journal of Narrative Technique* 22.1 (1992): 35–47.

Fletcher, John, and Malcolm Bradbury. "The Introverted Novel." *Modernism*. New York: Penguin, 1976.

Hyman, Suzanne Katz. "'A Painful Case': The Movement of a Story through a Shift in Voice." *James Joyce Quarterly* 19.2 (1982): 111–18.

Joyce, James. *Dubliners*. London: Minerva, 1992.

———. *Letters of James Joyce*. Vols. 1 and 2. Ed. Richard Ellmann. New York: Viking, 1966.

———. *Ulysses*. Ed. Seamus Deane. London: Penguin, 1992.

Lentricchia, Frank. *Modernist Quartet*. Cambridge: Cambridge UP, 1994.

Lindholm, Howard. "Shapes to Fill the Lack and Lacks to Fill the Shape: Fram-ing the Unframed in Modernist Narratives." Diss. Michigan State U.

Lowe-Evans, Mary. "Who Killed Mrs. Sinico?" *Studies in Short Fiction* 32.3 (1995): 395–402.

Mepham, John. "Mourning and Modernism." *Virginia Woolf: New Critical Es-says*. Ed. Patricia Clements and Isobel Grundy. London: Vision, 1986.

Miller, J. Hillis. *Fiction and Repetition*. Oxford: Oxford UP, 1982.

Nietzsche, Friedrich. *Untimely Meditations*. Ed. Daniel Breazeale. Trans. R. J. Hollingdale. New York: Cambridge UP, 1997.

Prince, Gerald. "The Disnarrated." *Style* 22 (1988): 1–8.

———. "Narratology, Narrative, and Meaning." *Poetics Today* 12.3 (1991): 543–52.

Shklovsky, Victor. *Theory of Prose*. Trans. Benjamin Sher. Elmwood Park, IL: Dalkey Archive, 1991.

Terdiman, Richard. "The Depreciation of the Event." *Remembrance of Things Past*. Ed. Harold Bloom. New York: Chelsea House, 1987.

POSTMODERN NARRATIVE
AROUND THE WORLD

Too often the misunderstanding exists that postmodernism is not a world literary movement/convention/craft. Authors around the globe struggle to break convention, to find new ways to tell the story. Christine Loflin's essay "Multiple Narrative Frames in R. R. R. Dhlomo's 'Juwawa'" discusses one of the first black South African short story writers, who published "Juwawa" in 1930. The complexity of life for black South African mine workers is reflected in this piece by the shifting narrative perspective and scene changes. The death of the white foreman, Loflin says, can be read in multiple ways: as a traditional revenge story, as an act of supernatural revenge, as an accident, or as an act of violent resistance to oppression. Loflin further states that Dhlomo cleverly reverses stereotypical racial roles, showing the white characters as ignorant and superstitious while the black protagonist is rational and cautious.

Allan Weiss, in his essay "Beyond Genre: Canadian Surrealist Short Fiction," explores one of the least-known postmodernist movements in the history of the Canadian short story: the small but active surrealist movement. Weiss discusses the history, themes, and techniques of surrealism, then traces the development of surrealist short fiction in Canada, especially on the west coast. Authors discussed include Michael Bullock, J. Michael Yates, Andreas Schroeder, and Eric McCormack. Weiss traces the roots to international surrealist beliefs and practices, and argues that surrealism has been one of the most revolutionary and enduring modes of postmodernist writing in Canada.

Fittingly, this collection ends with "Postmodernism in the American Short Story: Some General Observations and Some Specific Cases," Harold Kaylor's contemporary historical overview of postmodernism in the United States. Kaylor explores what he claims was a long overdue "shift in aesthetic consciousness" that had already swept much of the rest of the literary world, a shift in America brought on by great national stress due to the Cold War, Vietnam, Watergate, and political and racial assassinations. Kaylor discusses American postmodernism's general characteristics as well as specific writers including Vladimir Nabokov, Imamu Amiri Baraka, Kurt Vonnegut, Tim O'Brien, and Shirley Ann Grau.

Multiple Narrative Frames in R. R. R. Dhlomo's "Juwawa"

Christine Loflin

R. R. R. Dhlomo was the first black South African to publish a novel in English: *An African Tragedy* (1928). While his stature as an important figure in the history of black South African writing has been acknowledged, little attention has been paid to the specifics of his technique and style, especially in his short fiction. "Juwawa," published in 1930, is one of a number of English-language short stories he wrote in the 1920s and 1930s focusing on the experiences of black workers in the gold and diamond mines of South Africa. "Juwawa" is very brief; yet in its three pages it uses at least six different frames of reference, suggesting the complexity of Dhlomo's social vision and raising the question of how his work might fit into international modernist or postmodernist modes of writing.

Dhlomo was born in 1901 in Pietermaritzburg, South Africa. He was one of a small number of early-twentieth-century black journalists and writers, including his brother Herbert, the better-known short story writer, poet, and dramatist. There is very little research on Dhlomo's work. In 1975, *English in Africa* published some of his short fiction. In that issue, the primary emphasis was on Dhlomo's role as (possibly) the first black South African short story writer. In his introduction, Tim Couzens writes, "Any definitive histories, even assessments, of Black South African literature cannot fail to take the writings of R. R. R. Dhlomo into account. Many of the themes he raised are 'universal' to the Black South African condition and foreshadow the concern of present-day African writers" (1). Thus, Couzens makes a dramatic claim for Dhlomo's importance in black South African literary history. Yet he also says that "the formalists of literary criticism and the purists of New Criticism will miss the point if they dismiss this material as 'bad literature.' We are not here primarily concerned with evaluative criticism but with literary history" (1). This comment suggests that he does not find the stories to be significant in themselves, but rather for their role as inaugurating black South African short story writing in English. Couzens does say "care needs to be taken before snap judgements are made" (6).

Stephen Black, Dhlomo's editor at *Sjambok*, seems to have appreciated the art of Dhlomo's work, and encouraged him in both his journalism and his fiction writing. He says Dhlomo writes "with simple and direct force because he has not copied the established models" (qtd. in Couzens 4). Mbulelo Mzamane, who republished "Juwawa" in his collection of fiction, *Hungry Flames*, emphasizes a class analysis of the story: "Dhlomo employs bitter irony to convey the acrimony engendered by oppression and exploitation. . . . He depicts the working class as the vanguard of the African liberation struggle. In his class analysis and consciousness, Dhlomo is more revolutionary than many of his successors" (xi). Couzens, Black, and Mzamane all point to the significance of Dhlomo's work and career, but none provide a careful analysis of the complex narrative structure of "Juwawa."

Rolfes Dhlomo was Zulu, and was brought up in a traditional culture. He was educated at a missionary school, and later became the editor of the paper *Ilanga laseNatal*. His early journalism and short fiction is in English, as is "Juwawa." However, in 1934, he began writing in Zulu, and published several historical novels about the Zulu kings, including *Udingane* (1936) and *Ushaka* (1937), about the legendary Zulu kings Dingane and Shaka Zulu. These novels were among the first depictions of Zulu history in literature from a Zulu perspective.

The story of "Juwawa" is influenced by Dhlomo's cultural background, particularly the strategies of Zulu traditional storytelling. As N. N. Canonici points out in his article "Elements of Conflict and Protest in Zulu Literature," "Oral literature is multivocal; the surface or story level of a narrative can be followed and understood by any audience, even young children, but the deeper meanings, expressed at the symbolic level, are grasped through personal and group reflection, while the application to modern situations is derived from slight hints in the use of narrative details and language" (57). Literature in Zulu, Canonici contends, is influenced by this oral genre to express its values indirectly and to carry a double message: a surface message for casual readers, and a deeper, symbolic or moral message for a Zulu audience. Reading contemporary African short fiction in connection with traditional storytelling reveals that the stories benefit from a more thoughtful, integrated reading than simply a "close analysis" using Western readers' expectations.

"Juwawa" begins in the Survey Office of a South African gold mine. The white mine foremen are eating their lunch. They gossip about a recent death, and also talk about an absent foreman, George Garwin, who has been "beating his own men." The story then jumps to a scene in which Garwin is in bed, unable to sleep, after being reprimanded. There is a visual break marked in the story, followed by a scene in which Juwawa consults a witch doctor, Keleti. After another break, we learn there has been an accident; Garwin has been killed. This is reported to us through the white miners. The tone shifts to a journalistic perspective, reporting on an enquiry held by "The Commission." Although The Commission frees him, the white mine owners blacklist Juwawa, forcing him to leave. The final scene is of Juwawa headed for the train station, singing triumphantly. These different frames of reference in a three-page story signal the fragmented world that Dhlomo wishes to depict. Each scene suggests a different context for the plot— even a different understanding of what happens in the plot.

In the first scene, the white miners are presented through a third-person narrator. After the first two paragraphs, however, the scene consists primarily of dialogue, letting the white miners speak for themselves. One significant fact that emerges is that the white miners dislike their work, and claim that selling fish door to door would be preferable. So Dhlomo begins, not with whites enjoying their power, but with white characters who feel themselves to be trapped. Their conversation is about a recent accident on the mine, "involving the deaths of a miner and two natives" (1). This accident is not blamed on lack of attention to safety, but to the dangers of mine work itself. Raikes, the Chief Surveyor says "You never can tell what may happen underground. One minute a place looks as safe as a house, the next the darned thing is clattering about your ears—if you aren't killed, you are buried alive, so either way you get it in the neck!" (1). Their perspective is similar to white mineworkers in D. H. Lawrence's fiction; their lives are being absorbed into the machine, and their fates are no longer in their own hands but submitted to the chances of the mine work itself. This becomes the context for the major conflict of the story, between Garwin and his "Boss-boy" Juwawa.

The white miners are presented as fearful, almost superstitious. They are concerned about Garwin, not because he has been beating black workers—this is apparently acceptable—but because he has been "knocking *his* boys about" (emphasis added). This, they claim, needs to stop. Why? Because "some darned queer things happen underground"

(2). This superstitious phrasing repeats Raikes's warning that "you never can tell what may happen underground," and implies that the mine tunnels are in fact an underworld, where different rules apply. It also suggests the possibility of "queer" agency underground. Already, Dhlomo is setting up a dichotomy between the world aboveground, where whites are in control and can hit blacks with impunity, and the world belowground, where, alone with their own crew, "queer things" happen.

Their comment about the "queer things" that are possible underground also reveals their reluctance to attribute rational thought and resentment to blacks. It is not that the crew leader, Juwawa, will be reasonably angry, and might take revenge on Garwin for the beating aboveground, but that "things happen." Yet by taking refuge in a superstitious phrase rather than acknowledging the possibility of black revenge, the whites in Dhlomo's story prefer an almost magical reading of the underground mine to a rational analysis. In the 1920s and 1930s, the vast majority of whites in South Africa considered blacks to be racially and intellectually inferior; yet the white characters are the irrational, superstitious ones here.

Another indication of their fear and suspicion of their black workers is the question of language: Garwin, we are told, "can't speak their language, and they pretend they don't understand either English or Dutch, and so whatever suits them" (1). Again, expectations of racial superiority and authority are reversed here: the white character, we are told, is truly ignorant, unable to speak "their language" (black mine workers spoke a number of languages, including Zulu). But they say that the blacks *claim* not to speak English or Dutch. Thus, Garwin is the uneducated one, whereas the black workers are suspected of knowing two or three languages, but simply refusing to admit it. This, the white miners assert, is giving the black miners the upper hand with Garwin: they do "whatever suits them" (1). Garwin's violence is presented as a response to this reversal of power and authority, as shown in the next sentence: "As a matter of fact, he was knocking blazes out of his Boss-boy Juwawa when I passed him on 6 this morning" (1). The whites in this novel live fearful, superstitious, limited lives, afraid of accidents, and afraid of retribution for their savage physical acts.

These points are reinforced by the image of Garwin, unable to sleep, repeating the warning told to him by Raikes: "Never, if it possibly can be avoided, HIT ANY of YOUR OWN BOYS: hit any one else's, if you like, but not your own. SOME DARNED QUEER THINGS HAPPEN UNDERGROUND!" (2).

After this image there is a visual break (a blank line is left in the text; in the *English in Africa* version, a small colophon is added). The next scene is in the mine dumps. Juwawa, showing the effects of his beating, is consulting with Keleti, the "Shangaan witch-doctor." Here, Juwawa follows his own cultural practices. Beaten and angry, he does not strike back immediately, but consults with an elder about his course of action.

The setting, emphasizing the "towering waste-dumps" and the endless stamp of the mine batteries, crushing rock, place Juwawa and Keleti as small figures surrounded by the technology and waste of the mines. This again parallels Lawrence's mine stories, such as "Odor of Chrysanthemums," which opens with a scene of a woman pressing herself back into bushes to avoid the implacably advancing engine of a coal train. The landscape, and the human characters' roles within the landscape, are marked and circumscribed by the requirements of the technology.

While the white conversation in the first sections is represented as dialogue, here we do not know what Juwawa and Keleti say to each other. Instead, the scene is described as if a viewer is present who either cannot hear or cannot understand what they say. There are several possible explanations for this, the most obvious being to create suspense: What has Keleti suggested Juwawa should do? What will happen? Beyond this narrative suspense, however, Dhlomo's approach suggests a careful presentation of the interactions of different social and cultural worlds, which only come into contact in brief conflicts interspersed with silence and misinterpretations. The white and black characters have only partial understanding of each other, as a result of language barriers and dramatically different cultural readings of their situation. Throughout the story, Dhlomo limits the narrative point of view. The narrator shows us only what a white witness might have seen and observed—no black narrator, for example, would have been present in the Survey Office. A white witness would not understand this conversation between Juwawa and Keleti, which would not be in English or Afrikaans. Thus, the reader is kept at a similar distance, only able to watch, not hear, what happens.

An additional factor is the nature of the consultation itself—such conversations are private, personal communications; the witch doctor is Juwawa's intermediary with his ancestral spirits. Perhaps Dhlomo wishes to preserve a respect for the spiritual nature of this conversation by not revealing it to an outside audience.

After this scene, there is another visual break and the scene shifts back to the Survey Office. We are told that Garwin has been killed: "a jumper fell on his neck!" (3). Most readers reading this story for the first time conclude that Juwawa has taken his revenge, with the permission of Keleti: he has killed Garwin, and made it look like an accident. This reading produces a classic, predictable short story narrative: the revenge tale, or crime story. Several years ago, however, I had the privilege of having two South African students in my class. One of them, Lubabalo Bululu, suggested a dramatically different reading. He said, "Keleti told Juwawa to do nothing. The ancestors will take care of it." In this reading, Garwin is killed underground by the ancestral spirits, through the accidental fall of equipment. This reading opens up the story considerably; the story supports the traditional way of life, including its spiritual values, and shows it to be an effective agent in a Western-dominated, technological environment.

In the next few frames, we get a journalistic perspective on the accident, reporting the official conclusions of The Commission. The British-style court of inquiry examines the evidence and discharges Juwawa: there is not enough evidence to convict him. The white judicial reading of this story, then, is that Juwawa is not guilty. Interestingly, this accords with the black South African reading offered above—in both cases, Juwawa is not a criminal, although in the court version, the phrase *insufficient evidence* implies a reluctance to exonerate Juwawa completely. But this is not the end of the story.

After this verdict, Juwawa is sacked by the Mine as a troublemaker, and blacklisted. He will never be able to work in the mines again. Here, Dhlomo reveals the double standard of the white community. They ignore their own system of justice and apply a different rule to black workers: even the appearance of wrongdoing must be punished. Juwawa's behavior can be interpreted as consistent and rational, while the white characters are revealed as fearful, superstitious, and hypocritical—in only three pages.

The final scene shows Juwawa singing "Ya, Keleti! Ya, Keleti! That was good advice!" (3). Juwawa is now freed from the system that has been abusing him. Perhaps it is also a song of triumph at the revenge taken by the ancestors. The final word in the story, however, is deeply disturbing. Juwawa is identified, at the very end of this story, as "Juwawa, the savage" (3). Why would an elite black South African writer choose to identify his protagonist as "savage"?

There is a parallel to this ending in the conclusion of Chinua Achebe's *Things Fall Apart*, published thirty years later. The white district commissioner gets the last words of the novel, and tells us the title of the work he is drafting: *The Pacification of the Primitive Tribes of the Lower Niger*. Achebe's novel prepares the reader to read that title properly; we realize that the district commissioner is bringing conflict and destruction, not peace, and that the people in the novel are anything but primitive. A similar strategy is at work in "Juwawa." By the end of the novel, no reader, even a reader who believes Juwawa has taken his revenge and killed Garwin, can easily identify him as "savage." If he has acted, it is after repeated abuse in a system that offers no forum for complaint or redress for the sufferings of the black workers. The white workers, with their casual violence (Raikes tells Garwin, "hit anyone else's [boys], if you like"), their superstitious fears of the underground world, and their renunciation of their own justice system's conclusions, are much more savage or primitive in their beliefs and actions than Juwawa. Thus, it is parallel to Achebe's ending—readers are supposed to be disturbed by the word *savage* and we must reject it as a misrepresentation of the character of Juwawa. For Dhlomo's contemporary readers in the early 1930s in South Africa, that would be remarkable; blacks were still openly identified as savage. As J. M. Coetzee has said, "[W]hat is striking about the discourse of racism before 1945 is its nakedness, its shamelessness" (137). The story of Juwawa is a tremendous accomplishment, undermining and questioning the common language of the racist white population of South Africa.

Like oral folktales, this narrative, simple on the surface, reveals deeper meanings to a thoughtful audience. The story is also modern, even postmodern, in its form. Its depiction of working-class consciousness in the black and white mine workers parallels Lawrence's Welsh mine stories; its representation of different scenes in an extremely short story parallel Virginia's Woolf's techniques in "Kew Gardens" and "A Mark on the Wall." Further, the fragmented scenes, the gaps and silences in dialogue, and the shifts in frames of reference all create connections to a postmodern aesthetic.

For those who think of *postmodern* as a term in the periodization of literary history, a 1930 text may be too early. Frederic Jameson identifies the postmodern as a distinct cultural phase associated with late capitalism. (Historically, of course, it did begin as a reaction against the institutionalization of modernism in universities, museums, and concert halls against the canonization of a certain kind of architecture. This entrenchment is felt to be oppressive by the generation that comes of age, roughly speaking, in the 1960s [see Jameson in Stephanson 44]). Clearly, by this temporal designation, the Dhlomo story cannot be categorized as "postmodern."

The term *postmodern* has also been used more broadly: "[T]he postmodern displaces the rigidly periodized temporality that has hitherto governed the discourse of literary studies" (Readings and Schaber xiii); or, as Judith Butler has said, "[N]o postmodern could come after the modern, for the historical narrative that could secure the place of the 'before' and the 'after' had, through the collapse of temporal frames, lost its moorings" (234). Thus the "postmodern" collapses the "before" and "after" of literary periodicity; under this definition, a work can be postmodern in any period. The definition of *postmodern*, then, becomes a series of common features rather than the identification of a historical period.

Kwame Anthony Appiah warns against applying the term too easily to African literature and culture in his essay "Is the Post- in Postcolonial the Same as the Post- in Postmodern?" He points out in Jameson's articulation of postmodernity that "'postmodernism' is a name for the rejection of [modernism's] claim to exclusivity" (342). Appiah traces how African novels have moved from a first, nationalist phase into a postcolonial phase exemplified by Yombo Ouologuem's *Le Devoir de Violence*: "[Ouologuem] seeks to delegitimate the forms of the realist African novel" (349). This is distinct from the project of postmodernism, in Appiah's view, because it is "not an aesthetics, but a politics" (352–53). Thus, the postcolonial African novel and the products of postcolonial popular culture in Africa need to be considered apart from the postmodern, "for what the postmodern reader seems to demand of Africa is all too close to what modernism—in the form of the postimpressionists—demanded of it" (356). Rather than showing a rejection of a modernist culture, as in European postmodern texts, popular African culture is "not so much dismissive of as blind to, the issue of neocolonialism or 'cultural imperialism'" (348). He cites as an example a Yoruba sculpture of a man riding a bicycle; the bicycle can take its place as a part of an indigenous sculpture without implying an attitude toward the presence in Africa of this European invention.

Dhlomo's work does not fit neatly into either Appiah's first (national) or second (postcolonial) stage of fiction writing in Africa, because Appiah does not consider works written earlier than Achebe's *Things Fall Apart* (1958). Dhlomo, writing in 1930 within a Republic of South Africa that was itself considered part of the British dominions, is not yet outside of the colonial structures that Achebe analyzes and critiques. Yet he is part of the educated intellectual elite that will later produce writers such as Achebe and Ouologuem. Writing in English, Dhlomo's work has both a white and a black South African audience, and his work shows consciousness of this doubled position.

For example, his narrator only reports what would be known to a white observer. Yet within this perspective, the narrative voice shifts radically in tone and ideology. The original narrator reports the disaffection of the miners generally with some sympathy and without comment on their racist and violent culture. In reporting the inquiry's verdict on the accident, a magisterial voice is created: "Death, it appeared, was due to a terrific blow from an iron crowbar (jumper)" (3). This narrator does not assume that the reader will know what a *jumper* is, even though the term was used without definition previously: "yes, killed outright—a jumper fell on his neck!" (3). Thus, without warning, the narrative perspective has shifted. Knowing this, it is possible to read the earlier scene shifts as each representing a different narrative situation: the narrators of the opening scene, Garwin in bed, and Juwawa and Keleti may all be different voices. The white reader may blend these positions into one contradictory white perspective (simultaneously finding Juwawa not guilty yet firing him), while the black reader might gleefully recognize the deconstruction of the contradictions in white ideology in South Africa. Writing from within colonialism, Dhlomo is able to undermine and reverse the commonplace assessment of racial superiority, for the careful reader.

Butler in her "Skeptical Feminist Postscript" emphasizes the pleasure of the postmodern, using as her illustration a water aerobics class: "And here they were, entering the postmodern hybrid of 'hydrobics' to the 'remake' of an 'original' that belonged to an adolescent culture they never had. Now, happily, it reappeared in their present. They raised their huge thighs with obvious pleasure. I thought to myself that perhaps this was the collapse of temporal frames as the occasion for affirmation—and I dove in" (236). The fragmentation and playful secretiveness of "Juwawa" offer less of a fusion or hybridization than Butler's example, but the story still has parallels with works by postmodernist writers such as Roland Barthes or Thomas Pynchon. There is a potential for pleasure and affirmation in the reader's recognition of the author's accomplishment in "Juwawa," and the tacit creation of a community that recognizes the hypocrisy and superstition inherent in contemporary white ideology. If it asserts a "traditional" position (the ancestors will take care of things), it does so in a stylistically sophisticated and suggestive manner.

The reading also has political implications, as Mzamane suggests: Juwawa has freed himself from the oppressive, demeaning and dehumanizing life of the mines, and his jubilant singing at the end of the story is a call to African readers to reject the position that mine work has created for them. This social and political consciousness seems to go beyond the individual despair and individualized solutions of modernist fiction for soulless working conditions. The analysis in the story itself, suggesting that the white workers are also oppressed by their predicament, finds parallels in the socialist novels of the 1930s and 1940s in the United States. The racism of the white miners and their lack of solidarity with the black workers also reflects the failure of South African unions to unite white and black mine workers (Thompson 155). Thus, "Juwawa" is firmly linked to its historical context in its depiction of social relations on a South African gold mine.

The importance of the historical setting of the story and its realistic representation of landscape and event link it to traditional storytelling modes. However, the multiple readings of this narrative and the shifting spaces of the narrative suggest that the author of "Juwawa" was experimenting with an innovative mode of fiction in order to represent the complexity of black life in South Africa. That his story anticipates some of the elements of European and American postmodern experimental fiction only underscores the extraordinary nature of his accomplishment.

References

Appiah, Kwame Anthony. "Is the Post- in Postcolonial the Same as the Post- in Postmodern?" *Critical Inquiry* 17 (winter 1991): 336–57.

Butler, Judith. "A Skeptical Feminist Postscript. To the Postmodern." *Postmodernism Across the Ages*. Ed. Bill Readings and Bennet Schaber. Syracuse: Syracuse UP 1993. 233–37.

Canonici, N. N. "Elements of Conflict and Protest in Zulu Literature." *South African Journal of African Languages* 18.3 (Aug. 1998): 57–64.

Coetzee, J. M. *White Writing: On the Culture of Letters in South Africa*. New Haven: Yale UP, 1988.

Couzens, Tim. Introduction. *English in Africa* 2.1 (Mar. 1975): 1–7.

Dhlomo, R. R. R. "Juwawa." *Hungry Flames and Other Black South African Short Stories*. Ed. Mbulelo Mzamane. Essex, UK: Longman African Classics,1986. 1–3.

Mzamane, Mbulelo. Introduction. *Hungry Flames and Other Black South African Short Stories*. Ed. Mbulelo Mzamane. Essex, UK: Longman African Classics, 1986. ix–xxvi.

Readings, Bill, and Bennet Schaber. "The Question Mark in the Midst of Modernity." *Postmodernism Across the Ages*. Ed. Bill Readings and Bennet Schaber. Syracuse: Syracuse UP, 1993. 1–28.

Stephanson, Anders. "Regarding Postmodernism: A Conversation with Frederic Jameson." *Postmodernism/Jameson/Critique*. Ed. Douglas Kellner. Washington, DC: Maisonneuve, 1989. 43–74.

Thompson, Leonard. *A History of South Africa*. New Haven: Yale UP, 1990.

Beyond Genre: Canadian Surrealist Short Fiction

Allan Weiss

Among the least-known postmodernist "traditions" in the Canadian short story is the small but active surrealist one. The term *tradition* may not be appropriate; the history of surrealist fiction in Canada is short, and perhaps to talk of traditions violates the very spirit of post-modernism in general and surrealism in particular. Yet since the 1960s much exciting—and enigmatic—work in the Canadian short story has been accomplished by writers operating in the surrealist mode.

We need first to distinguish surrealism from magic realism. Magic realism refers to largely realistic narratives in which some element of the extreme or fantastic—the improbable—intrudes (Hancock, "Magic" 37). In surrealism, the fantastic element is more pervasive and, as we will see, accepted by the characters.

Surrealism's history can be traced to the post–World War I cultural reaction also embodied in Dadaism, Cubism, and the Lost Generation of writers (Chénieux-Gendron 12–25; Langford 249; Russell 124–28). These artists and writers saw the war as epitomizing everything that was wrong with bourgeois society, above all its systemization, restrictions, and inhibitions. They rejected conventional society's mores and codes of behavior in favor of greater freedom for the individual, and decried its faith in logic and the primacy of the conscious mind. Inspired, paradoxically enough, by the scientific researches of Sigmund Freud, they sought to tap into the unconscious for new sources of creative energy. One might expect such a philosophy to favor private visions over public responsibilities, but from its beginnings surrealism had a social purpose: to free humanity. The movement as it arose in

France during the postwar period was not seeking self-indulgent expression but liberation for the self and society as a whole from every restrictive and constricting force it could identify. As Mary Ann Caws says, "For [Breton], we should all be in permanent revolt against limits of all kinds" (*André Breton* 8). Surrealism's somewhat stormy relationship with Communism during the 1920s and 1930s illustrates both its revolutionary purpose and dissatisfaction with all ideological straitjackets (Caws, *André Breton* 6; Russell 154–63). Some surrealists looked to Oriental art and philosophy for a more holistic, antirational approach to thought and expression. One could say that in its rejection of any notion of defined form or limits as to subject matter, surrealism was one of the earliest expressions of postmodernism.

The leading figure and spokesman of the movement was André Breton (1896–1966). His two "Manifestoes of Surrealism" (1924, 1929) laid out the foundations of surrealist belief and practice, although during the intervening period he abandoned his faith in "automatic writing"—writing directed entirely by subconscious control. In his Second Manifesto he assigned a greater role to the author's active imagination as a shaping force for the work, in part because he feared the loss of individuality that seemed to attend the surrender of the self to the powers of the unconscious, in part because his reading of Leon Trotsky produced a more Hegelian, that is, dialectical, vision (Forest 55; Powrie 183). But what mattered was not so much the freedom of the author's mind as the freedom the reader would gain in his or her encounter with the text. Breton wanted the reading experience itself to be a liberating one, and the author's duty was to ensure that the work caused the reader to think in new ways, even if that meant conscious efforts to make the story seem more like the product of the unconscious (Langford 251, 254; Russell 142).

Thus, the "theme" of surrealist fiction, if it can be said to have one, is freedom, especially from rational thought and action. Surrealists portray a world of paradox and duality in which logical categories and distinctions are exploded. They seek integration rather than division, but not to the point of denying differences and thereby losing the dialectical tensions that result from the collision of opposites (Caws, *Poetry* 14–15; Powrie 185). Their works celebrate passion, nature, instinct—whatever bourgeois society tries to suppress or sublimate. Any passion, whether violent or erotic, is better than no passion at all (Chénieux-Gendron 2–3). The world they depict is that of dream, myth, and archetype, of images and symbols that appeal to the reader's imagination or spirit rather than his or her reason. As Russell puts it:

the surrealists sought to expand the possibilities of personal and collective behavior by breaking down what they felt to be the repressive barriers between
the unconscious and the conscious, between the irrational and the rational,
and between imagination and reason. From the resulting reconciliation of
these polarities, new forms of perception and behavior were to emerge which
would allow individuals to overcome their extreme alienation from their environment and other people. (122)

The quest was for a higher, integrated reality, or "surreality," beyond
our conventional fragmented existence (129). Here, we see a diver-
gence between surrealism and postmodernism, as the latter seeks to
celebrate rather than transcend that fragmentation.

Yet both strive to shock the reader into new perceptions and understanding through formal experimentation. Surrealists have offered
what is perhaps the most radical challenge we have seen to the conventions of short story form and content. The most characteristic feature of
a surrealist story is its "dreamlike" nature. This sense is achieved in two
main ways: by what takes place, and by how the characters react to
these events. First, the typical surrealist story, like surrealist painting,
involves vividly portrayed elements that are juxtaposed in surprising
ways (Caws, *Poetry* 19–20; Russell 146–47). Surrealist art is representational in the sense that figures and objects can be easily identified, but
they appear in odd combinations or with unreal characteristics—like
Dali's liquid clocks. In surrealist fiction, the scenes are also visually
striking thanks to the author's attention to detail, such as the precise
naming of plants. But wild animals appear in the midst of cities, or objects or events take on extreme dimensions in space and time. A character's actions and movements may be complete non sequiturs: there
seems to be no logic behind what a character does, except perhaps a
magical logic. Also, stories usually involve metamorphosis; as in
dreams, inanimate objects suddenly turn into animate beings and vice
versa. Humans and animals change into each other, but not without
some obvious symbolic meaning—for example, women with violent natures may become tigers. Women characters are often magical, and
seem to act as spirit guides or embodiments of nature (Russell 138–39).

The stories are usually short and move swiftly, maintaining a high
level of elemental energy. The events do not form "plots" so much as series of encounters with strange beings and events. Stories frequently
involve doubles, even doppelgangers; surrealists seek to undercut our
assumptions about logical oppositions, so characters, objects, and natural beings (organic and inorganic) turn out to be or end up becoming
each other.

The protagonist's reactions are a key element to the effect. Magical things happen in fantasy generally, but what distinguishes surrealist from other fantasy is that protagonists take the juxtapositions and transformations largely in stride. Protagonists in high fantasy usually understand the magical world in which they live, accepting its rules and operating within them. Protagonists in horror stories may or may not understand the rules, and respond with the same degree of terror we would in the same circumstances. In both cases, we accept and even share the characters' emotions. The protagonist in surrealist fiction, on the other hand, generally does not understand what is happening, but more importantly exhibits little emotional response to it. The protagonist's reactions are therefore at least as surprising to us as the events themselves, and constitute one of the main disorienting, or estranging, features of the work. In addition, the protagonist is often an isolated, alienated individual with little or no defined social role; therefore, he or she is both free to engage in bizarre journeys and experiences, and unable to share them (either during the events or after) with someone from "normal" society.

The language of surrealist fiction reflects the author's aim to attract and surprise the reader. The attraction, as we have seen, comes from precise, vividly descriptive prose that arouses sharp images in the reader's mind. The protagonist's acceptance of the inexplicable events is conveyed through a neutral, matter-of-fact tone; many surrealist stories are told in the first person, and the narrator recounts his or her experiences as if recounting an everyday incident. Language occasionally contributes to the surprise by playing with clichés—abstractions become concrete, so that "following a road" may turn into a literal pursuit. Such highlighting of language in order to jar the reader into rethinking its nature is another postmodern characteristic of the genre.

Canadian surrealism exhibits most if not all of these traits. Its particular history began in the 1960s; few examples of experimental or surrealist prose can be found before then. Of course, surrealists were not the first Canadian writers to challenge literary conventions. Writers of the 1930s like Morley Callaghan and Thomas Murtha sought to bring greater immediacy to their fiction by portraying marginalized characters, constructing less "well-made" plots, and using naturalistic diction; later, Modernist writers like Hugh Hood began to experiment with symbolist narratives. Surrealists like Michael Bullock, J. Michael Yates, Andreas Schroeder, and Eric McCormack similarly reject what they see as the artificiality of conventional form, but also reject social realism in order to depict a different kind of reality. Surrealism is thus a philosophy as well as a mode. It would therefore not be entirely true to say that these writers are entirely antirealist; rather, they are realists of a different sort, having a different concept of what is real.

The surrealist movement in Canada has largely been a west coast movement, for a variety of reasons. First, as scholars have shown, west coast culture has developed in very distinctive ways; generalizations about the "garrison mentality" and "survival" as themes in Canadian literature do not apply to a region where the climate is not so hostile. Indeed, west coast writing—like surrealist writing—takes a very positive view of nature and often emphasizes both the need for and the possibility of communion with it (Hancock, "Magic" 32; Pritchard 97). It is no coincidence that one of the first writers to experiment with a symbolist approach to nature and native mythology was west coast writer Sheila Watson. The primitivist and holistic spirit that we see in much British Columbia literature is the expression of a culture that proved to be fertile ground for the surrealists who arrived or emerged in the late 1960s. As Schroeder has said, "[B]eing who we are out there [in British Columbia] . . . almost *requires* that we be 'experimental'" (Hancock, "Interview" 55). Bullock has said, "I am . . . led to believe that it is B. C. itself which fosters the surrealist spirit" (Parkin 162).

The timing is also worth noting. Like the 1920s, the 1960s was a period of reaction against the repressive nature of bourgeois society. The revolt of the 1920s was triggered by World War I; the revolt of the 1960s was triggered by McCarthyism, the conformism of the 1950s, and the Vietnam War. Like their forebears, the cultural revolutionaries of the 1960s sought to liberate the individual from all that might oppress him or her, and writers sought to throw off what they saw as the literary shackles of realist fiction. Again like their earlier counterparts, many west coast writers in particular began to explore Eastern philosophy and culture, seeking nonrational, non-Western modes of thought and expression.

An additional factor was the rise of the university as the dominant institution supporting the writing, publishing, and reading of short fiction. With the decline of mass-market magazine publishing as a viable outlet for short story writers, the university emerged as the institution where writers could gather to share ideas, establish creative writing departments with distinctive aesthetic approaches, found and publish literary magazines and small presses, and provide or even create audiences for their work. The universities, above all the University of British Columbia, played a vital role in enabling the rise of Canadian surrealist fiction.

Perhaps the earliest manifestation of west coast surrealism was the literary magazine *Limbo* (1964–67?). Primarily a poetry magazine, it was published by the Neo-Surrealist Research Foundation in Vancouver and edited by Murray Morton. But the most important development was the arrival at the University of British Columbia's Creative Writing Department of J. Michael Yates in 1967 and Michael Bullock in 1969. Bullock has become Canada's André Breton: the country's major practitioner and theorist of surrealism. He encountered surrealist art in 1936, although he had been writing surrealist poetry before that (Parkin 164). He has published a number of surrealist stories, and articles explaining and defending the surrealist approach. His stories reflect much of what we have seen as the main characteristics of surrealist fiction, and operates from the point of view expressed by Breton in his Second Manifesto. Bullock rejects the notion that automatic writing can lead to true surrealist fiction. He argues in an article entitled "Surrealism and the Future of Fiction" (1981) that the whole point of surrealism is to combine opposites in vigorous tension—including the conscious and unconscious minds (cf. Parkin 143–45). Valorizing the unconscious over the conscious, he asserts, violates the spirit of surrealism; also, he believes in the author's responsibility to shape the text, and give it coherence, so that it will fulfill its designed ends of surprising and liberating the reader—not rationally, but through "free association" (Parkin 145). Above all, he seeks a higher integration of apparently opposing forces, especially inner and outer worlds (Parkin 149; Stewart passim).

His early stories, published in *Sixteen Stories as They Happened* (1969) and *Green Beginning Black Ending: Fables* (1971), are usually set in gardens and forests, and involve characters being drawn into strange encounters with metamorphosing creatures and mysterious humans, usually women. Bullock's is not a Romantic vision of nature; his primitive worlds are not idylls, but are full of violence or the threat of it. Yet all of nature is infused with spirit, reflecting an animist vision; "[t]his state of animism represents the breakdown of the barrier between inside and outside, mind and nature, that Breton describes as the aim of surrealism" (Stewart 93; cf. Parkin 148). Symbolizing that violence in many of the stories are crocodiles hidden in apparently placid rivers. Meanwhile, the women his narrators meet, like Selva in "The Green Girl" (*Green Beginning* 15–36), seem to be nature spirits; indeed, Selva's name means "forest" in Italian. In this story, a bull represents violent passion that the narrator is both attracted to and repelled by. The stories in this volume feature elements of the natural world violating their "normal" characteristics in order to show the dual, indeed paradoxical, quality of reality. Thus, in "The Trees and the Fish" logs enter the sea and become snakes, while sea creatures come onto the land and become inorganic objects (*Green Beginning* 45–46). Our simple categories of land and sea creatures, and of living and nonliving beings, are annihilated in an orgy of metamorphosis.

For Bullock, passion is both a constructive and a destructive force; neither aspect is better than the other, and passion of any kind is preferable to stasis and indifference. In "The Scent of Honey," a story that embodies very clearly the dialectical vision of surrealism, a group of beehives exudes a honey scent that arouses erotic passion in the women who live nearby. The bees are destroyed by invading anti-bees, who take over the hives and produce a scent that causes these same women to become violent. A new bee invasion leads to "a conflicting duality of emotion" (*Green Beginning* 103). In reaction, the people of the district have the hives destroyed altogether. But the result is "deadly tedium and monotony," and a sense of regret at lost emotional intensity (103–04).

Bullock's themes and techniques have remained consistent throughout his career. In his more recent volumes of short fiction, such as *The Man with Flowers through His Hands* (1985) and *The Invulnerable Ovoid Aura and Other Stories* (1992), he continues to portray isolated narrators experiencing visions in primitive settings. The title story of the first volume concerns a weeping man whose tears grow larger as they fall toward a lake, producing splashes whose spray causes holes to form in his hands. He inserts flowers in the holes, finds he cannot remove them, and is left both blessed and cursed by his very physical communion with nature. "Battle of the Characters" highlights the power of language; in this story, the Chinese characters for diseases and weapons are themselves able to inflict harm. Also, the technique of rendering the abstract concrete can be seen in "The Man and His Intuition"; the man's intuition is a separate character whom he pursues into a river, apparently in vain. Bullock's humor is illustrated in "By the Canal" in which a man has a quasi-Arthurian meeting with a Water Spirit who offers him a black stone he simply returns, oblivious to the gift's potential. Throughout, Bullock uses very precise language to convey a vivid portrait of his settings, naming specific plants and trees (Loeffler 37).

Bullock's stories contain a number of common images and symbols: rivers (symbolizing flux or the unknown), birds, crocodiles, secret gardens, labyrinths, mirrors, and gates, doors, and other means of entry and exit (Loeffler passim). "Roditi," from *The Invulnerable Ovoid Aura*, includes a number of these motifs. Roditi lives literally with his feet on the ground (he even creates vegetation where he walks) and his head in the clouds. There is no line between what he imagines and what is "real" in the story's context; whatever he creates in his mind exists or occurs, whether constructive or destructive. He walks to the end of his garden, finds no gate (although one used to exist), and creates an opening with a touch of his finger. After a number of adventures, including a meeting with a typical Bullockian female spirit guide named Ombra, he uses the same technique to return to his garden and, perhaps, to a higher form of innocence.

Throughout Bullock's corpus runs the figure of Noire, a character based on a real woman, who can be interpreted in a variety of ways but appears to be primarily the dark or hidden side of the narrator (Parkin 147). She may well be his anima, or, since she is so enigmatic, the incomprehensible basis of reality. More simply, she may represent Bullock's lost mother, who died when he was young (Parkin 158). In any case, her role is obviously to be an Other of some kind, one who provides the catalyst for the narrator's adventures and education.

Before Bullock's arrival, J. Michael Yates came from the United States to join the department. His interests were in Latin American magic realism, and his work reflects the influence of Jorge Luis Borges above all. His "Realia," for example, published in *Fazes in Elsewhen* (1976), is about a Borgesian library that contains, quite literally, everything. Unlike Bullock, Yates often sets his stories in cities; his themes are less about the dichotomy between man and nature than the dehumanizing effects of modern society. One of the best examples is "The Passage of Sono Nis"; the narrator leaves his apartment building to discover an endless stream of runners, who leave the dead bodies of the trampled lying crushed in his doorway. If he remains indoors he will be trapped, and starve, so the narrator joins the human river and its perpetual race that is, for everyone, without purpose or destination. "Smokestack in the Desert" is about industrialism gone mad: the workers in the "plant" endlessly stoke the furnace, thereby producing nothing but toxic fumes, and the smokestack stands in the middle of a wasteland of its own creation. In "The Sinking of the Northwest Passage," Commodore Eric F. F. Forrer is the captain of a ship he has built in his driveway, far from any body of water. When the *Northwest Passage* begins to sink into the asphalt—in an event whose scientific impossibility attracts little surprise from Forrer or his wife—he bravely goes down with the ship. He is an excellent example of a man who has found in fantasy the intense life that contemporary society denies him. To his glee, of course, fantasy becomes "reality" of a sort.

Yates also writes frequently about the role of the artist in society; in "The Broadcaster," a radio announcer speaks to an absent audience, while Sono Nis, Photographer, is a recurring character who uselessly tries to preserve the past and succeeds only in having no real life (see especially "An Inquest into the Disappearance and Possible Death of (the Late) Sono Nis, Photographer" [111–32]). The artist, Yates may be suggesting, has been rendered mute or irrelevant by society's indifference to his message, or by certain artists' determination to focus on superficial images of the real, rather than become part of what is alive and life affirming.

Andreas Schroeder studied with Yates and Bullock, receiving his M.F.A. in Creative Writing from the University of British Columbia in 1971. *The Late Man* is a collection of mostly surrealist stories published in 1972 by Yates's Sono Nis Press. In an article that appeared in the first issue of *Canadian Fiction Magazine*, he expresses his dissatisfaction with realism:

the short story must be able to accommodate a denser, tighter language, a more lyrical, alogical progression of events and thought, a greater number of realities. . . . The allegory, the parable, the amplified metaphor must be pulled back into play. ("The 'New' Short Story" 5)

His "The Roller Rink" is very much like Yates's "The Passage of Sono Nis," and may well have been inspired by it. In the story, a visitor to a small German city wishes to skate in a popular roller rink. As we have seen, surrealist stories often feature extreme dimensions; in this case, the narrator must wait months for his turn, and when he finally does join the crowds skating around the oval track he skates nonstop for a dozen years. He becomes a manager of the rink, and he strives to render the walls so featureless that people will not notice their circular path and become dizzy. The story's structure mirrors the rink's: at the beginning, the narrator notices a human-shaped hole in the building's wall—a hole that magically disappears—and at the end he loses his balance and crashes through the wall. Like Yates's story, "The Roller Rink" is about a mindless race to nowhere except death, perhaps commenting on the nature of modern life or life in general. As Schroeder has said of the story:

this was the perfect metaphor, an exact miniature replica of the shape of our lives; our endless, almost mindless repetition of our customs and traditions pursued day after day in safe predictable cycles, which few challenged and fewer escaped. ("Irresistible" 277)

Schroeder's stories are often about alienated characters, such as the fisherman in the title story of the volume, who finds his routine moving more and more out of synch with that of the other fishermen.

Other writers influenced by Yates and Bullock include Rikki Ducornet, George McWhirter, and Ernest Hekkanen. Later, and elsewhere, the short-lived literary magazine *Ichor: A Magazine of Surreal Prose* was edited by L. Andrew Coward out of Ottawa and appeared for two issues (1980–81). Some of the writers published in it were Beverley Daurio, Bruce K. Filson, and Don Austin.

A more recent surrealist writer to emerge is Eric McCormack. His story collection *Inspecting the Vaults* (1987) contains a number of nightmarish surreal tales; like Bullock, he is very much aware of the existence and power of violence. But the violence in McCormack is human violence—characters who are supposed to be civilized display an astonishing underside of viciousness (Alford 26; Manicom 151). The title story concerns a small settlement made up of cloyingly named cottages that house criminals in their "vaults," or dungeons. The civilized facades of the homes do not adequately conceal the horrors within— the narrator, the local Vault Inspector, refers frequently to the wailing that regularly breaks forth. He is supposed to be a representative of the established order, a repressive and self-righteous government. But as we learn he is not merely a simple bureaucrat or moral arbiter; he has apparently committed some horrific murders of his own, and the prisoners he oversees end up seeming far more benign than the Inspector or the government he represents. Civilization, we see, is a thin veneer covering truly horrible realities. In "Sad Stories in Patagonia," we cannot—are not allowed to—maintain the comfortable illusion that we are listening to nothing more than a campfire ghost story told within a conventional adventure tale.

Perhaps the most surreal story in the volume is "The Swath," in which a rectangular cut suddenly begins working its way around the globe. As in other surrealist stories, the characters' reactions are unexpected: people greet the oncoming swath with glee rather than fear or horror, and some even elect to disappear into it. Other than what disappears, nature remains largely unaffected: rivers continue to flow into the swath and out of it, but nothing exists in it. Objects are neatly divided, but no people or animals are dismembered—either one disappears entirely, or escapes entirely. When the swath completes its circumnavigation of the world, in exactly twenty-four hours, it vanishes, and everything but the people return unharmed and unaffected. Yet no one mourns those who disappeared, because the swath has become a quasi-religious experience for everyone, and victims are believed to have transcended life rather than lost it. Once the swath is gone, the authorities try to erase its memory, and the religious movements that it inspired, the way the swath had erased much of the globe for a day;

clearly, such transcendental thinking is seen as dangerous by those in power. Like Yates and Bullock, then, McCormack recognizes those aspects of our natures and of life in general that conventional society (especially government) denies and suppresses. Wisdom comes from accepting these less pleasant or less controllable realities, and freeing ourselves from the political, social, and cultural blinders we wear.

As we have seen, surrealists frequently label their stories "fables": tales designed to convey a moral of some sort (on modern fabulation, see Robert Scholes passim). Whereas realist fiction takes an "objective" stance, seeking to portray the world without overt comment, surrealist fiction continues to exhibit its social purpose by unabashedly striving to influence its readers. Canadian surrealists, like their French forebears, use fantasy to open their readers' eyes, appealing to our conscious and unconscious minds in order to liberate us from conventional thinking. Thus, Bullock exposes the yin-yang character of the natural and human realms; Yates and Schroeder depict the loss of human values in our dehumanizing society, and the meaninglessness of life; and McCormack reveals the violence and spiritual emptiness underlying our civilized facades.

Fantastic literature has become an increasingly important part of the Canadian literary scene in recent years. As part of that trend, and in keeping with the purposes and techniques of postmodernism generally, surrealism continues to provide a remarkable source of new approaches to form and content. Like other postmodern movements, it emphasizes continuing revolution in style, structure, and subject matter, defying conventions and unsettling the reader as it offers new insights into hidden realities that can only be seen in our literary dreams and nightmares.

References

Alford, Edna. "Art of Darkness." Rev. of *Inspecting the Vaults*, by Eric McCormack. *Books in Canada* May 1987: 26–27.

Balakian, Anna. *The Snowflake on the Belfry: Dogma and Disquietude in the Critical Arena*. Bloomington: Indiana UP, 1994.

Breton, André. *Manifestoes of Surrealism*. Trans. Richard Seaver and Helen R. Lane. Ann Arbor: U of Michigan P, 1969.

Bullock, Michael. *Green Beginning Black Ending: Fables*. Port Clements, BC: Sono Nis, 1971.

———. *The Invulnerable Ovoid Aura and Other Stories*. London, ON: Third Eye, 1992.

———. *The Man with Flowers through His Hands*. London, ON: Third Eye, 1985.

————. *Sixteen Stories as They Happened*. Vancouver, BC: Sono Nis, 1969.

————. "Some Thoughts on Writing." *Canadian Fiction Magazine* 1 (1971): 1–4; rpt. *Canadian Fiction Magazine* 50–51 (1984): 137–40.

————. "Surrealism and the Future of Fiction." *Canadian Fiction Magazine* 39 (1981): 17–23.

Caws, Mary Ann. *André Breton*. New York: Twayne, 1996.

————. *The Poetry of Dada and Surrealism: Aragon, Breton, Tzara, Éluard, and Desnos*. Princeton: Princeton UP, 1970.

Chénieux-Gendron, Jacqueline. *Surrealism*. Trans. Vivian Folkenflik. New York: Columbia UP, 1990.

Fogel, Stanley. "'McBorges.'" Rev. of *Inspecting the Vaults*, by Eric McCormack. *Essays on Canadian Writing* 37 (1989): 137–45.

Forest, Philippe. *Le mouvement surréaliste: poésie, roman, théâtre*. Paris: Vuibert, 1994.

Hancock, Geoff. "An Interview with Andreas Schroeder." *Canadian Fiction Magazine* 27 (1977): 47–69.

————. "Magic or Realism: The Marvellous in Canadian Fiction." *Magic Realism and Canadian Literature: Essays and Stories: Proceedings of the Conference on Magic Realist Writing in Canada*. Ed. Peter Hinchcliffe and Ed Jewinski. Waterloo: U of Waterloo P, 1986. 30–48.

Keefer, Janice Kulyk. "Daughters & Demons." Rev. of *Inspecting the Vaults*, by Eric McCormack. *Canadian Literature* 116 (1988): 218–19.

Langford, Michele K. "The Concept of Freedom in Surrealism, Existentialism, and Science Fiction." *Extrapolation* 26 (1985): 249–56.

Loeffler, Peter. "The Poet as Alchemist: Five Thoughts on Michael Bullock." *Canadian Fiction Magazine* 84 (1993): 34–47.

Manicom, David. Rev. of *Inspecting the Vaults*, by Eric McCormack. *Rubicon* 9 (1987): 150–52.

Matthews, J. H. *Surrealism and the Novel*. Ann Arbor: U of Michigan P, 1966.

McCormack, Eric. *Inspecting the Vaults*. Markham, ON: Penguin, 1987.

McMullin, Stanley E. "'Adams Mad in Eden': Magic Realism as Hinterland Experience." *Magic Realism and Canadian Literature: Essays and Stories: Proceedings of the Conference on Magic Realist Writing in Canada*. Ed. Peter Hinchcliffe and Ed Jewinski. Waterloo: U of Waterloo P, 1986. 13–22.

Parkin, Andrew. "An Interview with Michael Bullock." *Canadian Fiction Magazine* 50–51 (1984): 141–66.

Powrie, Phil. "Automatic Writing: Breton, Daumal, Hegel." *French Studies* 42 (1988): 177–93.

Pritchard, Allan. "West of the Great Divide: A View of the Literature of British Columbia." *Canadian Literature* 94 (1982): 96–112.

Richardson, Michael, ed. *The Dedalus Book of Surrealism (The Identity of Things)*. Sawtry, UK: Dedalus, 1993.

Russell, Charles. *Poets, Prophets, and Revolutionaries: The Literary Avant-Garde from Rimbaud through Post-Modernism*. New York: Oxford UP, 1985.

Scholes, Robert. *The Fabulators*. New York: Oxford UP, 1967.

Schroeder, Andreas. "The Irresistible Force and the Immoveable Object." *Transitions II*. Ed. Edward Peck. Vancouver, BC: CommCept, 1978. 275–77.
———. *The Late Man and Other Stories*. Port Clements, BC: Sono Nis, 1972.
———. "The 'New' Short Story." *Canadian Fiction Magazine* 1 (1971): 5.
Stewart, Jack. "The Surrealist Art of Michael Bullock." *Canadian Fiction Magazine* 59 (1987): 86–105.
Yates, J. Michael. *The Abstract Beast*. Port Clements, BC: Sono Nis, 1971.
———. *Fazes in Elsewhen: New and Selected Fiction*. Vancouver, BC: Intermedia, 1976.

Postmodernism in the American Short Story: Some General Observations and Some Specific Cases

Noel Harold Kaylor

Compared to postmodernism's development in other countries, its appearance in the United States came fairly late. Larry McCaffery (after respectfully mentioning literary experimentation by William Faulkner, Gertrude Stein, F. Scott Fitzgerald, Djuna Barnes, Kenneth Patchen, Nathaniel West, John Hawkes, and Jack Kerouac) says:

for whatever reasons in the United States from the period of 1930 until 1960 we do not find the emergence of a major innovator—someone equivalent to Beckett or Borges or Alain Robbe-Grillet or Louis Ferdinand Céline—except in the person of perhaps postmodern fiction's most important precursor, Vladimir Nabokov. . . . As a result, by the late 1950s the United States was just as ripe for an aesthetic revolution as it was for the cultural revolution that was soon to follow. (xiv–xv)

A sweeping statement such as this, of course, demands some further comment.

It was in the early 1960s that experimentation *in literary form* by U.S. authors converged with a receptive audience to facilitate the rise of postmodern fiction. Jerome Klinkowitz describes this phenomenon of coincidence in terms of "literary disruptions." Writing specifically about developments in the novel, he begins his first book with this rather tantalizing sentence: "Fiction breeds its own continuity." Up to about 1960, the *form* of the American novel had changed little from the time when it arose as a meaningful genre:

despite all the cultural and historical innovations in topic, it was the old-fashioned *form* for this content—in the guise of a mimetic pretense at life—which was the most debilitating thing of all. If the world is absurd, if what passes for reality is distressingly unreal, why spend time representing it? (Klinkowitz 32)

The salient points here are that the innovations through which post-modernism finally gained its success in the United States were in form and structure rather than content and in the postmodernists' inventive alternatives to realist representation of the "world outside of the work." Instead of drawing a reader's attention to conditions that prevail "out-side," in the mundane universe that surrounds a work, these innovations drew it "inward," toward the literary object itself, questioning the very principles by which fiction has been produced in the West since the invention of the written text.

What were some of the forces that led to the shift in aesthetic con-sciousness in the United States during the 1960s? The postmodern writ-ers and the postmodern audience had lived through a period of great stress: specifically, the era of the Cold War with its threat of nuclear an-nihilation. Then came the American War in Vietnam with its graphic, televised reporting, the Watergate scandal (culminating in the resigna-tion of a disgraced president), various political and racial assassinations (almost making of national mourning a national pastime), and the em-powerment of some minorities (further fragmenting national consensus and dispersing influence among newly established political groups).

What distinguished these sources of stress from those experienced earlier in the century? Perhaps a major difference was the loss of any sense of justification for the violence that surrounds us. Propaganda used during and after World War II stimulated a generally accepted sense of moral rectitude concerning U.S. action in Europe and to a lesser extent, due to exploding atomic bombs in Japan, in Asia. The ar-bitrariness of Cold War events and their aftermath, however, strained all notions of universal justice to the breaking point. After about 1960, the use of violence and force had lost the moral imperative that it seemed to have gained during the conflicts of the earlier half of the century. It also lost some of its sensational impact; violence and force gradually came to characterize the quotidian experiences on our na-tion's streets. The perception of order in the universe had changed. Events and the ordering of events appeared to be absurd.

The term *postmodernism* refers to a movement in the arts that gained definition during the latter half of the twentieth century. It does not designate the aesthetic agenda of any particular national tradition so much as that of a worldwide cultural movement, but the approach taken by each national tradition does distinguish it to some degree from the others. In an effort to define the movement, literally thousands of books and articles devoted to postmodernism, or various aspects of it, have appeared over the past several decades.

This study comprises a brief introduction to aspects of postmodernism in the United States.[1] The first part presents some prominent features of postmodernism in U.S. literature; the second part focuses on several significant short stories that variously manifest these characteristics. Together, the two parts present an overview of the theory and practice of postmodernism in the short story in the United States.

General Characteristics

The general features of postmodernism fall into five categories, which are all interrelated. First, an effort is made by postmodernists to emphasize the "surface" of the text. An examination of one of the early textual influences on many of the U.S. postmodern writers may help to bring this somewhat cryptic notion into focus.

In 1962, "The Circular Ruin," a short story by Jorge Luis Borges (1899–1986), an Argentinean writer, was published in English, and it has had tremendous influence on U.S. writers. It is written in even-paced, descriptive, and narrative prose that is interrupted only rarely by thoughts quoted directly from the mind of the protagonist. This protagonist has a curious mission: "He wanted to dream a man: he wanted to dream him with minute integrity and insert him into reality" (46). In this short story, it is the combination of Borges's insistence on a lyrically measured narrative and the subject's insistent pursuit of his mission that keeps the reader's attention fixed firmly on the narrative per se. Implications in the story for the universe outside the text indeed exist, but they arise only in retrospect, after one has finished reading.

The subject character arrives, in mythic time and amid a mythic landscape, at the site of a jungle temple long since destroyed by fire. After resting, he begins his step-by-step project. He makes a few false starts, but during the course of several years of intense dreaming, "He dreamt a complete man, a youth, but this youth could not rise nor did he speak nor could he open his eyes" (48). Then, finally, "In the dreamer's dream, the dreamed one awoke" (48). This "dreamed one" undergoes a thorough apprenticeship and eventually is sent out, unaware of his origin, to maintain another temple downstream.

The dreamer worries, however, that his dreamed one might someday discover that he is not a man but the "projection of another man's dream" (50), and also he remembers that "of all the creatures of the world, fire was the only one that knew his son was a phantom" (49).

Somewhat later, his own circular ruins are again threatened by fire. With stoic resignation, he walks into the flames to be destroyed with his temple, but he is amazed to discover that the flames do not harm him: "With relief, with humiliation, with terror, he understood that he too was a mere appearance, dreamt by another" (63). Thus, the circularity indicated in the title is transformed, through this final sentence, into the structuring device of the entire story. The reader's attention to the surface of the text is rewarded as the linearity of the narrative becomes, if not totally circular, at least spiral.

The textual effect in this story is similar to the visual effect of certain drawings by M. C. Escher (1902–1972), a Dutch graphic artist who has also exercised influence on U.S. postmodernists. In "Relativity," a lithograph of 1953, we see, for example, an architectural structure resembling a spacious, central stairwell with many sets of steps being ascended and descended by various individuals. Close inspection reveals, however, that the perspective of the drawing insists upon the flat surface of the medium and that none of the climbers escapes that plane. Climb as they may, they all arrive at the same geometric plateau, the surface of the drawing.

The architectural rules governing this type of drawing are determined by the flatness of the lithographer's stone, a two-dimensional rather than a three-dimensional surface. Any reference to rules existing in the universe beyond the drawing are incidental, to be pondered retrospectively. Similarly, in Borges's story, the reader's fascination remains fixed on the aesthetic object, the story with its narrative texture and circularity of plot, rather than on any laws governing a universe beyond the text. It is this direction of insistence that is referred to by "keeping the reader's attention focused on the surface of the text."

A second tendency of postmodern writers, "to deny the outside world," is related to the first. Mimesis, the theory stating generally that art should mirror nature, which has been the basis for creating Western fiction since the time of Homer, is flagrantly abandoned by the postmodernists, and some theoretical justification for such disregard has been developed. According to the linguistic theory expounded by Ferdinand de Saussure, a sign comprises two parts: the *signifier*, which is a phoneme or set of phonemes, chosen arbitrarily, and the *signified*, which is the concept signaled by the signifier. The linguistic sign depends, then, on a relationship between sounds and concepts rather than on a relationship between sounds or concepts and an object in the world. The literary text, seen as a whole, becomes itself such a sign, but an extended sign. In light of Saussure's theoretical construct, the external world disappears, leaving only the text and its significance for the reader. Thus, from this perspective, mimesis becomes, at least for post-modernists, a peripheral or coincidental, rather than a central, principle in the aesthetics of a literary work.

During the postmodern period, the theorists of structuralism and later of deconstruction have either built on or reacted to Saussure's linguistic theory. Their concerns have been focused on problems arising specifically from the text; respectively, they have either commented on structures operating in the text or on premises underlying the content of the text that support or subvert assumptions maintained by various readerships. In either case, the nature and potential of the text per se is the focus of theoretical discussion, and both structuralism and deconstruction have provided critics with vocabulary to describe the accomplishments of postmodern writers. In other words, postmodern writers found an audience, and they also have been blessed with critics prepared to discuss their innovations intelligently.

A third characteristic of postmodern fiction is an outgrowth of its denial of mimesis: that is, its defiance of the tenets of realism. In postmodern fiction, fictional characters move and develop in dream landscapes or through other realms of "fictional reality." The conventions of science fiction and of fantasy operate concomitantly with those of realism. Magic, supernatural entities, and extraterrestrials quite often appear as realities amid landscapes of imminent seriousness. In Borges's narration, for example, the presence of the dreamer's son is not apologized away in the fictional world of the story; the son, like the ghost of Old Hamlet, must be accepted as a "fact" in the fiction established in the text. This characteristic of demanding acceptance of the fictionality within fictional works will be seen as a prominent feature in several of the short stories I will discuss.

A fourth preoccupation of postmodern writers is to question the nature and significance of the "subject self." A brief interpretation of the story by Borges should make this fourth characteristic of postmodernism quite clear. The dreamer (an author) dreams a son (a character) into existence and inserts him into reality (a piece of fiction). That dreamer (the author), however, is but a summation of constructions and assumptions dreamed up by yet other dreamers (other writers the author has read). The uniqueness of the ego or the "myth" of the autonomy of the "subject self" of both characters and authors is thus seriously questioned, revised, or even undermined.

A theoretical basis for this sort of questioning originates in Nietzschean philosophy: those who do not, as Zarathustra attempts to do, escape the conventions imposed on them by history and culture are in fact creations of those very conventions. This Nietzschean notion of cultural determinism leads directly to Michel Foucault's later ideas on the nature of the self as a construct of roles imposed by social "inculturation." Postmodern writers tend to create characters whose thoughts and actions are determined, to a greater or lesser extent, by the dreams dreamed by others. Their personal agendas are scenarios received from or scripted by others and their individuality is often difficult or impossible to define. This is not so obscure a concept; postmodernists simply extend the application of the rule *ex nihilo nihil fit* (from nothing nothing is produced) to include the individual consciousness.

A fifth feature that characterizes postmodern fiction consists in the frequent demand that a reader closely consider the genre in which the author is working and the linguistic devices displayed in the text. Again, this is a device that draws the reader's attention to the surface of the text. Postmodern writers enjoy causing the readers to question what the text or aesthetic object before them really is: "Is this a short story?" or "Is this a romance?" By manipulating the linguistic and generic aspects of a work in this way, the writers are able to present the text as an object of interest in and of itself (and on its own terms)—an object that is inserted, like an extraordinary dream child, into a readership's mundane reality. Similarly, postmodern writers enjoy using puns and even etymologies that force the verbal play used in the telling of stories on the reader's attention. Words per se become significant aesthetic elements in the text and readers necessarily ask, "Why is the author punning here?" or "Why is the author inserting an etymology into this sentence?" Therefore, postmodernism in practice raises new questions about the literariness of texts that demand new answers.

Specific Cases

Vladimir Nabokov (1899–1973)

As pointed out in the first quotation in this essay, a survey of postmodern literature in the United States properly begins with works by Vladimir Nabokov. Many critics agree: "The crossover from modernist to postmodernist writing in the U.S. also occurs during the middle years of Vladimir Nabokov's American career, specifically in the sequence [of novels] *Lolita* (1955), *Pale Fire* (1962), *Ada* (1969)" (Nabokov, *Pale Fire* 18). These *novels* exhibit most of the characteristics of postmodern writing I have mentioned. Nabokov's short stories, some of which were written earlier than this sequence of novels, also clearly manifest various tendencies that characterize postmodern writing.

The narrator of Nabokov's short story "The Leonardo," speaking as an artist himself (even though he must be considered an unreliable narrator), opens his story by stating:

The objects that are being summoned assemble, draw near from different spots; in doing so, some of them have to overcome not only the distance of space but that of time: which nomad, you may wonder, is more bothersome to cope with, this one or that, the young poplar, say . . . or the singled-out courtyard which still exists today but is situated far from here? (589)

The narrator/artist then "sketches in" a rather unattractive tenement building with a dismal yard in front, which he populates to the need of his story:

two live people—Gustav and his brother Anton—already come out on their tiny balcony, while rolling before him a little pushcart with a suitcase and a heap of books, Romantovski, the new lodger, enters the yard. (589)

The title of the story, "The Leonardo," prepares the reader to enter into a fictional realm that concerns a work of art, and the opening paragraphs indicate that the narrator/artist is carefully choosing the elements to paint into his own work of art. The narrator's approach is that of a realist, almost in the tradition of Gustave Flaubert, except for the fact that he insists on imposing his own personality into the fiction. Expectations, seemingly, are thus established for a story that will adhere to the principles guiding Western art since the Renaissance in general and Western realism in particular—a realism that took as one of its tenets that characters should be brought together and allowed to interact without undue manipulation by the author.

However, apart from his title, and in spite of his narrator's introductory paragraphs, Nabokov is cleverly establishing a text that defies any realist expectations. In fact, the narrator/artist tells the reader very specifically that such expectations will be undermined, and then he repeats his statement with "transparently veiled" emphasis:

Now this is the way we'll arrange the world: every man shall sweat, every man shall eat.

•   •   •

Repeat: the world shall be sweaty and well-fed. Idlers, parasites, and musicians are not permitted. (590)

Thus, the reader is abruptly whisked away, almost unaware, from the conventions of a broad movement in the Western tradition in art into the narrowly defined conditions of art prevailing, for example, in a communist dictatorship of the proletariat. Later, in retrospect, the reader must come to realize that the opening scene sketched out earlier bears an unmistakable resemblance to "utopian" residences built under the Marxist regimes of Central and Eastern Europe.

In their "utopian" existence, the two brothers on the balcony live together because they cannot afford to do otherwise and Romantovski moves into their building because his circumstances afford him nothing better. With this backdrop and with these characters, the reader is far removed from the world painted by Leonardo and his fellow artists of Renaissance Italy.

In the sequence of events delineated in the story, the two brothers become more and more distressed by their inability to define their neighbor:

This cannot go on. He poisons the life of honest folk. Why, it can well happen that he will move at the end of the month—intact, whole, never taken to pieces, proudly strutting about. It is not enough that he moves and breathes differently from other people; the trouble is that we just cannot put our finger upon the difference, cannot catch the tip of the ear by which to pull out the rabbit. Hateful is everything that cannot be palpated, measured, counted. (593)

To understand him, the brothers attempt to make him reveal some secret aspect of his being by tormenting him. Unable to avoid his tormentors, Romantovski innocently goes to a movie with the fiancée of one of the brothers, hoping that this act of camaraderie will satisfy their demand for interaction. It provides, however, an excuse for them to kill him. After Romantovski is dead, the brothers discover during the police investigation that he had been a *leonardo*, a counterfeiter of currency. The police believe that he must have been killed by one of his accomplices, so the brothers do not become suspects. They literally "get away with murder."

The narrator/artist ends his story by reversing the process of bringing various physical elements together—he reverses that process by which he had initiated the story:

My poor Romantovski! It is all over now. Alas, the objects I had assembled wander away. The young poplar dims and takes off—to return where it had been fetched from. The brick wall dissolves. The house draws in its little balconies one by one, then turns, and floats away. Everything floats away. Harmony and meaning vanish. The world irks me again with its variegated void. (596)

By having his narrator end his story in this way, Nabokov raises a question in the mind of the reader that demands a second, and possibly a third, reading of the story: How can this story warrant such attention to theory at its beginning and ending when its intervening sequence of events delineate such dystopian squalor and corruption?

A solution to this problem can be found in the meaning of the title, which is understood only at the end of the story. Just as the title is shown to signal a counterfeit of the expectation established when the reader first encounters the word (or name) *Leonardo*, so too is the artistry, so insisted on by the narrator, shown to be a counterfeit of the expectation he establishes. The narrator, in his artistic theory and in his judgment of the unfortunate Romantovski, is discredited: he must be considered unreliable. However, because he is obviously unaware of his unreliability, Nabokov manages to question the very nature of the narrator's subject-self or of that consciousness that narrates the tale. The story, whose title suggests continuity with the long tradition of Western art and whose language initiates expectations of the principles of realism, becomes a counterfeit of both. The story itself is, therefore, a leonardo. Thus, Nabokov manages to make of the narrator himself and of the story the narrator tells the true subjects of interest for the reader. The events become "background" as the reader seeks answers to Nabokov's foregrounded questions. These answers are carefully "hidden," of course, directly on the surface of the postmodern story.

Imamu Amiri Baraka (1934–)

Imamu Amiri Baraka took his Muslim name in 1966, but it was under his original "slave name," LeRoi Jones, that he had published his earlier writings. Baraka works primarily as a neorealist, so he is not usually classified as a postmodern writer, but many elements in his works are postmodern. The short story "Answers in Progress," dated March 1967, was collected in *Tales*, and it exemplifies several postmodern elements that characterize much of the author's fiction.

The story presents the "projection of a revolutionary holocaust" (Baraka 758), and it is set in a semimythic past/present/future time. The title is intriguingly enigmatic: It suggests that *answers* to the social problems of inequality in the United States may have been in progress either (1) since some point in America's far-distant history, perhaps (2) since the period of social unrest and civil disobedience of the 1960s when the story was written, or even (3) "since" some potential beginning of progress in the future; the story also provokes questions about the nature of *progress* itself, that central concept in so many slogans that have been used to justify policies guiding America's growth out of a collection of East Coast, European colonies into a nation that spans a continent and comprises populations from all national and racial groups of the world.

Influenced by Marxism, Baraka sees violence as a "necessary corollary" to the social change needed to make the United States realize its so-often-stated principle of "liberty and justice for all." This particular short story derives, in some ways, from his Marxist thinking on this issue: the story relates events of great violence. The postmodern aspects of the story, however, draw the reader's attention away from the violence of the events of the story and back to the linguistic surface of the work—to the aesthetic cadences and unusual uses of words that relate Baraka's "revolution in progress." Thus, the surface of the text is foregrounded and the violence presented in the text is, to an extent, backgrounded.

Following a prelude of four verses, the story begins:

"Stick a knife through his throat,"
                    he slid
                 in the blood
            got up running toward
         the blind newsdealer. He screamed
      about "Cassius Clay," and slain there in the
   street, the whipped figure of jesus, head opened
eyes flailing against his nose. They beat him to
pulpy answers. We wrote Muhammad Ali across his
face and chest, like a newspaper, like a newspaper of bleeding meat.
                                                              (758)

Like blood spreading out from a freshly inflicted wound, staining everything in its path, Baraka's story proceeds from an emphatic initial directive to slit a man's throat. In death, the victim's error of referring to a prizefighter by his "slave name" is corrected, and he carries that correction into eternity, carved across his body. Thus, blood and death are the backdrop for the events against which the aesthetics of the story, if *story* indeed it is, unfold. These opening lines flow outward and downward into the rest of the story, and their verselike measures contrast with the more prosaic lines that follow. Apart from their form, however, both the verse and the prose passages are similar in their ungrammatical, cadenced, almost musical syntax: echoes of the rhythms of jazz lie behind both, as is typical in much of Baraka's writing.

In the middle of this short tale, Baraka introduces the lyrics of a song listened to by the characters who are his revolutionaries. A few verses of this song read:

You have brothers
you love each other, change up
and look at the world
now, it's
ours, take it slow
we've long time, a long way
to go,
we have each other, and the
world. (760)

The prose statement that immediately follows the presentation of this song indicates how Baraka's "revolution in progress" is actually "orchestrated," so that the actions of the characters become a macabre dance: "Boulevards played songs like that and we rounded up blanks where we had to" (760).

The story ends with "That's the way the fifth day ended" (761). This final line in the story brings into play a multitude of possible sources. In the Judeo–Christian Genesis narrative, animal life was created on the fifth day, and on the sixth day Human Beings were created to have dominion over them. This is one traditional source for the Western concept of progress that Baraka is considering. Whatever the source of Baraka's final phrase, behind the violence depicted in this story lies the model of the slave rebellions of one hundred years prior, in which African Americans attempted to erase unacceptable definitions imposed on them and initiate a new era.

Just as Baraka plays verse against prose in his text, he also plays several genres of narrative against each other (newspaper reporting, history, science fiction), creating a freshness of approach in the telling of his story, so his literary form becomes as revolutionary as his political message. Baraka's constant insistence on foregrounding the form or genre of the story keeps the reader's attention on the surface of the text. For his readers, the important questions raised by all postmodern writers are also raised here: "Is this narrative or verse?" "Is this the news or science fiction?" Other kinds of questions are also raised: "Is this a revolution or a dance routine?" "Is this a hallucination or a premonition?" Baraka's constant insistence on the music that animates and orchestrates the story frees him from moralizing. Still, a moral question is clear: "Is the United States truly united, or does alienation of the magnitude supposed by Baraka create national schizophrenia and disunity that only revolution can resolve?"

Baraka's postmodern style, which facilitates the crescendo of tensions experienced by the subject character and the series of questions arising in the consciousness of the reader, helps to make this peculiar short story effective postmodern fiction—fiction that causes readers to look at both literary and political realities in new, possibly revolutionary ways.

Kurt Vonnegut, Jr. (1922–) and Tim O'Brien (1946–)

Kurt Vonnegut, Jr. and Tim O'Brien are paired in this section because each, marked indelibly by one of America's wars, represents a generation of U.S. writers that has contributed significantly to the literature of postmodernism in the United States: the generation of World War II and that of the American War in Vietnam, respectively. Each author did service in his generation's war, and each survived to write about that experience.

No discussion of postmodernism in America is complete without mention of Vonnegut's *Slaughterhouse-Five or The Children's Crusade: A Duty-Dance with Death*. It is an innovative novel, and it, along with the film that resulted from it, caught the attention of Americans as no earlier postmodernist's work had. Some of Vonnegut's short stories manifest those postmodern qualities that define the uniqueness of his famous novel and of his style in general, and among these is his 1954 story "Unready to Wear."

In this short story, Vonnegut presents a what-if world in which evolution is making a change as great as that of the development through the transitional development of amphibians, of land-dwelling creatures out of sea-dwelling creatures. Dr. Ellis Konigswasser "discovered how people could do without their bodies" (Vonnegut 29), and he wrote a book on the process that allowed large numbers of people to separate their bodies and their minds, if not totally, then at least for lengthy periods of time. On the personal level, without a body:

Konigswasser didn't have to sleep any more, just because *it* had to sleep; or be afraid any more, just because *it* thought it might get hurt; or go looking for things *it* seemed to think it had to have. And, when *it* didn't feel well, Konigswasser kept out of it until it felt better, and he didn't have to spend a fortune keeping the thing comfortable. (28)

On the social level, the narrator finds even greater disadvantages to carrying one's body around:

When we get into bodies for the Pioneers' Day Parade, we take up over fifty thousand square feet, have to gobble more than three tons of food to get

enough energy to march; and lots of us catch colds or worse, and get sore because somebody's body accidentally steps on the heels of somebody else's body,
and get jealous because some bodies get to lead and others have to stay in
ranks, and—oh, hell, I don't know what all. (30)

As in the novel, *Slaughterhouse-Five*, there is utopian consideration behind some of the postmodern scientific anomalies that readers must
accept as fact within the text "Unready to Wear." However, instead of
positing the necessity of living part time on the planet Tralfamadore in
order to experience utopian conditions (as he did in *Slaughterhouse-
Five*), Vonnegut posits the possibility of living on earth on some type of
astral plane, at least part time. As seen in the passages quoted above,
this posited possibility allows the author opportunity to explore certain
problems that the condition of living in a body carries with it.

Toward the end of the story, when the "still-embodied population"
puts the "amphibious" narrator and his wife on trial "for desertion,"
the primary problem (within the strictures of Vonnegut's story) arising
from being entrapped in a body is articulated:

"Now I understand you poor fish," [says the narrator to his judge]. "You
couldn't get along without fear. That's the only skill you've got—how to scare
yourselves and other people into doing things. That's the only fun you've got,
watching people jump for fear of what you'll do to their bodies or take away
from their bodies." (37)

In "Unready to Wear," Vonnegut notes the very human problems that
arise from the fact that consciousness is embodied: it is care and repair
of a body that occupy most of our waking time, and it is fear of harm
to that bulky body that creates many of our social problems. As the
narrator points out: "When we're not in bodies, the Amphibious Pioneers can meet on the head of a pin" (30). The implication of this comment is that people without bodies are "more like angels" than they are
with bodies, and conditions prevailing within the narrative support
this inference.

It is important to note that this story is not science fiction. The
premises that define science fiction generally are of a "when" rather
that of a "what-if" nature. The story is also not fantasy, which generally
premises "once upon a time" conditions for the narrative. The story is
fiction, of course, but it is presented as reality, a reality that operates
purely within the frame of reference established within the work itself.
Thus, it is the consideration of genre definition, the denial of the laws
governing the outside world, and the defiance of the assumptions and

the conventions of realism that make of Vonnegut's "Unready to Wear" a good example of postmodern writing.

Tim O'Brien's novel *Going After Cacciato* appeared in 1978. Its treatment of the experience of America's War in Vietnam is, in its own way, as innovative as the treatment of experiences of World War II in Vonnegut's *Slaughterhouse-Five,* and it treats the absurdity of war in a way similar to that found in Vonnegut's work. The novel's main character Specialist-Four Paul Berlin, doing night duty in an observation post in Vietnam, *imagines* his way out of war in Southeast Asia and into the semblance of peace in Europe, as Billy Pilgrim had imagined his way to Tralfamadore. Indeed, careful consideration of the nature of human imagination characterizes much of O'Brien's fiction, including his short stories.

In his short story cycle of 1990, *The Things They Carried,* O'Brien portrays many characters and episodes from the American War in Vietnam so convincingly that he has to preface the collection with a note (almost a disclaimer) to the readers: "This is a work of fiction. Except for a few details regarding the author's own life, all the incidents, names, and characters are imaginary." Within the various intertwined tales that comprise the collection, "Sweetheart of the Song Tra Bong" shows a particular concentration of postmodern attributes. The story is reflective in many ways of Joseph Conrad's famous *Heart of Darkness*, even to its use of several levels of *mise-en-abîme*, which so characterizes Marlow's narrative. In O'Brien's what-if world, however, the Intended or "Sweetheart" comes directly into the heart of America's dark war, and she gradually becomes Kurtz herself. In this story, it is the boyfriend, Mark Fossie, who returns alone to the United States, and he is later given a medical discharge.

O'Brien's narrator in fact "retells" a story that he has heard earlier from Rat Kiley, who supposedly witnessed many of the events himself, but who also eventually must draw details he did not witness from the reports he has gleaned from others. As Rat recounts the events: "This cute blonde—just a kid, just barely out of high school—she shows up with a suitcase and one of those plastic cosmetic bags. Comes right out to the boonies. I swear to God, man, she's wearing culottes" (102). She comes to visit a regular army fire-base, a corner of which also serves as a Special Forces base. A few weeks after Mary Anne Belle's arrival and her rather quick acclimatization to Vietnam, she disappears from Fossie's camp. O'Brien's primary narrator informs his listeners:

When he first told the story, Rat stopped there and looked at Mitchell Sanders for a time.

So what's your vote? Where was she?

"The Greenies [Special Forces]," Sanders said.

"Yeah?"

Sanders smiled. "No other option. That stuff about the Special Forces—
how they used the place as a base of operations, how they'd glide in and out—
all that had to be there for a *reason*. That's how stories work, man." (112)

In this way, Sanders's literary criticism is integrated structurally into
the story. In the particular interpolation cited here, Sanders's "reading"
of Rat's narrative is accepted; Rat continues by saying that Mary Anne
has indeed been with the Special Forces unit: "Ambush. All night long,
man, Mary Anne's out on fuckin' *ambush*" (113).

Finally, Rat manages to conclude his narration of Mary Anne's adventures as he had witnessed them, and then he stops again, but without bringing any closure or resolution to the story.

"Jesus Christ, it's against the *rules*," Sanders said. "Against human *nature*.
This elaborate story, you can't say, Hey, by the way, I don't know the *ending*. I
mean, you got certain obligations."

Rat gave a quick smile. "Patience, man. Up to now, everything I told you is
from personal experience, the exact truth, but there's a few other things I heard
secondhand. Thirdhand, actually. From here in it gets to be . . . I don't know
what the word is."

"Speculation" [interjects Sanders]. (122)

Through Rat's speculation, but thanks primarily to Sanders's comments
from within or perhaps from "the far side" of the tale, the reader learns
that Mary Anne eventually disappears into the jungle, to be consumed
physically by the war that had already absorbed her psychologically.

Sanders's most telling metafictional comments appear at the mid-
point of Rat's telling of Mary Anne's transformation. Rat tends to interject his own commentary on the tale as he is telling it, and this practice
also offends Sanders' aesthetic sense. He complains:

That just breaks the spell. It destroys the magic. What you have to do,
Sanders said, is trust your own story. Get the hell out of the way and let it tell
itself.

But Rat Kiley couldn't help it. He wanted to bracket the full range of
meaning. (116)

The narrator of Rat's story interjects this conversation between Rat and
Sanders into his own narration; the conversation itself is between Rat,
the postmodern stylist, and Sanders, the auditor with realist expectations, but it allows O'Brien, the author, to underline his own postmodern defiance of realist conventions through adherence to an interesting

postmodern permutation of mimesis: he mirrors a conversation between a postmodern teller of tales and someone not necessarily prepared for postmodern practices, and thereby he makes the subject of
the content of the story the surface of the story itself. O'Brien, too, is a
postmodernist, more concerned with the surface of the story than with
any "narrative spell."

As in the case of Conrad's earlier work, in O'Brien's story the constant shifts from one narrator to another also draw the reader's attention repeatedly away from any "spell" O'Brien's primary narrator might
otherwise create and bring it directly to the surface of the text itself. In
"Sweetheart of the Song Tra Bong," the reader must constantly ask: is
this a story?—is this a reported conversation?—or is this literary criticism?—all of which is part and parcel with the postmodern precepts on
which O'Brien structures his work.

In a postmodernist context, O'Brien's early note, prefacing this
cycle of stories, increases in its significance. The note is more than a
simple "disclaimer," absolving the author of accusations of involving
any living people, other than himself, in his fiction. It is a signal of one
of the functions of this cycle of short stories: to question the assumed
distinctions between "factual" history or biography, on the one hand,
and "nonfactual" fiction, on the other. By inserting himself into some
of his stories in this cycle, he undermines the assumed distinctions,
and realism, as it has been understood for centuries, is redefined.

Both Kurt Vonnegut and Tim O'Brien subvert the conventions of
realism that have set reader expectations at least since the appearance
of Flaubert's *Madame Bovary* in 1857. Each author tells his tale in a
work that operates only on its own fictional terms and within the context of the postmodern conventions that each author manages either to
define or redefine. Both authors are important postmodern practitioners whose "literary disruptions" help bring to American fiction shifts in
the understanding of the nature of reality as readers experience it, and
they have been led, to some degree, to their own understanding of
these shifts by major disruptions in their lives and in the lives of many
of their readers: their very real experiences of two of America's devastating twentieth-century wars.

Shirley Ann Grau (1929–)

Shirley Ann Grau and her works frustrate most attempts at categorization, and she cannot be listed as a mainstream American postmodernist, if indeed she can be called "postmodern" at all. Among her

numerous short stories, however, there are some that lend themselves to examination in this study because they are read as "borderline post-modern." One such story is "The Black Prince," which she wrote while a student at Tulane. It first appeared in the *New Mexico Quarterly* "in a somewhat different form" under the title "The Sound of Silver."

Preceding the story is a quotation: "How thou art fallen from heaven, / O Lucifer, son of the morning" (38). This word *Lucifer* represents the only use of this name for Satan in the English Bible. One etymology of this Latin-based name reads:

Lucifer n.: Old English *Lucifer* Satan; also the morning star . . . ; borrowed from the Latin *lucidus* the morning star; literally, light bringing (*lux*, genitive *lucis* light + *ferre* carry).

This name for Satan comes from the Biblical passage [Isaiah 14.12] (translated from the *Vulgate*). (Barnhart 444)

Due to its etymology, and even to its use in Isaiah, the term is ambiguous, as is also the second title that Grau gave to her story, "The Black Prince." The author brings her readers into a mythic realm that is neither wholly good nor evil, but somehow both, simultaneously. The atmosphere of the story, however, definitely conjures up the supernatural, as does the second title (which could refer either to the African American ethnicity of the protagonist or to something else).

The atmosphere and the prefacing passage come together after Stanley Albert Thomspon makes his first appearance in the story:

[Alberta] pushed her hands in the pockets of her dress and looked him over. "Where you come from?"

"Me?" The little green twig went in and out of his teeth with each breath. "I just come straight out of the morning." (Grau 42)

As this initial conversation between the protagonist and his chosen lady continues, Alberta is amazed that Stanley Albert knows her name, and she asks him how so. He replies: "I done seen it in the fire and I read it clear" (42). Thus, the supernatural continues to be evoked in a story whose lyricism is almost hypnotic.

Evidence of the magic evoked by the story's earlier title is also still to be discerned in the retitled narrative:

Once when Willie [the owner] was standing behind the bar, shuffling a pack of cards with a wide fancy twirl—just for amusement—Stanley Albert, who had had a couple of drinks and was feeling especially good, got up and pulled a handful of coins out of his pocket. He began to shuffle them through the air, the way Willie had done with the cards. Stanley Albert's black hands flipped the coins back and forth, faster and faster, until there was a solid silver ring hanging and shining in the air. Then Stanley Albert let one of his hands drop to his side and the silver ring poured back into the other hand and disappeared with a little clinking sound. (52)

As in the case of the ghost of Hamlet's father, the elements of magic—ambiguously either of the black or of the white varieties—are an assumption in the story. This assumption sets the story in a realm apart from the mundane world "outside" and places its premises in opposition to the conventions that govern the literature of realism.

The supernatural qualities associated with Stanley Albert become clear one evening when Alberta is alone, asleep in the woods. She awakens to Albert's song:

The song went round in a circle, round and round, weaving in and out of the pines, passing invisible across the open moon filled spaces.
"*Alberta, let your hair hang low . . .*"
There wasn't a man alive could do that. Go round and round. (60)

Stanley Albert and Alberta do become a couple, and the supernatural qualities that had characterized Albert alone then come to characterize them both. Thus, they become even more conspicuous in their quiet and happy relationship than Albert had been earlier. Eventually Willie, the tavern keeper and would-be boyfriend of Alberta, collects some of Albert's silver coins and casts them as four bullets. He subsequently shoots Albert, and the couple disappear from the area, after Albert escapes, wounded.

To conclude her lyrically measured narrative, Grau does not demand of her readers their full acceptance of the fictionality of the supernatural elements that she structures into her story. She accounts for those elements, rather, by placing the story in the category of "folk legend." Grau writes toward the end of "The Black Prince": "All that was maybe eight or ten years ago. People don't see them any more—Stanley and Alberta. They don't think much about them, except when something goes wrong—like weevils getting in the cotton, or Willie's [tavern] burning down and Willie inside it—then they begin to think that those two had a hand in it" (70). It is in this attempt to "explain away" the supernatural in this lyrical story—by placing the story in an established genre—that it ceases to be postmodern and joins the much older, longer tradition to which belong certain works by such writers as Washington Irvine or Nathaniel Hawthorne. In this regard, Grau's short story remains "borderline postmodern," but it should also remain of great interest to the postmodern readership.

Conclusion

As mentioned briefly at the beginning of this essay, the period in the United States during which postmodernism developed has also been the period in which various minorities have become politically empowered and in which minority authorships have gained a voice. To a greater or lesser degree, postmodernism has provided the techniques used in conveying the messages of these voices to highly fragmented readerships, defined by their own special interests and political agendas. The selection of works I have discussed was made with this fact in mind. An attempt has been made to include representative authors from a variety of these U.S. authorships.

Nabokov hardly represents a newly empowered member of a minority, but he does represent an unusual class of Americans, and his story "The Leonardo" deserves first mention in this conclusion. Nabokov, as an intellectual, uses the techniques that characterize postmodernism to write a story about *delusion* on many levels, and in his story he never uses that word. The delusion is revealed from the inside of the characters only. As an international, born to social prominence and wealth in Russia and then—following the Revolution—making his career in American academe, he gives his short story an international dimension through his choice of narrator, setting, and political themes. Intellectually, "The Leonardo" is a very satisfying short story, and much of the satisfaction derives from Nabokov's masterful and effective use of postmodern elements—his plays on language, his questioning the nature of the subject-self, his emphasis on the surface of the text—all of which are sources of fascination to the postmodern reader.

Baraka, in "Answers in Progress," uses the techniques of postmodernism to create a short story that is semiautobiographical: a short story that tells of the experience of African Americans in a culture dominated by western European values—a culture that, in his view, fully enfranchises only white Americans while it alienates nonwhites. He posits as a possible solution to the problem the identification of American ethnic minorities with their own cultural roots, such as jazz, in this story: it is only by being true to one's own culture that authenticity of self can be developed. In his short story, Baraka uses the techniques of postmodernism to convey this theme of cultural authenticity: "The next day [after the revolutionaries had slit the throat of the man who referred to Muhammad Ali as Cassius Clay] the spaceships landed. Art Blakey records was what they were looking for. We gave them Buttercorn Lady and they threw it back at us. They wanted to know what happened to the Jazz Messengers" (Baraka 758–59). It is this culture of music that remains the dominant theme in the story, even as the streets flow with blood. The culture of music is important thematically in the story; death and destruction appear almost incidentally, as matters of fact.

Two postmodern voices representing white male Americans and their experiences are those of Kurt Vonnegut and Tim O'Brien, but their works transcend by far a narrow classification. Because the former mixes elements of science fiction and the latter elements of fantasy so freely with elements of realism, their "short stories" are difficult to catalog as to genre. This fact is not so unusual in postmodern fiction, but their approaches to achieving this effect are. Occasionally, they even interject themselves as characters into their fictions and interact with other characters. The "fiction of 'fact versus fiction'" sometimes breaks down completely in these particular stories.

In an article on feminism and postmodernism, Bonnie Zimmerman makes a point that at least in one way distinguishes male and female practitioners: "Feminist fiction seldom is as self-conscious and artificial as are male meta-fictions, and experimentation usually serves the ultimate end of realism" (177). It is difficult, therefore, to find feminist writers, or women writers in general, who make use of the methods of postmodernism in creating their fictional worlds. In "The Black Prince," Shirley Ann Grau blends the supernatural with the natural, but ultimately her use of these elements does serve a predominantly realist purpose. Grau is neither a mainstream postmodernist nor a mainstream feminist, but she is an author whose works deserve consideration by readers of both political persuasions.

The final paragraphs of Grau's story are significant in this context:

And when women talk—when there's been a miscarriage or a stillbirth—they remember and whisper.

And they all wonder if that's not the sort of work they do, the two of them. Maybe so; maybe not. The people themselves are not too sure. They don't see them around any more. (70–71)

Grau leaves the supernatural aspects of her story in a sort of netherworld, which is the proper realm of folk legend. This is also where the story lies in regard to literary movement: somewhere between the postmodern and the realist. It is partly through such ambiguity, however, that the truly lasting quality of her work is revealed. Grau does not lose the magic of her writing in adherence to any ideological persuasion.

Here we can ask: "Can postmodernism serve so many masters in the United States?" Judging from the success of postmodern works in the hands of the diverse writers I have discussed, the response must be "yes." In the twenty-first century, postmodernism may be approaching the end of its time of dominating the creative and artistic thought of the United States, but it has made its lasting mark in an important period of its literature, the latter half of the twentieth century.

Note

1. This essay has been adapted from an article I wrote ("Postmodernism in the United States") that treated the postmodern novel in the United States. For his permission to present this adaptation here, I thank Wlasyslaw Witalisz, the editor of the article.

References

Baraka, Imamu Amiri. "Answers in Progress." *Story to Anti-Story*. Ed. Mary Rohrberger. Boston: Houghton, 1979. 758–61.

Barnhart, Robert K. *The Barnhart Concise Dictionary of Etymology: The Origins of American English Words*. New York: Harper, 1988.

Borges, Jorge Luis. *Labyrinths*. Ed. Donald A. Yates and James E. Irby. New York: New Directions, 1964.

Grau, Shirley Ann. *The Black Prince and Other Stories*. New York: Knopf, 1955.

Kaylor, Noel Harold, Jr. "Postmodernism in the United States." *And Gladly Wolde He Lerne and Gladly Teche*. Ed. Wlasyslaw Witalisz. Kroków, Pol.: Wydawnictwo Uniwersytetu Jagiellonskiego, 2001. 83–99.

Klinkowitz, Jerome. *Literary Disruptions*. Chicago: U of Illinois P, 1975.

McCaffery, Larry, ed. Introduction. *Postmodern Fiction: A Bio-Bibliographical Guide*. New York: Greenwood, 1986. xi–xxviii.

Nabokov, Vladimir. "The Leonardo." *Story to Anti-Story*. Ed. Mary Rohrberger. Boston: Houghton, 1979. 589–96.

———. *Pale Fire*. New York: Putnam's, 1962.

O'Brien, Tim. *The Things They Carried: A Work of Fiction by Tim O'Brien*. Boston: Houghton Mifflin/Seymour Lawrence, 1990.

Rohrberger, Mary, ed. *Story to Anti-Story*. Boston: Houghton, 1979.

Vonnegut, Kurt, Jr. "Unready to Wear." *Super Fiction or the American Story Transformed: An Anthology*. Ed. Joe David Bellamy. New York: Vintage, 1975. 23–39.

Zimmerman, Bonnie. "Feminist Fiction and the Postmodern Challenge." *Postmodern Fiction: A Bio-Bibliographical Guide*. Ed. Larry McCaffery. New York: Greenwood, 1986. 175–88.

Selected Bibliography

Allen, Walter. *The Short Story in English*. New York: Oxford UP, 1981.

Anderson, Sherwood. *A Story Teller's Story*. New York: Huebsch, 1924.

Baldeshwiler, Eileen. "The Lyric Short Story: The Sketch of a History." *Studies in Short Fiction* 6.4 (1969): 443–53.

Bayley, John. *The Short Story: Henry James to Elizabeth Bowen*. Brighton, UK: Harvester, 1988.

Birbalsingh, Frank, ed. *Frontiers of Caribbean Literature in English*. New York: St. Martin's, 1996.

Bonheim, Helmut. *The Narrative Modes: Techniques of the Short Story*. Cambridge, UK: Brewer, 1982.

Brown, Suzanne Hunter. "'Tess' and *Tess*: An Experiment in Genre." *Modern Fiction Studies* 28.1 (spring 1982): 25–44.

Conde, Mary, and Thorunn Lonsdale, eds. *Caribbean Women Writers: Fiction in English*. New York: St. Martin's, 1999.

Crowley, Donald. *The American Short Story, 1850–1900*. Boston: Twayne, 1989.

Current-Garcia, E. *The American Short Story before 1850*. Boston: Twayne, 1985.

Dance, Daryl Cumber. *New World Adams: Conversations with Contemporary West Indian Writers*. Leeds, UK: Peepal Tree, 1992.

Dunn, Maggie, and Ann Morris. *The Composite Novel: The Short Story Cycle in Transition*. Boston: Twayne, 1995.

Exjenbaum, Boris. "O. Henry and the Theory of the Short Story." Trans. I. R. Titunik. *Readings in Russian Poetics*. Ed. L. Matejka and K. Pomorska. Cambridge: MIT P, 1971. 227–70

Ferguson, Suzanne. "Defining the Short Story: Impressionism and Form." *Modern Fiction Studies* 28.1 (spring 1982): 13–24.

Fusco, Richard. *Maupassant and the American Short Story*. University Park: Pennsylvania State UP, 1994.

Gerlach, John. *Toward the End: Closure and Structure in the American Short Story*. University: U of Alabama P, 1985.

Gordimer, Nadine. *Writing and Being*. Cambridge: Harvard UP, 1995.

Gullason, Thomas. "Revelation and Evolution: A Neglected Dimension of the Short Story." *Studies in Short Fiction* 10.4 (1973): 347–56.

———. "The Short Story: Revision and Renewal." *Studies in Short Fiction* 19.3 (1982): 221–30.

———. "The Short Story: An Underrated Art." *Studies in Short Fiction* 2.1 (1964): 13–31.

Hanson, Clare, ed. *Re-editing the Short Story*. New York: St. Martin's, 1989.

———. *Short Stories and Short Fictions, 1880–1980*. London: Macmillan, 1985.

Head, Dominic. *The Modernist Short Story*. Cambridge: Cambridge UP, 1992.

Hemingway, Ernest. *Death in the Afternoon*. New York: Scribner, 1932.

Iftekharrudin, Farhat, Mary Rohrberger, and Maurice Lee, eds. *Speaking of the Short Story*. Jackson: UP of Mississippi, 1997.

Ingram, Forrest L. *Representative Short Story Cycles of the Twentieth Century: Studies in a Literary Genre*. The Hague: Mouton, 1971.

James, Louis. *Caribbean Literature in English*. New York: Longman, 1999.

King, Bruce. *The New English Literatures: Cultural Nationalism in a Changing World*. New York: St. Martin's, 1980.

———, ed. *New National and Post-colonial Literatures: An Introduction*. Oxford: Clarendon, 1996.

———. *West Indian Literature*. Hamden, CT: Archon, 1979.

Lane, Dorothy F. *The Island as Site of Resistance: An Examination of Caribbean and New Zealand Texts*. New York: Lang, 1995.

Levy, Andrew. *The Culture and Commerce of the American Short Story*. Cambridge: Cambridge UP, 1993.

Lohafer, Susan. *Coming to Terms with the Short Story*. Baton Rouge: Louisiana State UP, 1983.

Lohafer, Susan, and Jo Ellyn Clarey, eds. *Short Story Theory at a Crossroads*. Baton Rouge: Louisiana State UP, 1989.

Lounsberry, Barbara, Susan Lohafer, Mary Rohrberger, Stephen Pett, and R. C. Feddersen, eds. *The Tales We Tell: Perspectives on the Short Story*. Westport: Greenwood, 1998.

Mann, Susan Garland. *The Short Story Cycle: A Genre Companion and Reference Guide*. New York: Greenwood, 1989.

Mansfield, Katherine. *Journal of Katherine Mansfield*. Ed. J. Middleton Murry. New York: Knopf, 1946.

Markham, E. A. Introduction. *The Penguin Book of Caribbean Short Stories*. Ed. E. A. Markham. London: Penguin, 1996.

Matthews, Brander. *Philosophy of the Short-Story*. New York: Longmans, 1901.

May, Charles E. *Edgar Allan Poe: A Study of the Short Fiction*. Boston: Twayne, 1991.

———. "The Nature of Knowledge in Short Fiction." *Studies in Short Fiction* 21.4 (1984): 327–38.

———, ed. *The New Short Story Theories*. Athens: Ohio UP, 1994.

———. *The Short Story: The Reality of Artifice*. Boston: Twayne, 1995.

———, ed. *Short Story Theories*. Athens: Ohio UP, 1976.

———. *Twentieth Century European Short Story: An Annotated Bibliography*. Pasadena: Salem, 1989.

McClave, Heather, ed. *Women Writers of the Short Story*. Englewood Cliffs: Prentice, 1980.

Nagel, James. *The Contemporary American Short-Story Cycle: The Ethnic Resonance of Genre*. Baton Rouge: Louisiana State UP, 2001.

O'Connor, Frank. *The Lonely Voice*. London: Macmillan, 1963.

Pascoe, Allan H. "On Defining Short Stories." *New Literary History* 22.2 (spring 1991): 407–22.

Pattee, Fred Lewis. *The Development of the American Short Story*. New York: Biblo, 1970.

Poe, Edgar A. *The Complete Works of Edgar Allan Poe*. Ed. J. A. Harrison. New York: AMS, 1965.

Reid, Ian. *The Short Story*. London: Methuen, 1977.

Rohrberger, Mary. *Hawthorne and the Modern Short Story*. The Hague: Mouton, 1966.

Rohrberger, Mary, and Dan Burns. "Short Fiction and the Numinous Realm: Another Attempt at Definition." *Modern Fiction Studies* 28.1 (1982): 5–12.

Shaw, Valerie. *The Short Story: A Critical Introduction*. London: Longman, 1983.

Shklovsky, Viktor. *Theory of Prose*. Trans. Benjamin Sher. Elmwood Park, IL: Dalkey Archive, 1990.

Smitten, Jeffrey R., and Ann Daghistany, eds. *Spatial Form in Narrative*. Ithaca: Cornell UP, 1981.

Tallack, Douglas. *The Nineteenth-Century American Short Story*. London: Routledge, 1993.

Voss, Arthur. *The American Short Story: A Critical Survey*. Norman: U of Oklahoma P, 1973.

Welty, Eudora. "The Reading and Writing of Short Stories." *Atlantic Monthly* Feb. 1949: 54–58; Mar. 1949: 46–49.

Wright, Austin. *The American Short Story in the Twenties*. Chicago: U of Chicago P, 1961.

Index

telling the truth. *See* essays, personal, imaginative leaps in

text: defined, 5

theory of donnée (deconstruction), 4, 5

tipping of the hand. *See* essays, personal, imaginative leaps in

title(s), 26, 60, 107, 109–18

Tralfamadorian clumps, 7, 8

Vonnegut, Kurt, Jr., 7, 257–59, 261, 265; *Slaughterhouse-Five*, 7, 257–59. *See also* Tralfamadorian clumps

White, Edmund: "Skinned Alive," 144–57

Wolff, Tobias: "Firelight," 37–38; *This Boy's Life*, 37–38

women's identity in the postmodern world, 63–105; for works discussed, *see* Cisneros, Sandra; Moore, Lorrie; Oates, Joyce Carol; Silko, Leslie Marmon

Woolf, Virginia: "Street Haunting," 29

writing: defined, 5

Yates, J. Michael, 236, 238, 240–41, 242, 243; "Broadcaster, The," 240–41; "Passage of Sono Nis, The," 240, 241; "Realia," 240; "Sinking of the Northwest Passage, The," 240; "Smokestack in the Desert," 240

About the Contributors
and Editors

Contributors

Marilyn Abildskov teaches writing and literature courses in creative nonfiction at the University of Iowa. Her fiction, poetry, and personal essays have recently appeared in such magazines as *Black Warrior Review*, *Puerto del Sol*, *Fourth Genre*, *Quarterly West*, and *Alaska Quarterly Review*. She is the recipient of a Pushcart Prize nomination, a Yaddo fellowship, and a 1998 Rona Jaffe Writers' Award, which is awarded to eight writers of national promise each year.

Rose Marie Cutting is chair of the Department of English and Communication Studies at St. Mary's University in San Antonio, Texas. She received her M.A. from the University of Michigan and her Ph.D. from the University of Minnesota. She has published a G. K. Hall reference guide to early American writers and a similar reference guide to Anaïs Nin. In addition, she has published articles on early American literature, Texas female poets, pioneer Texas businesswomen, the Texas fiction of Shelby Hearon, and the fiction of Sandra Cisneros. She asks us to mention her gratitude to Sandra Cisneros for her many public readings and support of the arts in San Antonio. Professor Cutting has a special interest in short fiction set in locations that students in her classes can explore, and she has a passion for pondering how and why authors create closure in their works.

Peter Donahue (Ph.D., Oklahoma State University) is an assistant professor of English at Birmingham-Southern College. He has published critical articles on Henry James, James Welch, Sherman Alexie, John Updike, Andre Dubus, Dagoberto Gilb, Peter Taylor, and Raymond Carver. In addition to his critical work, he has published a short story cycle titled *The Cornelius Arms* (Seattle: Missing Spoke, 2000) and more than twenty-five short stories in various literary periodicals. He regularly reviews fiction for the *Review of Contemporary Fiction*. He is also coeditor (with John Trombold) of *Reading Seattle: The City in Prose* (forthcoming from University of Washington Press in 2004), an anthology of fiction and nonfiction.

J. Scott Farrin received his M.F.A. from the University of New Orleans where he currently teaches. He has published fiction in such journals as *Puerto del Sol* and *South Carolina Review* and creative nonfiction in publications such as *Hermenaut*.

Brewster E. Fitz is an associate professor of English at Oklahoma State University. His teaching and research interests include cross-cultural literature, Native American literature, short story, detective-mystery narrative, and literary theory. He has recently published articles on Tony Hillerman, Diane Glancy, and Leslie Marmon Silko. He is currently completing a book on Leslie Marmon Silko.

Raymond-Jean Frontain is professor of English and interdisciplinary studies at the University of Central Arkansas where he teaches courses in religion and culture, world drama, and the Bible as literature. Among his publications are *Reclaiming the Sacred: The Bible in Gay and Lesbian Culture* (New York: Harrington Park, 2003) and articles on the construction of homosexuality in James Baldwin, D. H. Lawrence, and Allen Ginsberg. He is completing a book-length study of homoerotic representations of the biblical David figure in Western art and literature.

Larry D. Griffin, an Oklahoman, serves as professor of English and dean of arts and sciences at Dyersburg State Community College, Dyersburg, Tennessee. More than sixty of his essays have been published. His short stories appear in *A Gathering of Samphire and Other Stories* (Norman, OK: Poetry Around, 1990). More than 250 of his poems have appeared in journals, e-zines, and magazines in the United States and abroad. His poetry books include *The Jane Poems* (Winston, OR: 9Muses, 2002), *Larry D. Griffin: Greatest Hits: 1968–2000* (Johnstown,

OH: Pudding House, 2000), *New Fires* (Edmond, OK: Full Count, 1982), *The Blue Water Tower* (Norman, OK: Poetry Around, 1984), and *Airspace* (Austin, TX: Slough, 1989). He exhibits his paintings and photographs throughout the United States.

Noel Harold Kaylor, originally a Kentuckian, has been a student of various national literatures, though his primary academic work is in the area of medieval studies. He served as a medic in the American War in Vietnam, has taught languages and literature at many schools and on four continents, and he has developed study-abroad programs for students, both international and domestic, who are interested in learning about the world's cultures. He is currently professor and chair of the Department of English at Troy State University in Troy, Alabama.

Richard E. Lee is presently employed as an assistant professor of English at the State University of New York–College at Oneonta. He has lectured and taught in China, South Africa, and the United States. His academic specialty is nineteenth- and twentieth-century world literatures. His most recent publications include essays on American short story writers Robert Bausch and Barry Hannah; he edited (and wrote the introduction for) the *Dictionary of Literary Biography (Volume 234, Third Series): American Short-Story Writers since World War II.*

Paul R. Lilly is a professor of English at the State University of New York–College at Oneonta, and the author of *Words in Search of Victims: The Achievement of Jerzy Kosinski* (Kent: Kent State UP, 1998), as well as essays on contemporary American writers such as John Updike, Mary Gordon, and Richard Bausch. He has published fiction in the *Virginia Quarterly Review*, the *New England Review*, and other journals.

Howard Lindholm earned an M.Phil. in English at the University of Glasgow and a Ph.D. at Michigan State University. His dissertation "Shapes to Fill the Lack and Lacks to Fill the Shape: Framing the Unframed in Modernist Narratives" focuses on how William Faulkner, James Joyce, Virginia Woolf, and Gertrude Stein both create and conceal narrative "windows"—frames of speculative possibility based on the disnarrated gaps generated by stylistic and perceptual variation. He has published short fiction and poetry, and his "The Instance of There Being More: Cubist Narratives in *Run Lola Run* and *Memento*" will appear in a forthcoming book on post-punk cinemas. Originally from Los Angeles, he now lives in Chicago, where he is writing his first novel.

Christine Loflin is the author of *African Horizons: The Landscapes of African Fiction* (Westport: Greenwood, 1998) and essays on Ngugi wa Thiong'o, Flora Nwapa, Zaynab Alkali, Nadine Gordimer, Mongane Serote, Sindiwe Magona, and South African literary history. She teaches postcolonial literature at Oxford College of Emory University.

Michele Morano is a visiting assistant professor in the English Department of Skidmore College and a practicing writer of both nonfiction and fiction. Her essay collection *Grammar Lessons* is forthcoming from the University of Iowa Press.

Michael Orlofsky is an associate professor of English at Troy State University where he teaches courses in contemporary fiction and creative writing. He is a graduate of the writing programs at Penn State and the Iowa Writers' Workshop. His applied knowledge concerning historiografiction extends to the novel he is currently writing, *Michelangelo in Rome*, set in fifteenth- and sixteenth-century Italy.

Brenda M. Palo is a Ph.D. candidate in comparative literature at the University of North Carolina at Chapel Hill. She is completing her dissertation on melancholia and death in the literature of Franz Kafka, Marie Redonnet, and Richard Brautigan, employing the critical writings of Walter Benjamin and Julia Kristeva. Her master's thesis explored orality in the short fiction of Katherine Mansfield and Guy de Maupassant. During her course of study at the university, she has written on French, German, American, and English literature and has begun a study of the Czech and Slovak languages. She appreciates both psychoanalytic and feminist theories as critical approaches to literature and is particularly interested in the short story and in the expanding discourse on short story theory.

Wayne Stengel is professor of English at the University of Central Arkansas. He has published a book on Donald Barthelme and essays on Joyce Carol Oates, E. L. Doctorow, Don DeLillo, John Cheever, Robert Coover, Alfred Hitchcock, Oliver Stone, and Brian DePalma. He teaches American modernism, postmodernism, and film studies and is currently researching a book on the concept of history in the American postmodern novel.

Karen Weekes is an assistant professor of English at Penn State Abington, near Philadelphia. She received her Ph.D. from the University of Georgia in 2000. Her publications include work on ninteenth-

and twentieth-century figures in American literature, including Susan Minot, Constance Fenimore Woolson, and Edgar Allan Poe. She is currently completing a manuscript on contemporary American females' short story cycles.

Allan Weiss is a freelance writer in Toronto. He is a part-time instructor at York University, teaching courses in science fiction and fantasy, and chair of the Academic Conference on Canadian Science Fiction and Fantasy. He has had stories—both mainstream and science fiction—published in a number of periodicals and anthologies, including *Fiddlehead*, *Short Story*, *Windsor Review*, *Tesseracts 4*, *Tesseracts 7*, and *On Spec*. His first story collection, *Living Room*, a mainstream story cycle, was published by Boheme Press in 2001. He is currently working on a historical novel and a sequel to *Living Room*.

Editors

Joseph Boyden was born and raised in Ontario, Canada. He received his undergraduate degree in Humanities and Creative Writing from York University in Toronto and his M.F.A. from the University of New Orleans. His first collection of stories, *Born with a Tooth*, was published by Cormorant Books in the spring of 2001.

Jaie Claudet received a B.A. in mass communication from the University of New Orleans in 1999. He is currently taking a hiatus from the academic world to work on a few literary projects, such as this one. He hopes to produce a novel sometime before the next millennium.

Farhat Iftekharrudin is associate professor of English and dean of the College of Liberal Arts and Sciences at the University of Texas at Brownsville. He is the editor of the literary journal *Short Story*. His research interests include postmodernism, minimalism, magic realism, and feminist issues in contemporary literature. He has published articles and papers on such authors as Salman Rushdie, Isabel Allende, Bharati Mukherjee, and Rudolfo Anaya.

Mary Rohrberger, adjunct professor of English at the University of New Orleans, received her Ph.D. from Tulane University with a dissertation on the short story called "Hawthorne and the Modern Literary Short Story." In 1966, her dissertation was published as *Hawthorne and the Modern Short Story: A Study in Genre* (The Hague, Mouton). Since then, she has published or has currently in press more than a dozen books and some 350 articles. She has received both teaching and research awards and was recently honored with a Festschrift presented to her by her colleagues in the field of the short story. During her career she has been both teacher and administrator. She is the executive editor of the journal *Short Story*, director of the Society for the Study of the Short Story, and founder and executive director of a series of international conferences on the short story in English.